THE WORLD RELIGIONS
COOKBOOK

THE WORLD RELIGIONS COOKBOOK

Arno Schmidt and Paul Fieldhouse

GREENWOOD PRESS
Westport, Connecticut • London

Library of Congress Cataloging-in-Publication Data

Schmidt, Arno, 1937–
    The world religions cookbook / Arno Schmidt and Paul Fieldhouse.
        p. cm.
    Includes bibliographical references and index.
    ISBN 978–0–313–33504–4 (alk. paper)
    1. Cookery, International. 2. Cookery—Religious aspects. I. Fieldhouse, Paul. II. Title.
    TX725.A1S42155 2007
    641.59—dc22   2007002974

British Library Cataloguing in Publication Data is available.

Library of Congress Catalog Card Number: 2007002974
ISBN-13: 978–0–313–33504–4
ISBN-10: 0–313–33504–4

First published in 2007

Greenwood Press, 88 Post Road West, Westport, CT 06881
An imprint of Greenwood Publishing Group, Inc.
www.greenwood.com

Printed in the United States of America

∞

The paper used in this book complies with the
Permanent Paper Standard issued by the National
Information Standards Organization (Z39.48–1984).

10 9 8 7 6 5 4 3 2 1

Copyright Acknowledgments

The authors and the publisher gratefully acknowledge permission for use of the following
material:

Illustrations by J. Susan Cole Stone.

The publisher has done its best to make sure the instructions and/or recipes in this book
are correct. However, users should apply judgment and experience when preparing
recipes, especially parents and teachers working with young people. The publisher
accepts no responsibility for the outcome of any recipe included in this volume.

To Margaret
To Corinne, Emma, and Veronica

CONTENTS

List of Recipes	ix
Glossary	xvii
Measurement Conversions	xxix
Acknowledgments	xxxi
Introduction	xxxiii
1. Buddhism and Shintoism	1
2. Christianity	33
3. Hinduism and Sikhism	97
4. Islam	145
5. Judaism	189
Bibliography	233
Index	235

LIST OF RECIPES

Buddhism and Shintoism

B-1	Pounded Rice Cakes (*Omochi*)	4
B-2	Basic Soup Stock (*Dashi*)	5
B-3	New Year's Day Soup (*O-zoni*)	5
B-4	Kanot-Style New Year's Day Soup	6
B-5	Pickled Daikon, Cucumber, and Carrot	6
B-6	Burdock Pickle (*Tataki Gobo*)	7
B-7	Chilled Buckwheat Noodles (*Toshikoshi Soba*)	8
B-8	New Year Sweet Potato Balls (*Kuri Kinton*)	8
B-9	Hot and Spicy Walnuts	9
B-10	Tibetan New Year's Eve Soup with Dumplings (*Guthuk*)	10
B-11	Rice and Potato Stew (*Droma*)	11
B-12	Sweet Saffron Rice (*Dresi*)	12
B-13	Kapse Fritters	12
B-14	Monastery Bread	13
B-15	Barley with Mushrooms and Onions	14
B-16	Rice Soup	15
B-17	Crispy Duck Breast with Vegetables	16
B-18	Steamed Dumplings (*Jao Tze*)	17
B-19	Dumpling Dipping Sauce	17
B-20	Eight Precious Pudding (*Nian Gao*)	18
B-21	Potato Stew (*Dum Alu*)	19
B-22	Udon Miso	19

B-23 Indian Pancakes (*Malupa*)   20

B-24 Thai Pork and Bamboo Shoot Soup (*Gaeng Chud No Ma*)   21

B-25 Dried Dates   21

B-26 Myanmar Tomato Soup with Lemongrass   22

B-27 Vegetable Stock for Soup   22

B-28 Malaysian Coconut, Tapioca, and Melon Soup   23

B-29 Beef Sukiyaki   24

B-30 Rice Cooked in Milk (*Kheer*)   25

B-31 Shrimp with Spices   26

B-32 Zongzi   27

B-33 Hot and Sour Shrimp Soup (*Dom Yam Gung*)   28

B-34 Adzuki Beans and Rice with Sesame   29

B-35 Potato Stew with Asafetida   29

B-36 Chinese Aromatic Fried Rice   30

B-37 Stir-Fried Shrimp with Jasmine Tea Leaves   31

B-38 Spiced Rice with Lotus Root and Mango   32

Christianity

C-1   Tyrolean Dried Fruit Bread (*Kletzenbrot*)   36

C-2   Amish Apple Tarts on Cabbage Leaves   37

C-3   Candy Crisps (*Zuckerstangen*)   38

C-4   German Gingerbread (*Lebkuchen*)   39

C-5   Santa Claus Almond Cookies   40

C-6   Serbian Beans in Tomato Sauce   40

C-7   Mexican Chicken and Vegetable Soup (*Caldo Tlalpeño*)   41

C-8   Mexican Chicken Broth (*Caldo de Pollo*)   42

C-9   Mexican Pork Soup (*Pozole*)   42

C-10 Pineapple and Banana Dessert (*Cajeta de Piña y Plátano*)   43

C-11 Anise Star Cookies   44

C-12 Slovakian Bread Soup (*Velija Lokšy*)   45

C-13 Ukrainian Dumplings with Sour Cream (*Varenyky*)   45

C-14 Polish Sweet Sour Carp   46

C-15 Spanish Shortcakes (*Polverones Navideña*)   47

C-16 Broiled Oysters   48

C-17 Scandinavian Liver Spread (*Leverpastej*)   49

C-18 Dill-Cured Salmon (*Gravad Lax*)   49

C-19 Mustard and Dill Sauce (*Gravlaxsås*)   50

C-20 Mexican Cactus Salad (*Ensalada de Nopales*)   50

C-21 Italian Christmas Salad (*Insalata di Rinforzo*)   51

C-22 Christmas Sauerkraut Soup (*Kapustnica*)   52

C-23 French Hearty Soup (*Pot au Feu*)   53

C-24 Louisiana Gumbo with Sassafras   53

C-25	French-Canadian Pork Pie (*Tourtière*)	55
C-26	Baked Virginia Ham	55
C-27	Elizabethan Venison with Fennel	56
C-28	Czech Bread Dumplings (*Knedliki*)	57
C-29	Hungarian Stuffed Kohlrabi (*Töltött Kalarábá*)	58
C-30	Scandinavian Poached Preserved Cod (*Lutfisk*)	59
C-31	French Christmas Log (*Bûche de Noël*)	60
C-32	English Steamed Date and Fig Pudding	62
C-33	Gingerbread Pudding	62
C-34	Lemon Curd	63
C-35	German Baked Apples Filled with Almonds (*Bratäpfel mit Mandeln*)	63
C-36	Norwegian Christmas Cake (*Julakaka*)	64
C-37	Moravian Christmas Cookies	65
C-38	Greek Christmas Cake (*Vassilopitta*)	66
C-39	Three Kings Sweet Bread (*Roscón de Reyes*)	67
C-40	Greek Pork in Lemon and Vinegar Jelly (*Zalatina*)	68
C-41	Bulgarian Beef Soup with Meatballs (*Supa Topcheta*)	69
C-42	Lebanese Meat Turnovers (*Sambousik*)	69
C-43	Rasstegai with Fish	71
C-44	Pork Chops Baked with Apples and Sauerkraut	72
C-45	Honey Cakes (*Petruska*)	72
C-46	Apple Walnut Cake	73
C-47	Laotian Papaya Salad	74
C-48	Moravian Clear Beef Soup with Cream-of-Wheat Dumplings	74
C-49	Greek Cheese Pie (*Tiropitta*)	76
C-50	Amish Doughnuts (*Fastnacht*)	77
C-51	Brazilian Seafood Pie	78
C-52	Spanish Fried Cheese (*Queso Frito*)	78
C-53	Emperor's Shredded Pancake (*Kaiserschmarren*)	79
C-54	Potato Fritters (*Draniki*)	80
C-55	Ukrainian Easter Eggs	81
C-56	Mexican Squash Flower Soup (*Sopa de Flor de Calabacita*)	81
C-57	Venetian Rice and Peas (*Risi e Bisi*)	82
C-58	Roman-Style Easter Lamb (*Abbacchio alla Romana*)	83
C-59	Chicken Chili (*Aji de Gallina*)	84
C-60	French Alsatian Easter Cake (*Gâteau de Paque*)	84
C-61	Russian Easter Cheese Bread (*Syrnyk*)	85
C-62	Greek Roast Leg of Lamb in Paper (*Arni Psito Sto Hart*)	86
C-63	Mormon Baptism Buns	87
C-64	Holy Spirit Soup (*Sopa do Espírito Santo*)	88
C-65	Spanish Honey Cakes (*Galletas de Miel*)	89
C-66	Scallops with Anise and Oranges	89
C-67	Day of the New Bread (*Kalács*)	90

C-68   Sfingi Fritters   91
C-69   Mayan Mexican Graveyard Pie (*Bil Pollo*)   92
C-70   Barley Bread   94
C-71   Stuffed Dates   95

Hinduism and Sikhism

H-1   Saffron Rice Cooked in Milk (*Sarkkarai Pongal*)   100
H-2   Chickpea Soup (*Karhi*)   101
H-3   Cauliflower with Ginger and Cilantro (*Dum Gobi*)   101
H-4   Basmati Rice (*Chawal*)   103
H-5   Basmati Rice with Spices and Saffron (*Chawal Pullao*)   103
H-6   Garam-Spiced Chicken Strips   104
H-7   Flat Bread (*Paratha*)   105
H-8   Spiced Chickpeas (*Channa Masaledar*)   106
H-9   Spiced Milk Drink (*Thandai*)   106
H-10   Cumin Seed Cooler (*Jal Jeera*)   107
H-11   Sweet Tomato Chutney   107
H-12   Stewed Lentils (*Masur Dal*)   108
H-13   Split Pea–Filled Griddle Breads (*Puranpoli*)   109
H-14   Tandoori Baked Chicken (*Tandoori Murgha*)   110
H-15   Fried Turnovers (*Gunjiya*)   110
H-16   Sweet Fritters (*Malpuas*)   111
H-17   Besan Flour Chapattis (*Papri*)   112
H-18   Caribbean Lamb Curry with Pecans   112
H-19   Punjab Fried Wheat Bread (*Poori* or *Puri*)   113
H-20   Green and Red Lentil Soup (*Dal Shorba*)   114
H-21   Dried Nut Toffee (*Gajjac*)   115
H-22   Sour Mango Soup (*Mampazhapachadi*)   116
H-23   Fruit and Mint Chutney (*Podina* Chutney)   116
H-24   Samosas   117
H-25   Sweets (*Pedhas*)   118
H-26   Punjabi Mixed Spice (*Garam Masala*)   119
H-27   Lamb Masala (*Chaamp Masala*)   119
H-28   Peas with Farmer Cheese (*Mattar Paneer*)   120
H-29   Chickpea Flour Pancakes (*Besan ka Cheela*)   121
H-30   Lentil Stew (*Masoor Dal*)   122
H-31   Vegetable Puree (*Avial*)   122
H-32   Chicken Curry with Tomatoes (*Murgha Kari*)   123
H-33   Almond Milk (*Badam Phirni*)   124
H-34   Carrot Halwa   125
H-35   Chicken in Foil   125
H-36   Butter-Broiled Bananas   126
H-37   Cottage Cheese and Fruit Dessert   127

H-38 Sea Bass in Green Chutney   127
H-39 Green Mint and Cilantro Chutney (*Podina Dhania Ki*)   128
H-40 Dessert Dumplings (*Modakas*)   129
H-41 Coconut Rice (*Kheer Ade*)   129
H-42 Steamed Rice in Banana Leaves (*Potali*)   130
H-43 Banana Fudge (*Kele Ka Halwa*)   131
H-44 Potatoes and Rice (*Aloo Pulao*)   131
H-45 Sweet Pumpkin Curry (*Kaddu Ki Sabzi*)   132
H-46 Chicken Dilruba   133
H-47 Bengali Cabbage Curry (*Bandhakopir Dalna*)   133
H-48 Chickpea Dal (*Chana Masaledar*)   134
H-49 Frozen Milk (*Kulfi*)   135
H-50 Tamarind Sauce (*Imli Ke* Chutney)   135
H-51 Five-Jewel Creamed Legumes   136
H-52 Caribbean Black-Eyed Peas (*Urhad Dal Sabat*)   138
H-53 Sesame Halwa   138
H-54 Almond Rice Dessert (*Badam Phirni*)   139
H-55 Ricotta Dessert (*Roshogolla Rasgulla*)   139
H-56 Diwali Ladoos (*Besan Ke Ladoo*)   140
H-57 Mawa Ladoos   141
H-58 Potatoes with Poppy Seeds (*Aloo Posto*)   141
H-59 Sweetened Semolina (*Kahara Prasad*)   142
H-60 Collard Greens (*Haak*)   143

Islam

IS-1   Baked Goat and Rice (*Gosht Biryani*)   148
IS-2   Sweet Lamb Stew (*Mrouzia Tajine*)   149
IS-3   Smoked Eggplant Puree (*Baba Ghannooj*)   149
IS-4   Fish Roe Dip (*Tarama*)   150
IS-5   Lamb with Figs, Grapes, and Almonds   151
IS-6   Stuffed Lamb Shoulder (*Kabourga*)   151
IS-7   Lamb Curry (Lamb *Korma*)   152
IS-8   Barbecued Lamb Breast   153
IS-9   Sweet Vermicelli Pudding (*Seviyan/Savia/Sewian*)   153
IS-10 Almond Ice Cream   154
IS-11 Cherry Bread Pudding   154
IS-12 Millet Porridge   155
IS-13 Tunisian Terabilesi Bread   156
IS-14 Malaysian Roast Lamb   156
IS-15 Indonesian Spiced Shrimp (*Sambal Goreng Undang*)   157
IS-16 Lemon Chicken   157
IS-17 Honey-Baked Shredded Dough (*Tel Kadayif*)   158

IS-18   Pomegranate Mint Tea   159
IS-19   Millet Pancakes   159
IS-20   Lentils with Rice (*Moujadara*)   160
IS-21   Persian Lamb Stew   160
IS-22   Persian Sweet Rice (*Shekar Polo*)   161
IS-23   Fritters in Syrup (*Gulab Jamin*)   162
IS-24   Chard and Lentil Soup   163
IS-25   Semolina Cooked in Water (*Lâässida*)   163
IS-26   Stewed Fish over Rice and Noodles   164
IS-27   Yam Patties   164
IS-28   Algerian Roast Chicken with Sweet Stuffing   165
IS-29   Iranian Fruit Rice with Fish   166
IS-30   Malaysian Chicken in Coconut Cream (*Rendan Santan*)   166
IS-31   Date Sweetmeat (*Holwar Tamar*)   167
IS-32   Benne Cookies   168
IS-33   Fig and Date Bread   169
IS-34   Syrian Flat Bread   169
IS-35   Agras   170
IS-36   Iranian Almond and Pistachio Loaf   170
IS-37   Sweet Cardamom Rice (*Sevaiyya Kheer*)   171
IS-38   Oxtail and Okra Soup   172
IS-39   Bosnian Apricot Soup   172
IS-40   Moroccan Lentil Soup (*Harira*)   173
IS-41   Fava Bean Fritters (*Taamiya*)   174
IS-42   Turkish Spiced Liver Rice (*İç Pilâl*)   174
IS-43   Semolina Cake (*Basbousa*)   175
IS-44   Peanut Stew   175
IS-45   Chicken in Nut Sauce (*Cerkez Tavuğu*)   176
IS-46   Hilbeh Dip   177
IS-47   Egyptian Mazza Dip   177
IS-48   Egyptian Chickpea Fritters (*Falafel*)   178
IS-49   Lamb and Lentil Soup (*Abgooshth*)   178
IS-50   Stir-Fried Scallops with Chicken, Mushrooms, and Cucumbers   179
IS-51   Iranian Lemon Chicken with Roasted Garlic (*Tahsreeb Dijaj*) 180
IS-52   Lamb in Almond Sauce (*Roghan Josh*)   180
IS-53   Rainbow Rice Dessert   181
IS-54   Quince Sorbet   182
IS-55   Peach Condiment   183
IS-56   Shiebiat Pastry   184
IS-57   Malaysian Rice Flour Dessert   184
IS-58   Tharid   185
IS-59   Hais   186
IS-60   Fruit Refreshment   186

Judaism

J-1	Chicken and Date Patties	191
J-2	Braised Brisket with Pomegranate	192
J-3	Carrots and Prunes Tzimes	193
J-4	Kasha Varnitchekes	194
J-5	Farfel	195
J-6	Frosted Grapes	196
J-7	Stuffed Cabbage (*Holishkes*)	196
J-8	Unstuffed Cabbage	197
J-9	Fillet of Perch with Almonds and Avocados	197
J-10	Date Nut Loaf	198
J-11	Mandelbrot	199
J-12	Rugelach	199
J-13	Sufganiyot	200
J-14	Chicken Legs with Kumquats	201
J-15	Potato Latkes	202
J-16	Stuffed Kishke or Derma	202
J-17	Zucchini Flower Fritters	203
J-18	Carciofi alla Giudea	204
J-19	Hamantaschen	205
J-20	Breakfast Matzo Fritters	207
J-21	Ashkenazic Charoset	207
J-22	Sephardic Charoset	208
J-23	Beet Horseradish	208
J-24	Chickpea Dip (*Nahit*)	209
J-25	Stuffed Chicken	209
J-26	Pineapple Carrot Soufflé	210
J-27	Azerbaijani Roasted Eggs	211
J-28	Eastern European Seed Cake	212
J-29	Brazilian Cashew and Guava Cake	212
J-30	Blintzes	213
J-31	Crisp Cornmeal Waffles	214
J-32	Challah	214
J-33	Cholent	215
J-34	Hungarian Sólet (Bean and Goose Cholent)	216
J-35	*Powidltascherln*	217
J-36	Nahit with Rice	218
J-37	Honey Cake	219
J-38	Chopped Herring	220
J-39	Gefilte Fish	220
J-40	Chopped Liver	221
J-41	Lamb and Eggplant Matzo Pie	223
J-42	Bagels	223

J-43	Matzo Brei	224
J-44	Sephardic Leek and Feta Fritters	225
J-45	Matzo Omelet	226
J-46	Vegetable Cutlets	226
J-47	Zucchini Frittata	227
J-48	Lokschen Noodle Kugel	227
J-49	Matzo Kugel with Apples	228
J-50	Baked Pears with Walnuts and Honey	229
J-51	Tabbouleh	229
J-52	Millet Flat Bread	230
J-53	Lentil Stew	231

GLOSSARY

Boldface terms in definitions refer to main entries in the glossary.

Achiote: Seed of the annatto tree. Achiote dye, prepared by stirring the seeds in water, is used to color butter, cheese, and rice.

Adzuki: Small, dark, reddish-brown bean from Japan.

Allspice: Dried berry of a tree of the myrtle family. Called allspice because the flavor resembles a combination of **cloves**, **cinnamon**, and **nutmeg**. Ground allspice is used in baking and pickling.

Almond extract: Concentrated almond flavor made either synthetically or from bitter almonds. Widely used in food manufacturing and baking.

Almond paste: Paste made with ground peeled almonds and sugar. Available canned as pastry ingredient.

Amchoor: Acidic powder made from unripe **mangos**; used primarily in East Indian cooking.

Anchovy fillets: Small salty fish fillets usually purchased canned, packed in oil.

Anise: Annual herb of the parsley family. Often sold as fennel in supermarkets.

Anise seeds: Licorice-flavored seeds of anise plant are half-moon-shaped and have been used for centuries in European, Middle Eastern, and Indian cooking. Main ingredient in Chinese **five spice powder**.

Arrowroot: Starch extracted from dried tuber of arrowroot plant, ground to a white powder to make thickener for sauces. Name came from Arawak Indian practice of rubbing root into arrow wounds in belief that it would absorb poison.

Artichoke (globe artichoke): Vegetable from perennial thistle plant that will grow up to five feet tall. Unopened flower of plant is eaten.

Asafetida/Asafoetida: Smelly resin paste or powder used in small quantities in East Indian vegetarian dishes.

Avocado: Fruit from tree in laurel family, ranging from two to eight inches in length. Pulp between peel and single large seed is soft and buttery when ripe. Avocados sold in stores are typically midsized and weigh from 10 to 16 ounces.

Baker's cheese: Cream cheese made without addition of gum arabic.

Baker's chocolate: Semisweet chocolate used in baking.

Baking powder: Leavening agent consisting of sodium bicarbonate and acid salt mixture invented in the mid-1850s. **Cornstarch** is used to keep mixture dry.

Baking soda: Leavening agent without acid salt. Used in cakes and batters with high acid content, such as gingerbread and fruitcakes.

Bamboo shoots: Young shoots of bamboo plant, grown from underground root stock. Popular vegetable in Japan and China. Available canned and, occasionally, fresh.

Basmati rice: Fragrant, high-quality, East Indian long-grain rice from foothills of Himalayas.

Bay leaves: Important culinary seasoning. Leathery, dark green, aromatic leaves of bay tree can be used fresh or dried to flavor soups, marinades for meat or fish, and other dishes.

Bay scallops: Small, sweet-flavored scallops, mostly from China, usually sold by weight.

Bean sprouts: Mung bean sprouts. Available fresh, or canned in brine.

Beet: Root vegetable that is usually deep red, though some varieties can be white or gold. Served cooked or raw. Boiling or roasting beets in skin preserves color.

Besan: Pale yellow East Indian flour, also called gram flour or *channa*, made from **chickpeas**.

Blintzes: Jewish pancakes usually filled with pot cheese.

Bonito flakes: Dried shredded tuna; also called *Katsuobushi* in Japanese cuisine.

Borlotti beans: Italian bean variety, pinkish with red speckles; usually sold dry.

Broccoli rabe: Bitter variety of broccoli.

Buckwheat grits (kasha): Dried seeds with high protein content. Seeds are light green or brown, have a mellow flavor, and are used in cooking. Should be toasted to improve flavor.

Bulgar/Bulghur: Steamed, dried, crushed wheat kernels.

Burdock: Long, slender, root vegetable with brown skin resembling salsify. Both root and leaves are eaten.

Buttermilk: Milk that remains after butterfat has been removed from full-cream milk. Cultured buttermilk is made by adding lactic bacterial cultures to pasteurized skim or low-fat milk. Cultures change milk sugars into lactic acid to give buttermilk its tart flavor and thickness.

Capers: Pickled blossoms of hardy shrub growing on mountain slopes around Mediterranean.

Caraway seeds: Among oldest known spices. Half-moon-shaped seeds are used in bread, especially in Germany, where they are called *kümmel.*

Cardamom: Green, white, or black varieties grow in pods. Whole or ground cardamom is used as spice in curries. Crushed cardamom is used in Middle East to flavor coffee.

Carob beans: Sweet, succulent, long brown pods, used as human and animal food since ancient times. Also known as locust beans or St. John's bread, owing to belief that they may have been Biblical "locusts" eaten by John the Baptist.

Cayenne pepper: Powerful spice made with dried hot peppers of the genus *Capsicum.* Named after town where it is grown in French Guiana, South America.

Chana: East Indian name for small beans resembling **chickpeas**; used in many dishes whole or ground.

Chana dal: Dried, split **chana** beans.

Chapatti: Indian flat bread made with whole-wheat flour.

Chard: Leafy vegetable in **beet** family. Only leaves and stalks are eaten.

Chickpeas: Plant seeds originally from around Mediterranean region. Large peas shaped like hazelnuts are beige, yellow, or brown. Staple in Middle East and India.

Chili: Also known as chile or chili pepper: Seedpod of capsicum plant in nightshade family. Eaten raw or cooked in dishes to impart varying degrees of hotness. Remove seeds and inner membranes to reduce heat.

Chili bean sauce: Very hot bottled sauce made with **chilies**, apricots, lemons, and garlic.

Chili powder: Blend of powdered **chili** peppers and other spices such as **cumin** seeds.

Chili sauce: Tomato sauce simmered with **chili** peppers and spices. Available bottled or canned.

Chinese cabbage: General name for Oriental *brassica* vegetables. **Napa cabbage** family, which includes bok choy, is best known in the West.

Chives: Mild-flavored herb of onion family. Slender stalks can be chopped to use as garnish.

Cholent: Jewish term for slow-cooked casserole dish served on Sabbath.

Chrysanthemum leaves: Grown as leaf vegetable; used in Asian cooking.

Cilantro: Leaves of coriander plant, also known as Chinese parsley. Often used as garnish and flavoring in **curry** dishes.

Cinnamon: Reddish-brown inner bark from tropical tree, used in baking, desserts, and South Asian cooking. Most cinnamon used in U.S. is *cassia* variety from Southeast Asia sold as sticks or ground as powder. West Indian variety of cinnamon is *canela.*

Cloves: Unopened dried buds from evergreen myrtle tree, whole cloves are shaped like tacks or nails, and used whole or ground in East Indian cuisine. Most is grown in Zanzibar off East African coast.

Coconut milk: Cloudy liquid pressed from ripe coconut flesh steeped in boiling water. Flesh can be pureed and liquefied in blender. Dried, unsweetened coconut flakes can also be used to make coconut milk. Available canned, sweetened, and unsweetened.

Collard greens: Dark green leafy vegetable in kale family.

Confectioners (icing) sugar: Superfine sugar containing small amount of **cornstarch** to prevent caking.

Coriander seeds: Mild-flavored seeds of coriander plant, available whole and ground. Main ingredient in **curry** powders. Seeds should be roasted to enhance flavor.

Corn syrup: Thick syrup, used in baking and as sweetener in soft drinks because it is less expensive than sugar. Light and dark syrups are available.

Cornstarch: Starch extracted from corn. Added as **slurry** to thicken boiling liquids.

Cream of tartar: Organic crystalline powder, its most common uses in kitchen are as baking powder when blended with **baking soda**, and as beaten egg-white stabilizer.

Cream of wheat: See **Farina**.

Cumin: Aromatic spice, with hot taste, popular in Middle Eastern, East Indian, and Mexican cuisines.

Currants: Small, edible, red and black berries growing in clusters on shrubs. High in vitamin C. Term also applied to small, dark, seedless dried grapes used like raisins.

Curry: Indian spice blend varying greatly in composition from region to region and cook to cook. Can be sharp or mild, yellow or red, dry or available as paste. Most Indian cooks blend curry powder when needed and according to dish.

Curry leaves: Leaves of kari plant, member of citrus family used in Indian, Sri Lankan, and Thai cooking. Leaves are not used in **curry** mixtures but are added, fresh or dried, to cooking oil.

Daikon: White radish used either raw or cooked in Japanese and Indian dishes.

Dashi: Basic Japanese soup stock made with kelp and **bonito flakes**.

Dates: Fruits of the date palm. Come in many varieties, available fresh or dried.

Denver ribs: Spareribs trimmed of fat and connective tissue.

Derma: Jewish sausage casing. Called stuffed derma, or *kishke*, when stuffed with flour or **matzo meal**, suet, and seasonings.

Dill: Delicate, feathery green annual herb.

Dried red seedless dates: Small red shriveled fruits, most made from jujube, fruit native to Southeast Asia.

DUTCH OVEN

Dutch oven: Heavy, cast-iron cooking pot with tight lid, used for slow cooking.

Enoki: Tiny, white, long-stemmed Japanese mushrooms, grown at snowline in mountainous regions. Mild-flavored and crunchy.

Farfel: Jewish pasta in small odd-shaped pieces, often used in soups.

Farina: Ground wheat, coarser than flour, made from germ and endosperm. Also brand name of breakfast wheat cereal.

Fava beans: Broad beans resembling lima beans. Staple of Mediterranean cookery.

Fenugreek seeds: Flat, yellow, rather bitter seeds available whole and ground. Used extensively in Asian cuisine.

Feta: Tangy, salty-tasting Greek cheese, made from either sheep's or goat's milk. Cheese is marinated in brine and sold in brine or as dry product. Texture ranges from soft and creamy to almost dry.

Figs: Rounded tree fruits, pointed at stem end. Vary in color when ripe, from bright green to deep purple, depending on variety. One of oldest domesticated crops. Can be eaten fresh, made into paste, or dried.

Filé powder: Powdered dried sassafras leaves used for thickening and seasoning Cajun gumbos.

Filo (Phyllo): Paper-thin pastry dough made with wheat flour and water, used in Greek and Turkish cooking. Available as frozen sheets in 16-ounce packages.

Fish roe: See **Tarama**.

Fish sauce: Seasoning ingredient made from sun-dried or fermented fish. Strong smelling and salty. Common in Southeast Asian cuisine.

Five-spice powder: Chinese seasoning spice blend, usually of fennel, **cloves**, **cinnamon**, **star anise**, and Szechuan peppercorns.

Fowl: Mature chicken; boiling chicken.

FRENCH KNIFE

French Knife: Sharp, tapered knife used for chopping, slicing, and dicing. Designed so it rocks on cutting board as it cuts. Also known as a chef's knife.

Ganache: Rich chocolate cream used as filling or icing.

Garam masala: Indian blend of hot spices, available dry as powder or as paste.

Garbanzos: Hispanic name for **chickpeas**.

Garland chrysanthemum: Leafy vegetable resembling **Chinese cabbage**. Basically same plant as used for ornamental flowers; leaves are bluntly lobed and rough.

Gefilte fish: Jewish term for ball or cake of chopped fish.

Ghee: Clarified butter used in Indian cooking.

Ginger: Rhizome with spicy, hot, and pungent flavor. Essential to Oriental cookery.

Gluten: Natural protein component in some grains, primarily in hard wheat.

Glutinous rice: Also called sticky rice, this Asian short-grain rice is "glue-like." Will stick together when cooked. Can be easily eaten with chopsticks.

Gobō (Burdock): popular vegetable in Japan.

Guava: Tropical fruit with shiny yellow skin, native to South America.

Hazelnuts: Reddish-brown, sweet-tasting nuts, also called filberts. Filberts are actually an English variety of hazelnut. Thus, all filberts are hazelnuts, but not all hazelnuts are filberts. Oregon and California are major producing states in U.S.

Heavy cream: Cream with at least 36% butterfat content.

Herring: Fatty fish harvested in Atlantic and Pacific Oceans. Bismarck herring are large herring pickled with vinegar.

Hoisin sauce: Sweet, sour, and spicy Chinese seasoning sauce made from soybeans or wheat.

Hominy: White corn kernels with hulls and germs removed. Whole hominy is available dried, precooked in cans, or packaged in plastic.

Horseradish: Root vegetable with strong and sharp flavor, often used as relish to accompany beef. Not related to radish despite name.

Hummus: Middle Eastern dip made from mashed **chickpeas** flavored with **tahini**, lemon juice, and garlic.

Italian parsley: Parsley variety with flat leaves.

Jalapeño: Small, hot green **chili**.

Jasmine rice: Long-grain, fragrant rice popular in Asian cooking.

Jasmine tea leaves: Tea leaves blended with jasmine flowers. Very aromatic.

Juniper berries: Berries of juniper tree used for seasoning in marinades and sauces, particularly with game.

Kataïfi: Finely shredded **filo** (phyllo) dough used in Greek desserts. Available frozen.

Katsuobushi: Dried **bonito flakes** used for making **dashi**, basic Japanese soup stock.

Kefalotori cheese: Hard Greek cheese with strong flavor and sharp aroma, made from goat's or ewe's milk. Used for grating on pasta and other cooked dishes.

Khoa: Concentrated milk solids used as basis for East Indian desserts. Also called *mawa*.

Kishke: Jewish term for sausage made with fat and cereal, same as **derma**.

Konbu: Edible dried kelp used in Japan for making the basic soup stock called **dashi**.

Kugel: German word for ball. Refers to variety of Jewish savory and sweet side dishes made with noodles or potatoes.

Kumquats: Small orange citrus fruits with edible skin. Used as decorations, candied fruits, or in syrup. Often served during Chinese celebrations such as Chinese New Year to symbolize plenty.

Kutya: Eastern European dish made from whole wheat, **poppy seeds**, and honey. Served as part of Christmas Eve meal.

Leek: Vegetable of onion family, with distinctive flavor. Rich in calcium and potassium. White stalk is usually cooked but can be eaten raw in salad.

Legumes: Generic name for two-valved seedpods. Best-known are peas, beans, **lentils**, and peanuts. High protein and starch content. Important staple in many diets.

Lemongrass: Tall, slender **scallion**-like grass varieties native to Southeast Asia. All contain citric oils released when smashed or cut. Stem base can be peeled off its tough exterior and finely minced or pressed to yield lemongrass oil. Lemon rind can be substituted for a similar but somewhat less authentic taste.

Lentils: Tiny **legumes** in variety of colors. Ancient staples of Middle Eastern and East Indian cooking where they are referred to as *dal*.

Light cream: Cream with 18% butterfat content.

Lotus root: Vegetable used in Chinese and Japanese cooking. Available both fresh and canned.

Lotus seeds: Small oval seeds eaten raw when fresh, boiled with sugar as candy, and used as nuts when dried.

Mace: Filmy red membrane covering of **nutmeg**. Mace is removed from shell and broken into pieces or ground into powder. Inside is sold as nutmeg. Little difference in flavor, though mace is somewhat stronger.

Manchego: Ewe's milk cheese from Spain's La Mancha region.

Mango: Intensely flavored, succulent tropical fruit, with slightly acidic sweet taste, although flavor of inferior ones has hint of turpentine.

Marjoram: Perennial herb in mint family, closely related to **oregano**.

Maror: Bitter herbs used as part of Jewish Seder meal, representing bitterness of slavery. Grated **horseradish**, or *chrain*, is commonly used.

Masa harina: White corn flour made of hulled corn treated with lime. Has finer texture than cornmeal.

Masoor dal: East Indian name for red **lentils**.

Matzo: Jewish unleavened wheat cracker.

Matzo meal: Ground **matzo**.

Millet: Drought-resistant grain-bearing grass, cultivated for human food use since ancient times.

Mirin: Sweet Japanese rice wine or syrup.

Miso: Japanese bean paste used for thickening sauces and soups. Classified as red (pungent) or golden (mild and white with touch of sweetness).

Mochi gomé: Japanese **gluten**-free rice, usually served steamed.

Molasses: Syrupy by-product in processing of cane or beet sugar. Available in blackstrap, dark, or light varieties. Unsulfured product also available.

Moong dal: East Indian yellow split **legumes**.

Mustard oil: Distinctive aromatic oil made from pressed **mustard seeds**.

Mustard seeds: Small seeds of black, brown, or yellow mustard plant. Ground seeds, blended with spices and vinegar, make mustard.

Napa cabbage: Most popular family of **Chinese cabbages**, with celery-like stalks. Can be eaten raw or cooked.

Nopales: Mexican edible cactus, grilled or used in salads. Thorns are removed from paddles before being sold.

Nori: Thin sheets of Japanese seaweed. Many cooks toast sheets over open flame before use.

Nutmeg: Fruit of the tropical nutmeg tree. See **Mace**.

Okra: Also called lady's-finger, long fruit pod of this native African plant is popular vegetable in the southern United States.

Omochi: Steamed **glutinous rice** pounded and formed into cakes. Japanese New Year celebration food.

Oregano: Tender perennial herb with many culinary uses in Mediterranean cuisine. Blossoms are also edible. Also called **marjoram**.

Osechi ryori: Japanese New Year food.

Oyster sauce: Chinese seasoning sauce.

Palm sugar: Dark-brown coarse sugar, also known as jaggery, made from reduced sap of date or palmyra palm.

Pan spray: Commercial vegetable oil product for spraying on pans or into molds to prevent food from sticking.

Panir/Paneer: East Indian fresh soft cheese. Can be sliced and fried or added to **curry** dishes.

Papaya: Tropical fruit, also known as tree melon. While Mexican variety can grow up to 20 pounds, smaller Hawaiian papaya is what is sold in most supermarkets.

Paprika: Dried hot spice made from red peppers. Best is made in Hungary.

Parmesan cheese: Hard cow's milk cheese, originally from Parma area of northern Italy, but now made in many countries. Although mostly sold grated, it is also an excellent dessert cheese.

Pearl barley: Barley processed to remove tough inedible outer hull and pearled or polished. Cooked as side dish, like rice, or added to stews and casseroles.

Pepper: Dried, ground product of fruit (peppercorn) of black pepper plant. Made from whole unripe peppercorns. White pepper uses seed only.

Perch: Freshwater and ocean fish with scales. Considered kosher in Jewish cuisine.

Pine nuts: Mediterranean pine seed kernels. Cones are heated to spread scales and allow nuts to be extracted.

Pistachio: Nut native to southern Europe and Asia Minor. Kernels are light green. Those sold in shell are often tinted red for eye appeal.

Pomegranates: Fruits about size of oranges and containing many seeds, red pulp, and juice. Dried seeds are used as decoration. Juice and pulp are used in desserts and jellies.

Poppy seeds: Tiny slate-blue seeds used in baking. Popular in Eastern Europe and Austria as filling for strudel and Danish pastry.

Proof: To let yeast dough rise.

Prune butter: Concentrated fruit pulp; available canned.

Pulses: See **Legumes**.

Puranpoli: East Indian stuffed griddle cakes.

Quince: Acidic fruit native to western Asia. Related to apple and pear, but most often used in preserves rather than eaten fresh.

Red bean paste: Sweet paste made from cooked **adzuki** beans, used as bun or dumpling filling in Asian cookery. Not to be confused with another red bean paste, a highly odoriferous product made with fermented soybeans.

Red date: Fruit of the Chinese jujube tree. When candied, often eaten as snack.

Rice flour: Finely ground rice used as thickening agent. Rice is pulverized in blender, but sifted flour can be substituted.

Rice vinegar: Mild white vinegar made from fermented rice.

Rice wafer paper: Edible paper made with rice flour. Used for baking soft batters.

Ricotta cheese: Soft, low-fat cheese resembling fine cottage cheese; often used in desserts. In Italian, *ricotta* means recooked: Cheese is made from whey drained from other cheeses and is therefore, strictly speaking, a cheese by-product.

Rose water: Aromatic liquid made from rose petals, widely used throughout Middle East for cooking and as an ingredient in perfume.

Rose water essence: Similar to **rose water**, but more concentrated.

Rosemary: Perennial herb with needle-like leaves and tiny blue flowers. Good accompaniment for lamb.

Russet potatoes: Potato variety high in starch and low in moisture. Good for baking and mashed potatoes.

Rye flour: Flour made from rye cereal grain. Has less **gluten** than wheat flour and makes darker, denser bread. Used blended with wheat flour in baking.

Saffron: World's costliest spice. Made from dried stigmas of crocus plant. Prized for intense color and flavor.

Salted codfish: Staple product in Mediterranean countries and Caribbean.

Sauerkraut: Shredded, salted, fermented cabbage, usually sold canned in the U.S.

Savoy cabbage: Mild green cabbage with curly leaves.

Scallions: Slender onions with small bulbs and long green stalks, commonly used in salads. Also called green onions or spring onions.

Schmaltz: Jewish term for rendered chicken fat.

Seitan: Wheat **gluten** or wheat-meat, made by washing starch out of wheat dough. Used as meat substitute.

Semolina: Coarse flour made from hard durum wheat, used for pasta and gnocchi. Non-durum semolina is sold as Cream of Wheat.

Sesame oil: Seasoning oil. Can be light and mild, or dark and pungent.

Sesame seeds: Flat seeds of sesame plant dried and toasted to give nutty flavor.

Shallot: Small onion-like plant with mild and delicate flavor.

Shiitake: Large black or brown umbrella mushroom widely used in oriental cooking. Cultivated mushrooms grown on hardwood logs, originally those of *shii* tree, from which they get their name.

Shortening: Solid vegetable fat used for baking short-crust pastry. High fat-to-flour ratio makes pastry crumbly and soft.

Slab bacon: Unsliced bacon.

Slurry: Flour and water mixture used to thicken stews, soups, and sauces.

Snow mushrooms: Silver ear mushrooms available in U.S. in dried form, or may be found canned in syrup in Chinese stores.

Snow peas: Edible flat pea pods, also called sugar peas. Good in salads or stir-fried dishes.

Soba: Japanese noodles made with buckwheat flour.

Soy: Key ingredient derived from soybean and used in food products.

Soy sauce: Seasoning sauce made from fermented soybeans and grain, used extensively in Chinese and Japanese cookery. Light soy sauce is used more in cooking, while dark sauce is used to marinate meats and in stronger-tasting dishes.

Star anise: Licorice-flavored star-shaped spice used in oriental cooking.

Striped bass: Firm-textured, mild-flavored fish. Good for grilling.

Sultanas: Seedless, large, light-colored raisins. Some of the best come from Smyrna or Izmir in Turkey, where they are known as Smyrna raisins.

Sweet potato: Nutritious starchy root tuber with orange flesh. Different plant from **yam**, although terms are often used interchangeably.

Tabasco sauce: Commercial condiment made with hot **chili** peppers, salt, and vinegar.

Tahini: Sesame paste used in Middle Eastern cooking. Main ingredient in **hummus**.

Tamarind: Tropical fruit pods with sour taste, native to Africa or Asia. Used in southern Indian cooking. Pulp made into chutney or sold as compressed fibrous slab that can be reconstituted with hot water.

Tandoor: East Indian clay oven.

Tapioca: Dried starch extracted from cassava, yucca, or manioc root. Used as thickener in puddings, soups, and sauces.

Tarama: Salted fish eggs, usually from carp, mullet, or cod. Used in Greek cuisine to make *taramosalata*, central feature of Lenten meal.

Thai-style hot curry sauce: Bottled hot sauce with **curry** flavor. Hot sauce and some curry powder could be substituted.

Thyme: Perennial aromatic herb native to Mediterranean used to season soups and stews. Common thyme is easily grown in garden or in pots.

Tofu: Soybean curd available in many shapes and degrees of firmness.

Turmeric: Spice made from tropical rhizome related to **ginger** and **arrowroot**. Turmeric powder is bright yellow in color; principal ingredient in **curry** powder. Also used to color Indian sweets.

Tzimes: Traditional Jewish meat, fruit, and vegetable stew cooked slowly over low heat.

Udon: Flat, wheat flour noodles available fresh in Japanese grocery stores.

Vanilla extract: Liquid flavoring used in desserts and sauces. Pure vanilla extract is made by soaking cured vanilla beans in alcohol; final product must contain 35% alcohol by volume.

Varenyky: Ukrainian dumplings filled with potato, cheese, meat, or fruit. Similar to *perogi*, also of Eastern European origin.

Vark: Edible silver foil used for decorating Indian desserts.

Vermicelli: Thin, string-like pasta (literally "little worms"). Asian vermicelli is often made with rice flour.

Water bath: Pan containing hot water in which smaller containers of food are placed to cook food gently.

Water chestnut: Root of freshwater aquatic plant, resembling chestnut in color and shape. Widely used in Chinese cuisine. Usually sold canned, but fresh water chestnuts may be available in some ethnic stores.

Watermelon seeds: Nutritious seeds, rich in protein and fat. Can be eaten as snack food. Often available in health food stores.

Wood ear (wood tree ear): Dried mushroom used in Chinese and Japanese cooking.

Yam: Starchy root. Important staple in West Africa. See also **Sweet potato**.

Yeast, dry: Cells of minute fungi that convert starch and sugar into carbon dioxide and alcohol. Used in baking to produce "bubbles" trapped in dough, causing it to rise. Must be added to liquid at about 100 degrees to dissolve.

Yogurt: Smooth-textured fermented milk product, low in fat, high in calcium, potassium, and protein. Fat content varies, but most yogurt is marketed as low-fat diet food. Made with two strains of bacteria that curdle milk and give it a slightly acidic taste.

Zucchini: Prolific squash with edible skin and soft seeds. Easy to grow, inexpensive, and available year-round. Used in both savory and sweet dishes. Zucchini blossoms are served stuffed or fried.

MEASUREMENT CONVERSIONS

3 teaspoons	=	1 tablespoon
2 tablespoons	=	1 liquid ounce
4 tablespoons	=	$\frac{1}{4}$ cup
8 tablespoons	=	$\frac{1}{2}$ cup
1 cup	=	$\frac{1}{2}$ pint
2 cups	=	1 pint
4 cups	=	1 quart
2 pints	=	1 quart
1 stick butter	=	4 ounces

ACKNOWLEDGMENTS

I am grateful to so many people that have helped me in my sixty-year career in the kitchen. Very special thanks go to my wife, Margaret, who is a font of culinary knowledge and who has endless curiosity about cooking. She had patience when I took over her kitchen to test the recipes, and cheerfully used up the leftover ethnic ingredients in family dinners.

—Arno Schmidt

Thanks to Wendi Schnaufer of Greenwood Press for her patient support in the preparation of this book, and to Arno Schmidt for his indomitable spirit.

—Paul Fieldhouse

✈ INTRODUCTION

Religion and Food Choice

The food choices that we make reflect a multitude of social, economic, political, and cultural influences as well as ethical codes and personal preferences. Religion is one such influence, and the food practices of religious believers around the world are shaped by the teachings of their chosen faith. For most people in North America, eating is an everyday act; without food the human body cannot survive for more than a few weeks. Yet, from a religious standpoint, food is also a culturally and spiritually powerful substance that affects human relationships, promotes an understanding of the world, and is at the heart of human interactions with the divine. Religious teachings about food include both dietary laws and guidelines for what may be termed usual or customary practice. Religious dietary laws can serve a number of different functions.

- They can provide a way for people to demonstrate their faith, showing that they accept religious authority by unquestioningly following the food rules laid down by religious leaders or in sacred texts: ''I am a Hindu; the cow is sacred''; ''I am a Jew; I do not eat pork.''
- They strengthen feelings of religious identity—of belonging to a group that has in common not only beliefs but also ways of living in the world. The act of eating and drinking together is a symbol of fellowship and mutual obligation. It is a powerful feeling to know that all over the world, on a particular day of religious celebration, people are performing the same rituals or eating the same symbolic food.
- Dietary rules may be used to demonstrate or preserve separateness by clearly marking cultural boundaries between religions, and to protect against assimilation by others. The Muhammadan prohibition against pork is thought by some to have been a way of reminding Muslims that they were

different from their Christian neighbors. In the eighth century CE Pope Gregory III prohibited Christians and Christian converts from eating horseflesh to set them apart from the horse-eating Vandals of northern Europe.

- Food rules may restrict or prohibit certain types of social interaction and behavior. Notably, in the Hindu religion, the caste system imposes strict rules as to what may be eaten, with whom, and by whom. High-caste Brahmins may eat only "pure" food and thus cannot eat with, or accept, food from lower castes.
- Giving up particular foods during religious fasts is a form of self-denial, showing that one is more interested in spiritual than in worldly values.
- Through sacrifices or sacrificial meals, food is used as a means of communicating with the divine. Offerings may be made to placate one's god and so forestall disaster, or to seek favors and good fortune.
- Religious practices may serve, incidentally or purposefully, to encourage ecological sustainability through conservation and judicious use of scarce resources. Some scholars believe that the Hindu prohibition on eating cows was a practical measure to ensure that farmers did not kill their means of livelihood during times of hardship.
- Food marks the boundary between ordinary time and religious or sacred time. For example, in the Orthodox Christian calendar, Cheese Sunday marks the last day one can eat dairy products and the last food consumed is an egg, which is eaten accompanied by the phrase "With an egg I close my mouth, with an egg I will open it again," referring to the breaking of the fast with red-dyed Easter eggs. In a similar vein, the Jewish Pesach or Passover is preceded by a clearing out of leavened food products from the house, while the end of the Islamic fast of Ramadan is marked with the festival of Eid al-Fitr, which means, literally, the festival of breaking the fast.

Religious food practices often require the use of specific foods in specific situations, especially during special celebrations such as feasts or fasts, where particular foods often have important symbolic values. Conversely there are many examples of foods that are not allowed for consumption though they are freely available, and religious codes often exclude whole categories of foods from consumption. What must not be eaten may be determined by characteristics of individuals such as age, gender, and social or physiological status, or by external constraints such as time of day or time of year. Prescriptive rules of what must be eaten, when and how, are the counterpart of prohibitions.

About This Cookbook

In *The World Religions Cookbook* we explore some of the practices, beliefs, and customs of faith communities as reflected in food served on significant days in the religious calendar of some of the major world faiths. There are many religious traditions found around the world and many subgroups or sects within these main categories. Listings of the major world religions most commonly include the Bahá'í faith, Buddhism, Christianity, Confucianism, Hinduism, Islam, Jainism, Judaism, Shintoism, Sikhism, Taoism, and Zoroastrianism. There are many other religions that are not included in such lists, either because they are relatively new, are concentrated in single countries, or lack a unifying central organization or scripture. The United States has a greater number of

---

Comparative Religious Dietary Laws

Judaism	Eat only animals with cloven hooves who chew cud
	Eat only forequarters of animals
	Eat only fish with scales and fins
	No blood
Islam	No blood
	No pork
	No intoxicating liquor
Sikhism	No beef

Days of the Year

Christianity	No meat or dairy products during Lent (Orthodox)
Judaism	No food preparation on the Sabbath

Time of Day

Islam	No eating between sunrise and sunset during Ramadan
Buddhism	Monks do not eat after midday

Preparation of Food

Judaism	Ritual animal slaughter
	Separate utensils for meat and dairy products
Islam	Ritual animal slaughter
Hinduism	Ritual bathing and donning of clean clothes by Brahmins before eating

Fasts

Christian	40-day great Lent fast before Easter; 40-day Advent fast (Greek Orthodox)
Islam	Month of Ramadan

---

religious groups than any other country in the world, of which the leading five in order of size (number of believers) are Christianity, Judaism, Islam, Buddhism, and Hinduism.

We have chosen to focus on the major world religions that are dominant in the United States: Buddhism and Shintoism, Christianity, Hinduism and Sikhism, Islam, and Judaism. It is important to note that this does not imply that the religions that have been excluded are any less important. For example, the Bahá'í faith is strong in the U.S.; however, because Bahá'ís come from all countries and cultures, there are no distinctively "Bahá'í" food customs or recipes. Zoroastrianism, Confucianism, and Taoism all have some particular food traditions but do not have major followings in the U.S. Nor are Native American religions covered. On the other hand, Shintoism is covered along with Buddhism in chapter 1, because both are usually included in lists of the classical world religions and they have overlapping cultural boundaries. In the end, the choice of what to include has to be limited by space constraints. A selection of cookbooks focusing on specific religions is included in the bibliography for those who may want to explore further.

Chapters begin with brief introductions to the history and beliefs of the religions covered. Each recipe section is organized by major events in the religious calendar and includes brief descriptions of religious festivals as well as particular food meanings and uses. It is important to understand that the relationship between food and religion is constantly changing. The way in which dietary laws are interpreted or obeyed may vary considerably between different communities of believers on a national, regional, community, family, or even individual level. Changes may occur as result of religious reform or revisionism, acculturation, and individual, family, or community adaptations. Immigration provides a good example of how changing circumstances may result in changing attitudes to food as people adapt to new customs and environments. Continued compliance with traditional rules depends on social contexts. Believers who are strict when with members of their own religious group may be willing to be more lax when alone or with a different social group. Thus it is generally not possible to make blanket statements such as ''Jews eat this'' or ''Hindus do not eat that.'' If you do, someone is sure to point out an exception!

When it comes to food at religious celebrations, the same is true. There are some foods that are crucially symbolic to some religious occasions and that are always eaten—no matter what the ethnic origin or cultural background of the believer. However, in many instances it is culture that is decisive. At Christmastime, for instance, there are distinctive food traditions in many countries—dishes that are traditionally prepared and eaten during the holiday season—but these are far from being universal Christian food traditions. Conversely, many dishes eaten on a particular religious occasion may also appear on the table at other times of year. Their use as celebration dishes is related as much to their elaborateness and cultural value as to any specific religious meaning. The Judaism chapter contains recipes for life-cycle events as well.

Many of the world religions have identifiable historical figures who are considered to be founders of the faith responsible for introducing the ideas of the new religion to humankind. (In some instances, such as Hinduism, there is no single human founder.) At the end of each chapter we speculate on what the religious founders may have eaten. In most cases there is no documented evidence of actual recipes or meals consumed, but based on common foods of the era and knowledge of general food customs, we have provided some ''historic'' recipes.

This book is first and foremost a cookbook, not a work of history or religion. It offers 231 recipes from many different countries that we hope you will find enjoyable to make and which will provide you with a taste of diverse cuisines. Because this cookbook draws on cultural practices from around the world, it does not stay only with the familiar, but invites you to explore different taste traditions and different flavor sensations. Preparing and eating the food of other cultures and religions is one way of getting to know more about the rich diversity of our world, and is a step toward mutual understanding and respect built on a common human need for food and sociability.

Recipes are chosen to reflect a wide variety of cultural and religious traditions. The recipes include appetizers, main dishes, side dishes, and desserts. Each recipe includes:

- A brief description of its origins or religious/cultural significance
- A list of ingredients, including quantities and types (e.g., fresh, canned)
- Simple step-by-step instructions for making the recipe; in many recipes, serving hints and suggestions are also provided
- Yield information, indicating how many people the recipe will serve

Some recipes require ethnic ingredients not always available in supermarkets. These can usually be obtained through speciality ethnic stores and markets—particularly in larger urban centers. You can usually purchase nonperishable items through mail-order suppliers if they are not available locally. A glossary is found in the front matter, and substitutes are identified for some of the more exotic ingredients in the recipes. Some recipes will require pre-preparation (e.g., soaking overnight), while others may have several stages of preparation (e.g., partially prepared item must be refrigerated)—so careful planning is needed to ensure that adequate time and storage facilities are available.

All recipes have been adapted and tested by Arno Schmidt.

Safety, Cooking, and Hygiene Tips

- Use only sharp knives.
- When cutting poultry, wash the cutting board and knife immediately with hot water and dry with a paper towel.
- When washing greens, fill a large bowl with water, add greens, then rinse and remove; sand will sink to the bottom. Repeat the process.
- When deep-frying, make sure the pot is wide and high. Fat can boil over and possibly start a fire.
- Turn off heat and leave pots containing hot fat on the stove until the fat has cooled.
- Cover all food in the refrigerator.
- Remember that all measurements are approximate. Ingredients have varying characteristics based on origin, season, storage, and many other factors.
- Baking and roasting times are approximate and depend not only on the accuracy of the oven thermometer but also on the size of the container, air circulation, and many other factors.
- Remember that 1 cup of a dry ingredient might not weigh 8 ounces.
- Measurements for flour are given before sifting.
- Cooking is a skill and an art. Two cooks using identical ingredients and recipes may produce different results.
- Taste food during the cooking process to adjust flavors if necessary. Use a disposable plastic spoon.
- Keep spices in closed containers in a dry, dark place.

1

BUDDHISM AND SHINTOISM

Buddhism originated in India in the sixth century BCE, with Prince Siddhartha Gautama. Born into a wealthy family in what is now called Nepal, the prince was disturbed by the suffering he saw in the ordinary world around him. Renouncing his life of ease, he decided to travel in search of truth and understanding. For six years he wandered the country, following a life of self-denial and near-starvation—sometimes eating only a little bean soup or a single grain of rice. After six years he still had not achieved what he sought—an escape from the sufferings of the world. He realized that starvation was no more the means to spiritual contentment than was wealth. Instead, he embraced the "Middle Way," avoiding extremes of both self-denial and self-indulgence. One day, while meditating under the shade of a bodhi tree, the prince finally achieved the spiritual understanding he sought. From then on he was known as Buddha, the enlightened one, and spent the rest of his life spreading his teachings.

Buddhism is a religion and a philosophy—a way of life that focuses on personal spiritual development and on understanding the true nature of life. Buddhists do not believe in a creator god, and there is no central religious authority. In fact, a buddha is not a specific single person at all, but a term applied to one who has attained wisdom through meditation and contemplation, thus achieving enlightenment. Buddhists believe in reincarnation, seeing life as a cycle of birth and rebirth that continues until enlightenment is achieved. Buddhism teaches that everything is interconnected and that one should always do good and avoid harmful actions. The five basic precepts of Buddhism are: Do not take life; do not steal; do not tell untruths; do not consume liquor or other intoxicants; and do not commit adultery.

From its birthplace in India, Buddhism spread throughout Southeast Asia. The two major branches are known as Theravada and Mahayana, although their fundamental teachings are similar. Zen Buddhism is a mixture of Mahayana and Taoism. It began in China, spread to Korea and Japan, and has become increasingly popular in Europe and North America in the last century. Currently, the world population of Buddhists is about seven hundred million. The greatest concentrations of followers are in China, Japan, Thailand, and Vietnam, with an estimated three to four million in North America. The first Buddhists to arrive in the United States were Chinese. Hired as cheap labor for the railroads and other expanding industries, they established temples in their settlements along the rail lines. Many Buddhists now living in North America are Asian immigrants, although Buddhism has also attracted many adherents who are not of Asian descent. In the Chinatowns of large cities, Buddhist shrines can be seen in businesses and homes. Buddhist monks are easily identified by their saffron-colored robes and shaven heads and can occasionally be seen praying and singing on city streets.

Shintoism

Shintoism, meaning "way of the spirits," is a belief system that seeks to promote harmony between the human and supernatural worlds. In Japan, Shintoism can be traced back to at least 300 BCE. Often considered a way of life rather than a religion, it has no specific founder, no holy books, and no religious laws. The essence of Shintoism is devotion to supernatural "kami" or divine spirits. These spirits are found in all things in heaven and earth and, if treated properly, will intervene to bring success in human affairs. Shinto rituals, held in thousands of public and private shrines throughout Japan, enable people to communicate with the kami. Shinto practitioners make daily offerings and prayers at home shrines and attend regional or national shrines on annual festival days. Before praying, worshippers and casual visitors are asked to purify themselves by washing their hands and mouths. (Most large shrines have a stone washbasin in front.) Salt is another purifier and is used in many ceremonies. In sumo wrestling, a Shinto ritual where prayers are offered for a bountiful harvest, salt is scattered before each bout to purify the contestants and the sumo ring. Shinto rituals close with a ceremonial meal or a ritual drinking of sake, a fermented beverage made with rice (often erroneously referred to as rice wine). In the U.S., most Japanese practice both Shintoism and a form of Mahayana Buddhism.

Food, Diet, and Cooking

There are not very many dietary rules in Buddhism, but fasting or feasting on holidays is common. Buddhists believe in reincarnation, including the possibility of humans being reborn as animals and vice-versa. Consequently, they do not wish to harm living creatures, and many Buddhists are vegetarians. However, meat is not completely forbidden in Buddhist doctrines. Buddha advised monks that meat should be eaten only when the animal had not been specifically killed for consumption. Meat is eaten in small quantities in some Buddhist countries, where it may be obtained from Muslim butchers. Buddhists in Thailand, Myanmar, and Malaysia are more likely to eat meat than Buddhists in India. In maritime countries, fish and seafood are generally accepted as being valuable sources of protein; the issue of not killing animals is rationalized because the fish are not killed but merely removed from the water. Some Mahayana Buddhists in China and Vietnam also avoid eating strong-smelling plants such as onions, garlic, chives, shallots, and leeks, believing that the strong flavors of these vegetables may excite the senses and present a challenge to Buddhists seeking to control their desires. Rules are generally stricter for monks and nuns than for lay people. For example, monks may eat only twice a day—in the morning and at noon, fasting for the rest of the day and night. Lay people can gain merit for themselves and for their dead relatives by preparing food and offering it to the monks.

Southeast Asian recipes are prepared with ingredients cultivated in a wet, tropical climate. Many dishes are highly seasoned. Widely used basic ingredients include lemongrass, ginger, and a variety of fermented fish sauces or fish pastes. Fresh spices are ground when needed. Traditionally this was done with mortar and pestle, but today blenders or small electric grinders are quicker and more efficient. Unlike Western cooking, where ground spices are sprinkled into food, here they are cooked in a little fat over moderate heat to develop flavor. It is left to the cook to determine the amount of hot peppers in each dish!

Zen cooking, developed by monks as a meditative art, focuses on achieving harmony, delicacy, and balance. Buddhist vegetarian chefs have become extremely creative in using gluten, tofu, agar, and other plant products. Soy and pressed wheat gluten (*seitan* or wheat-meat) are very versatile materials and can be manufactured into various shapes and textures. Although they have little flavoring of their own, with the proper seasonings these plant products can mimic various kinds of meat quite closely.

Rice is a long-standing staple of the Japanese diet. Having strong symbolic value, rice is offered in prayer and praise to Shinto deities throughout Japan. Traditionally, it is boiled or steamed. In many Shinto ceremonies, pounded rice cakes called *mochi* are offered to the deities on behalf of the local community by the priest. Shintoism has no dietary restrictions.

Celebration Recipes

Since Buddhism has spread to many countries with diverse climates, traditions, and lifestyles, not all celebration days are universally recognized, nor is it surprising that Buddhist holiday food varies greatly. Calendars are based on a lunar or solilunar year; thus dates of celebrations may differ from country to country.

While the traditional Japanese calendar dates from 660 BCE, the year of the accession to the throne of Emperor Jinmu, Japan's legendary first emperor and descendent of the sun goddess Amaterasu, modern Japan uses the Gregorian solar calendar, the same as in the Western world. In Japan, there are two categories of holidays: *Matsuri* are festivals, mainly of Shinto origin, that relate to the cultivation of rice and the spiritual well-being of the community. *Nencho gyo* are annual events of Chinese or Buddhist origin.

Shogatsu (January 1–3)

This Japanese New Year's Festival is the most important national holiday in Japan, when most businesses close and families gather together. Although of lesser significance outside of Japan, the holiday is commonly observed by Japanese families in North America. On New Year's Eve and New Year's Day many people go to a Buddhist shrine or temple to pray for good health and prosperity in the coming year. In Japan, at midnight on New Year's Eve, Buddhist temple

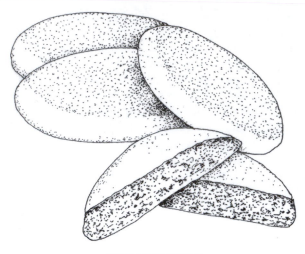

MOCHI RICE CAKES

bells are rung 108 times to purify the 108 sins described in the Buddhist belief system. Homes are decorated with two flattened mochi rice cakes, one large and one small, stacked on top of each other and topped with a tangerine. This edible decoration is displayed in a prominent place in the home and is shared by the whole family after the New Year. While food is an important part of the celebrations, no food preparation takes place on the three holidays. Instead, traditional dishes known as *osechi ryori*, presented in lacquered food boxes known as *jubako*, are prepared ahead of time or purchased from stores and are eaten throughout the three days of the holiday. They symbolize health, longevity, and good fortune.

B-1. Pounded Rice Cakes (*Omochi*)

Omochi, steamed glutinous rice pounded and formed into cakes, are either grilled or served in a soup called *o-zoni*. Bamboo mallets are used to pound the rice, a Shinto New Year's tradition that sometimes takes place at community shrines. Assembled on top of each other, sometimes in graduated sizes, the cakes are decorated with leaves and small oranges or tangerines. Mochi cakes are available year-round in the refrigerated section of most Japanese supermarkets. The cakes are unsalted and stay dry because they do not attract moisture.

Yield: 6 to 10 pieces

Equipment needed: Colander, one-quart saucepan with lid, potato masher, wooden mallet

Ingredients

1 cup mochi gomé (glutinous rice)

10 ounces water

Method

1. Put rice in colander and wash thoroughly.
2. Combine rice and water in saucepan. Cover and bring to a boil over moderate heat.
3. Continue at slow boil 15 minutes.
4. Remove from heat and let stand 10 minutes before lifting lid.
5. When rice is cool enough to handle, mash, then pound and knead it with wet hands into a smooth mass resembling taffy.
6. Shape into patties. Store in refrigerator until ready to use.
7. Mochi cakes can be cooked on the griddle or heated in a toaster oven.

B-2. Basic Soup Stock (*Dashi*)

Dashi is a basic stock made with *katsuobushi* (dried bonito flakes) and *kombu* (kelp) that is used in many soup preparations. Bonito flakes are available packaged in 1-ounce bags and kelp in 4-ounce packages.
Yield: 1 quart
Equipment needed: Soup pot, skimmer or slotted spoon, ladle, strainer

Ingredients

1 piece kombu (about postcard-size)	4¼ cups water 1 ounce bonito flakes

Method

1. Combine kombu and water in pot. Bring to a boil. Remove kombu and discard.
2. Add bonito flakes and bring to a boil again.
3. Steep 20 minutes. Do not stir; let flakes settle to the bottom.
4. Carefully strain through fine sieve, trying to keep stock as clear as possible.

B-3. New Year's Day Soup (*O-zoni*)

There are many regional variations on this most important dish of the New Year's meal. This version is made with miso (fermented soybean paste).
Yield: 6 servings
Equipment needed: 2-quart soup pot

Ingredients

½ cup potatoes, diced 1 quart dashi ½ cup carrots, diced 1 cup daikon, diced (white radish)	4 ounces miso (white) 2 small mochi cakes 3 tablespoons scallion greens, finely sliced

Method

1. Combine potatoes, carrots, and daikon, cover with dashi, and simmer 30 minutes.
2. Cut mochi into bite-size pieces and add to soup. Simmer 5 minutes.
3. Add miso and stir to dissolve. Remove from heat and serve hot, sprinkled with scallions.

B-4. Kanot-Style New Year's Day Soup

This is a more substantial variation of the basic New Year's Day soup. Mirin is a Japanese sweet rice cooking wine.
Yield: 4 to 6 servings
Equipment needed: Cutting board, French knife, 2-quart soup pot

Ingredients

1 quart dashi	1 teaspoon sugar
2 cups napa cabbage, shredded	2 tablespoons miso (white)
1/2 cup carrots, diced	4-ounce enoki mushroom cluster
2 tablespoons soy sauce	4 small mochi cakes
1 tablespoon mirin	1/4 cup scallion greens, sliced
1 teaspoon salt	

Method

1. Combine dashi with cabbage and carrots and bring to a boil. Simmer 15 minutes.
2. Add all spices.
3. Cut rice cakes into quarters and add to soup. Bring to a boil and set aside.
4. Dissolve miso in soup.
5. Wash mushrooms, removing root cluster. Add mushrooms and scallions to soup.
6. Serve hot.

B-5. Pickled Daikon, Cucumber, and Carrot

The most popular vegetables for fermenting are pickled daikon (white radish), cabbage, red and green peppers, cucumbers, and cauliflower. In traditional pickling, the vegetables are salted then placed in a lidded wooden vat. The lid is weighted down with stones, and the salt combines with the moisture in the vegetables creating the pickling brine. Fermented vegetables are served as condiments.
Yield: 1 quart
Equipment needed: Cutting board, French knife, grater, 2-quart stainless steel container, weights

DAIKON

Ingredients

1 pound daikon, peeled	4 ounces red peppers, seeded and sliced
1 pound cucumber, peeled, seeded, and thinly sliced	1 tablespoon salt
1/2 cup carrots, thinly sliced	2 tablespoons soy sauce
	1 teaspoon mustard seeds

Method

1. Thinly slice or grate daikon. (Grated daikon will ferment faster than sliced daikon.)
2. Combine all ingredients in a large bowl, then tightly pack into a non-reactive container.
3. Place plate on top of vegetables and weigh down.
4. Refrigerate and allow to ferment for three or four days. Eventually the salt will draw out moisture from the vegetables.

B-6. Burdock Pickle (*Tataki Gobo*)

Burdock root, or gobo, is well-liked in Japan. Although usually cooked, it can be added raw to salads. Vinegar water helps to keep it from darkening. A popular New Year's condiment, tataki gobo can be prepared ahead.

Yield: 6 to 8 servings

Equipment needed: Large bowl, cutting board, peeler, knife, 1-quart saucepan, frying pan, electric blender

Ingredients

2 pounds gobi (burdock roots), peeled
2 quarts cold water
1/4 cup vinegar
2 cups dashi

2 tablespoons mirin
2 tablespoons soy sauce
1 teaspoon salt

Dressing

4 tablespoons sesame seeds
2 tablespoons sesame paste
2 tablespoons dashi
2 tablespoons sugar

2 tablespoons vinegar
1 teaspoon soy sauce

Method

1. Fill bowl with 2 quarts cold water and add vinegar.
2. Cut burdock into 2-inch sections. Split roots if very thick.
3. Soak burdock in vinegar water for 5 minutes.
4. Remove burdock from vinegar water, add to pan, and cover roots with water. Simmer for 10 minutes. Drain and set aside.
5. Combine dashi with mirin, soy sauce, and salt. Add burdock, bring to a boil, and simmer 30 minutes. Remove from heat and allow to cool.
6. Combine dressing ingredients in blender.
7. Drain cooked burdock, saving cooking liquid.
8. Coat cooked burdock with dressing. If too dry, add some cooking liquid.
9. Refrigerate at least 24 hours before serving.

B-7. Chilled Buckwheat Noodles (*Toshikoshi Soba*)

Representing a long, healthy life, toshikoshi soba uses pressed and dried seaweed called *nori*. Some families serve this dish on New Year's Eve, when soba noodles are available fresh in Japan.

Yield: 4 servings

Equipment needed: 2-quart pot, colander, tongs, cutting board, paring knife, French knife, mixing bowl

Ingredients

10 ounces dried soba noodles
3 sheets nori seaweed
1/2 cup scallions, greens only,
    thinly sliced
1 tablespoon ginger, chopped
1/2 cup cold dashi

2 tablespoons mirin
3 tablespoons dark soy sauce
2 tablespoons hot sesame oil
2 tablespoons oil
1 teaspoon salt

Method

1. Boil noodles about 5 minutes; do not overcook. Rinse and drain to remove excess starch. Chill noodles.
2. Using tongs, carefully hold nori over a low flame to toast. Do not burn. Set nori aside; crumble when cooled.
3. Combine all remaining ingredients to make dressing. Toss noodles with small amount of dressing.
4. Sprinkle with toasted nori. Serve remaining dressing in small bowls.

B-8. New Year Sweet Potato Balls (*Kuri Kinton*)

This substantial dessert can be made ahead of time. It is garnished with kumquats, fruits that symbolize good luck. Fresh kumquats are available during the New Year season, but must be stewed with sugar to become edible. Canned kumquats are available year-round at Asian markets.

Yield: 20 pieces

Equipment needed: 2-quart saucepan, paring knife, ricer, 2-quart heavy saucepan, heavy wooden mixing spoon, 1-quart saucepan, small bowl, cutting board, ladle, small ice cream scoop, deep serving dish with rim

Ingredients

2 pounds sweet potatoes
1/2 cup sugar
1 teaspoon cinnamon
4 tablespoons instant mashed
    potatoes

20 walnut or pecan halves
kumquats, fresh or canned, for
    garnish

Syrup

1 cup sugar
1 cup water
1 tablespoon lemon juice

$1/2$ cup orange juice
1 tablespoon grated orange peel
1 teaspoon arrowroot

Method

1. Wash and scrub potatoes. Bake in 375-degree oven about 40 minutes, or until done.
2. Once potatoes are cool, peel and press through ricer to make puree.
3. Place puree in heavy saucepan; add $1/2$ cup sugar, cinnamon, and instant mashed potatoes.
4. Cook over moderate heat, stirring vigorously. The mix should be very thick; add more instant mashed potatoes if necessary. Set aside to cool.
5. When potato blend is cool enough to handle, use an ice cream scoop to make 20 balls.
6. Put one nut in the center of each ball. Place balls in deep serving dish.
7. Bring sugar, water, lemon juice, orange juice, and orange peel to a boil. Simmer 10 minutes.
8. Make slurry with arrowroot and 2 tablespoons cold water. Add to simmering syrup. Bring to a boil and set aside.
9. When cooled, ladle syrup over potato balls. Serve cold, garnished with kumquats.

Buddhist Mindfulness Days

Throughout the year, Zen Buddhists designate certain days of partial fasting when they honor the peace, joy, and beauty of the moment. Some people eat only a small snack.

B-9. Hot and Spicy Walnuts

The hot curry sauce gives this snack a bite.
Yield: About 4 cups
Equipment needed: Mixing bowl, baking sheets, wok

Ingredients

2 tablespoons Thai-style hot curry sauce
1 teaspoon ginger powder
$1/4$ cup rice vinegar
2 tablespoons sugar

2 tablespoons soy sauce
1 pound walnut halves or pieces
4 tablespoons oil

Method

1. Combine all ingredients except oil. Using gloved hands, blend well so walnuts are evenly coated.

(continued)

2. Spread walnuts on baking sheets and place in 175-degree oven until spices are dry (about an hour).
3. Heat oil in wok; fry walnuts over moderate heat until crisp and brown. Spread out to cool.

Gutor: Day before Tibetan New Year's Eve (February)

Gutor is celebrated on the last two days of the twelfth lunar month, when Tibetans drive away the evil spirits from the old year and prepare to welcome the new. After houses are thoroughly cleaned, festivities include fireworks, dances, and religious ceremonies.

B-10. Tibetan New Year's Eve Soup with Dumplings (*Guthuk*)

This traditional soup features nine large dumplings containing items such as a sugar cube, raw bean, small piece of wood, wool string, piece of charcoal, folded paper, pebble, hot chili pepper, or cotton ball, that predict the diners' New Year's fortune. Wool, for example, is considered to symbolize good-heartedness, while charcoal represents meanness. The dumplings are not eaten but discarded after their contents are revealed.

Yield: 9 servings

Equipment needed: 4-quart saucepan, cutting board, knife, electric mixer with dough hook, work surface, wide soup pot, skimmer, large platter, soup bowls

Ingredients for soup

2 pounds lean beef stew meat	2 teaspoons salt
3 quarts water	1 bay leaf
1 cup onions, sliced	1 teaspoon turmeric seeds
1 cup leeks, sliced	1 teaspoon mustard seeds
1 cup celery, sliced	1/2 teaspoon hot pepper flakes
2 cups napa cabbage, sliced	

Ingredients for dumplings

4 cups flour	1 cup water
1/2 teaspoon salt	Flour for dusting

Method for soup

1. Cube meat; place in large pot. Add 3 quarts water. Bring to a boil and simmer for an hour.
2. Add remaining ingredients and simmer one more hour. Keep soup hot.

Method for dumplings

1. Sift flour into mixing bowl. Add salt.
2. Using mixer with dough hook, at slow speed add enough water to form stiff dough.

3. Move dough to floured work surface; knead and shape into long roll.
4. Divide roll into nine pieces and flatten each piece with the palm of your hand.
5. Place one fortune symbol in each dumpling, moistening dough edges with water to seal.
6. Fill wide soup pot with water. Add dumplings and simmer 15 minutes.
7. Transfer dumplings to large platter and let each participant pick one at random.
8. Serve soup after dumplings are opened and fortunes are revealed.

Losar (February)

Known as *Losar*, the Tibetan New Year is celebrated from the first to the third day of the first lunar month of the year, usually in February of the Western calendar. Tibetans around the world begin preparations for this most popular festival a month in advance. Houses are cleaned and gingko barley seeds are set in water to sprout. On New Year's Day, these seedlings, placed on the family shrine, represent hopes for an abundant harvest. Sheep's heads are fashioned out of colored butter (a porcelain substitute may be used in urban households). In the Tibetan language, "sheep's head" and "the beginning of a year" sound the same, and the sheep has traditionally been regarded with importance. On New Year's Day, people rise early, put on new clothes and their finest jewelry, and make offerings of barley flour mixed with butter and sugar at the family shrine before visiting the temple. After exchanging greetings of "Tashi Delek" with neighbors and offering gifts to the deities, the day is spent feasting on food and drink.

B-11. Rice and Potato Stew (*Droma*)

Although potatoes are not native to Tibet, they are now extensively cultivated because they adapt well to the cool climate. This dish, a traditional combination of two starches, should be slightly sweet and oily. The fat of choice is yak butter, though regular butter is used here.

Yield: 6 servings

Equipment needed: 3-quart heavy saucepan, stirring spoon, peeler, French knife, cutting board

Ingredients

4 ounces (1 stick) butter, melted	1/2 teaspoon garlic, chopped
1/2 cup onions, sliced	1/4 cup rice
1/2 tablespoon paprika	1 cup Maine or new potatoes, diced
1/4 teaspoon coriander, ground	1 quart water
1 teaspoon salt	2 tablespoons cilantro, chopped
1 teaspoon sugar	

(*continued*)

Method

1. Sauté onions in butter until light brown.
2. Add spices, garlic, rice, potatoes, and water. Bring to a boil and simmer 30 minutes.
3. Serve sprinkled with cilantro.

B-12. Sweet Saffron Rice (*Dresi*)

Usually served at weddings and New Year's, this sweet buttered rice with raisins is traditionally flavored with saffron to give it a brilliant yellow color. Due to saffron's high cost, turmeric can be substituted.

Yield: 6 to 8 servings
Equipment needed: 2-quart heavy saucepan, wooden stirring spoon

Ingredients

3 cups milk
1/2 cup plus one teaspoon sugar
1/2 cup rice
1 teaspoon salt
1/4 teaspoon cardamom, ground

1/2 teaspoon saffron (or turmeric), ground
4 ounces (1 stick) butter
1/4 cup raisins

Method

1. Bring milk and 1 teaspoon sugar to a boil. (The sugar helps prevent the milk from scorching.)
2. Wash rice and add to milk with salt and spices. Simmer over low heat, stirring frequently until rice is very soft, about 45 minutes.
3. Add butter and raisins. Serve hot.

B-13. Kapse Fritters

Kapse is a fried sweet made in different shapes and forms. Ambitious cooks shape the dough like lotus flowers.

Yield: 30 to 40 pieces
Equipment needed: Electric mixer with paddle, sifter, work surface, frying pan, skimmer

Ingredients

1/2 cup sugar
4 eggs
4 ounces (1 stick) butter, melted
1 teaspoon grated lemon rind
1/2 cup milk, warmed
Few drops red food coloring

3 1/2 cups flour
1 teaspoon baking powder
Flour for dusting
Fat for frying
Powdered sugar
Honey

Method

1. Combine sugar, eggs, melted butter, lemon rind, milk, and food coloring. Blend at slow speed.
2. Sift flour with baking powder and gradually add to batter at slow speed. A stiff dough will result.
3. Dump dough onto table and knead briefly with floured hands.
4. Shape into small, flat balls, or more elaborate shapes.
5. Deep-fry fritters at around 375 degrees until golden brown.
6. Sprinkle liberally with powdered sugar and drizzle with honey.

Monlam (February or March)

Celebrated in temples worldwide from the fourth to the seventeenth day of the first lunar month, the Tibetan Buddhist Prayer Festival of Monlam is the greatest annual religious activity. Every year since 1409, a carefully crafted butter statue of Buddha has graced the Jokhang Temple in the Tibetan capital of Lhasa. Monks from many monasteries gather to pray in front of the statue, which may tower as much as thirty feet tall. The Chunga Choepa memorial service, or ''Butter Lamp Festival,'' falls on the fifteenth day and is the highlight of Monlam celebrations. Butter is shaped into symbolic forms and lamps fueled with melted butter are lit.

B-14. Monastery Bread

Resembling a large pizza without any toppings, this buttered bread is eaten by monks and served with *bho-cha*, a salted, buttery tea.
Yield: 4 disks
Equipment needed: Sifter, electric mixer with dough hook, rolling pin, baking sheets, pastry brush

Ingredients

4 cups bread flour	2 teaspoons salt
1 package instant dried yeast	$\frac{1}{2}$ teaspoon hot pepper flakes
$1\frac{1}{4}$ cups water	$\frac{1}{2}$ teaspoon cardamom, ground
4 tablespoons sesame seeds	Flour for dusting
4 tablespoons poppy seeds	4 ounces (1 stick) butter, melted
2 tablespoons cumin seeds	

Method

1. Sift flour into mixing bowl.
2. Make well in center; add yeast and $\frac{1}{4}$ cup water.
3. Let stand in warm place until yeast dissolves, about 10 minutes.
4. Add remaining ingredients, except butter.
5. Blend with dough hook at slow speed to smooth dough.

(continued)

6. Knead briefly on floured work surface. Form dough into large ball and cover with flour-dusted kitchen towel.
7. Let rest 1 hour.
8. Divide dough into quarters and roll each into a ball.
9. With rolling pin, flatten each ball into a ½-inch-thick disk.
10. Place disks on baking sheet and brush with melted butter.
11. Bake at 400 degrees until brown and crisp.

B-15. Barley with Mushrooms and Onions

Barley is cultivated in the high mountain valleys. This vegetarian main course uses stock flavored with dried mushrooms.
Yield: 6 servings
Equipment needed: Cutting board, French knife, 2-quart saucepan with lid

Ingredients

4 ounces (1 stick) butter
1 cup pearl barley
2 cups onions, sliced
3 cups vegetable stock (see recipe on page 22)

1 teaspoon hot pepper flakes
1 teaspoon salt

Method

1. Sauté onions in butter until soft.
2. Add remaining ingredients and bring to a boil.
3. Cover pot and simmer over low heat about 40 minutes.

Chinese New Year (January or February)

Chinese New Year, celebrated on the first day of the Chinese Lunar Calendar, is the most important and best-known annual festival for many Asians. Preparations begin about a month beforehand when people start buying presents, decorations, food, and clothes. Houses are cleaned from top to bottom to remove any traces of bad luck; cleaning a house on New Year's Day runs the risk of symbolically sweeping away good luck or even a family member. Doors and windows are often painted, usually red, and decorated with paper scrolls and squares inscribed with blessings and auspicious words such as ''happiness,'' ''wealth,'' and ''longevity.'' On Kitchen Gods' Day, the twenty-fourth day of the month, it is time to appease these gods before they head up to heaven to report on the family's activities. Images of kitchen gods are burned to symbolize their departure. Brushing the images' lips with honey or sugar improves the chances of a good report. On New Year's Eve houses are brightly lit and a family meal is prepared. Doors and windows are sealed to keep in good luck. Fireworks and firecrackers are set off to scare away evil spirits and to welcome back the traveling kitchen gods. Seals are broken on New Year's Day when people head out to visit family and friends.

No single dish is representative of Chinese New Year, but much of the festival food has symbolic meaning. Some names sound similar to characters with lucky connotations, while the shapes or colors of other foods symbolize happiness, prosperity, and good fortune. Kumquat plants, popular as presents, are considered lucky because of their little golden fruits. Trees decorated with red ribbons and kumquats are displayed in many public buildings and private homes like Christmas trees in Western countries.

Foods with Special New Year Meanings

Apples = peace
Candied coconut = togetherness
Candied fruits such as lotus seeds, kumquats, and dates = plenty
Candied melon = good growth and health
Eggs = rebirth and good fortune
Gold foil-wrapped chocolate coins = a wish for riches
Jade = youth and rebirth
Noodles = longevity
Oranges = sweet life
Peanuts = birth and long life
Pomelos = abundance
Sliced lotus root lets the good luck through
Tangerines = good luck
Tomatoes = joy and virtue
Water chestnuts = a wish for many children
Watermelon seeds = a wish for many sons

B-16. Rice Soup

Warming foods, such as hot rice soup containing dried lotus seeds, dried dates, and red beans, are popular during this cold season. Eating rice soup is thought to purify the body for the New Year.

Yield: 6 servings
Equipment needed: Small bowls, 3-quart soup pot

Ingredients

6 ounces dried lotus seeds
6 ounces dried red seedless dates
1/4 cup glutinous rice
3 cups water
2 cups canned chicken stock

1 can (16 ounces) red kidney beans, drained
1/2 tablespoon light soy sauce
2 teaspoons salt

(continued)

LOTUS SEEDS

Method

1. Cover lotus seeds and dates with cold water and let soak for 15 minutes.
2. Bring to a boil and simmer 20 minutes. Set aside.
3. Combine rice and water, bring to a boil, and simmer 10 minutes. Stir frequently.
4. Add chicken stock, beans, and cooked lotus seeds and dates.
5. Continue simmering 20 minutes longer. The rice should be very soft and almost dissolved. Set aside.
6. Add soy sauce. Season with salt if needed.

B-17. Crispy Duck Breast with Vegetables

Chinese cooking is famous for many duck dishes. This one uses a single duck breast.

Yield: 2 servings

Equipment needed: Small bowl, cutting board, French knife, small cast-iron skillet, wok, spatula for wok

Ingredients

½ teaspoon chili powder
½ teaspoon cinnamon
½ teaspoon turmeric
½ teaspoon curry powder
1 single duck breast, boneless, about 10 to 12 ounces
1 tablespoon vegetable oil
1 teaspoon hot sesame oil

¼ cup celery, sliced on bias into slivers
¼ cup onions, sliced
¼ cup canned snow mushrooms, drained
2 ounces red pepper, sliced
2 ounces snow peas, cleaned
2 tablespoons soy sauce

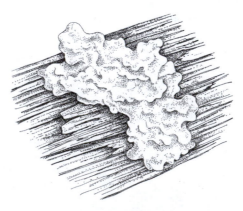

SNOW MUSHROOM

Method

1. Combine all dry spices.
2. Diagonally score duck skin and cover with dry spices on both sides. Chill to let spices penetrate meat.
3. Place duck breast skin side down in skillet. Brown on both sides.
4. Finish cooking in 400-degree oven for 10 minutes. Remove and keep warm.
5. Heat wok and add oils. Quickly stir-fry vegetables.
6. Slice duck breast and serve with vegetables.

B-18. Steamed Dumplings (*Jao Tze*)

A traditional North Chinese dish, these dumplings are served with a soy, ginger, and garlic dipping sauce (recipe follows).
Yield: 30 dumplings
Equipment needed: Electric mixer with dough hook, cutting board, French knife, 1-quart saucepan, colander, mixing bowl, rolling pin, 3-quart saucepan

Ingredients

2 cups flour
$^1/_2$ cup cold water
$1^1/_2$ teaspoons salt
Flour for dusting
8 ounces Chinese cabbage
8 ounces ground pork

1 teaspoon cornstarch
1 tablespoon mild sesame oil
1 tablespoon soy sauce
$^1/_2$ teaspoon sugar
1 cup chopped scallions, including green tops

Method

1. Combine flour with cold water in mixing bowl until stiff dough forms. Put dough on work surface and knead until smooth. Cover with damp kitchen towel and set aside to rest.
2. Chop cabbage into $^1/_2$-inch pieces, boil for about 5 minutes, and drain.
3. Rinse with cold water and squeeze dry.
4. Combine all remaining ingredients.
5. Flour hands and shape dough into a roll. Divide into 30 pieces, flattening each with a rolling pin.
6. Put a teaspoon of filling into each dumpling. Moistening edges, fold over, and seal.
7. Boil dumplings in large saucepan until they float.

B-19. Dumpling Dipping Sauce

Yield: 1 cup
Equipment needed: Bowl, stirring spoon.

(continued)

Ingredients

³/₄ cup mild soy sauce
1 tablespoon ginger, chopped fine
1 tablespoon garlic, chopped fine

1 teaspoon mild sesame oil
1 tablespoon chili sauce

Method

1. Combine all ingredients with wire whisk.

B-20. Eight Precious Pudding (*Nian Gao*)

A traditional South Chinese dish, this steamed, sticky-sweet glutinous rice pudding is named for the eight (or more) colorful, candied fruits it contains, each representing a precious stone.
Yield: 10 to 12 servings
Equipment needed: 2-quart saucepan, 1-quart stainless steel bowl, aluminum foil, large steamer to accommodate the bowl, serving platter

Ingredients

1¹/₂ cups glutinous rice
1 can (14 ounces) coconut milk
2 cups water
1 teaspoon salt
¹/₂ cup sugar

1 tablespoon oil
¹/₂ teaspoon anise, ground
Pan spray
1 cup canned red bean paste
2 cups assorted candied fruits

Method

1. Wash rice; combine with coconut milk. water, and salt. Bring to a boil; simmer 25 minutes.
2. Remove from heat. Stir in sugar, oil, and anise.
3. Pan-spray bowl, fill halfway with cooked rice.
4. Add layer of bean paste and remaining rice, enclosing bean paste completely.
5. Cover with aluminum foil.
6. Place in steamer and steam for 1 hour. Let stand 25 minutes before removing foil.
7. Unmold on platter and sprinkle with candied fruits to resemble precious jewels. Serve warm or cold with fruit syrup.

Nirvana Day (February 15)

Known in India as Parinirvana, this festival celebrates Buddha's death when, at the age of 80, he finally attained nirvana and was released from the cycle of death and rebirth. Mahayana or Theravada Buddhists meditate or visit temples or monasteries, and the day is treated as a social occasion. Nirvana Day celebrations vary throughout the world but usually include food preparation and the exchange of gifts such as money, household goods, or clothing.

B-21. Potato Stew (*Dum Alu*)

Potatoes are cultivated in the northern regions of India and are more popular there than the rice typical of southern Indian cooking. This vegetarian main course is flavored with yogurt and poppy seeds.

Yield: 6 servings

Equipment needed: Baking pan to accommodate the potatoes, cast-iron pan for toasting spices, 2-quart heavy saucepan, wooden stirring spoon

Ingredients

2 pounds Maine or white potatoes	2 tablespoons oil
5 tablespoons ghee or oil	1/2 cup onions, chopped
1/2 teaspoon turmeric	1 tablespoon garlic, chopped
1 teaspoon cumin seeds	1 tablespoon ginger, chopped
1 tablespoon coriander seeds	2 teaspoons salt
1/2 tablespoon peppercorns	2 cups yogurt
1 teaspoon cayenne pepper	1 tablespoon fresh green chilies,
6 cloves	sliced
5 cardamom	1/4 cup poppy seeds
1/4 teaspoon nutmeg	2 tablespoons cilantro, chopped

Method

1. Wash potatoes, leaving skin on. If large, cut into walnut-size chunks.
2. Rub with 3 tablespoons oil and bake at 375 degrees until tender, about 45 minutes.
3. Toast dry spices in frying pan over moderate heat to develop flavor. Set aside.
4. Brown onions, garlic, and ginger in remaining oil.
5. Combine all ingredients except cilantro in heavy 2-quart saucepan.
6. Add enough water to cover potatoes and simmer 10 minutes.
7. Serve sprinkled with cilantro.

B-22. Udon Miso

These flat, wheat-flour noodles are available fresh in Japanese grocery stores.

Yield: 4 servings

Equipment needed: 2-quart soup pot

Ingredients

1 pound fresh udon	1 teaspoon mild sesame oil
1 teaspoon salt	4 tablespoons miso (white)
1 cup dashi	

(continued)

Method

1. Boil noodles in 2 quarts salted water for about 8 minutes.
2. Drain and toss with remaining ingredients.
3. Serve hot as vegetarian main course.

Maka Puja (March)

One of the most important Buddhist celebrations in Sri Lanka and India, Maka Puja day is held on the full moon of the third lunar month (about the last week of February or early March). This festival commemorates the day when 1,250 disciples spontaneously gathered at the Indian city of Rajagaha to hear Lord Buddha preach.

B-23. Indian Pancakes (*Malupa*)

These can be served for dessert or as a meatless brunch dish.
Yield: 8 pancakes
Equipment needed: Flour sifter, bowl, whisk, strainer, 1-quart wide pot, 6-inch frying pan, spatula, tongs, serving platter

Ingredients

½ cup flour, sifted	1 teaspoon salt
½ cup milk	½ teaspoon anise seeds
½ cup light cream	Ghee or oil for frying pancakes

Syrup

1 cup sugar	2 tablespoons rose water
1 cup water	6 cardamom, crushed
2 tablespoons honey	

Method

1. Sift flour and combine with milk, cream, and salt into smooth batter.
2. Put small amount of ghee or oil in frying pan.
3. When hot, ladle in about 2 ounces of batter and swirl to coat bottom of pan.
4. When pancake is brown, flip over and brown on other side.
5. Combine syrup ingredients and bring to a boil. Simmer 5 minutes. Keep warm.
6. Slide pancakes into syrup to coat before serving.

Songkran (April 12 to 15)

The New Year is an important celebration throughout Southeast Asia. In Thailand, it is marked by four days of festivities called Songkran. After the

April harvest is safely in, homage is paid to Buddha with temple offerings of cooked food and fresh fruit. During the traditional ceremony of lustration, images of Buddha are purified and elders are sprinkled with water, ritually cleansing the soul and washing away the old year. Today, this custom has developed into a fun event where anyone venturing into the streets is likely to get a thorough dousing, all in good fun, and quite welcome at the peak of the hot season.

B-24. Thai Pork and Bamboo Shoot Soup
(*Gaeng Chud No Ma*)

Even though Lord Buddha allegedly died from eating tainted pork, it is still a popular ingredient. This dish, influenced by the northern Chinese, features bamboo shoots. Grown from underground root stock and harvested as soon as they poke through the earth, bamboo shoots must be carefully prepared. Fine black hairs at the base of the shoots are irritating to the skin and highly poisonous if consumed. Available canned, fresh bamboo shoots may be purchased at ethnic markets.

Yield: 8 servings

Equipment needed: 3-quart heavy soup pot, mixing spoon, cutting board, knife

Ingredients

2 tablespoons oil
1 tablespoon garlic, chopped
1 teaspoon coriander seeds, crushed
1 teaspoon peppercorns, crushed
1 teaspoon green chilies, sliced
1 teaspoon salt
1 pound boneless pork chops, cut in small cubes

2 tablespoons rice
2 quarts water
1½ tablespoons brown sugar
1 tablespoon fish sauce
1 can (14 ounces) bamboo shoots, braised, drained, and diced
4 scallions, cut in fine strips

Method

1. Sauté garlic, coriander seeds, peppercorns, and chilies in oil over medium heat.
2. Add pork, rice, and water. Bring to a boil and simmer 25 minutes.
3. Add brown sugar, fish sauce, and bamboo shoots.
4. Garnish with scallions and serve with bread.

B-25. Dried Dates

Unlike those available in U.S. markets, these dried dates—popular in Thailand and South China—are hard and resemble brown pebbles. They must be soaked and simmered to become edible.

Yield: 4 servings

Equipment needed: 1-quart saucepan

(continued)

Ingredients

16 ounces dried dates   2 tablespoons lemon juice

Method

1. Cover dates with water and soak 1 hour.
2. Bring to a boil and simmer 25 minutes. Add lemon juice.
3. Serve ice cold.

B-26. Myanmar Tomato Soup with Lemongrass

Although they originated in South America, tomatoes are an established ingredient in Southeast Asian cooking. Lemongrass is another popular flavoring component. This soup can be made with chicken broth or with vegetable stock (recipe follows).
Yield: 5 to 6 servings
Equipment needed: Cutting board, French knife, 2-quart heavy saucepan, stirring spoon, fine strainer, 1-quart saucepan, small bowl, chopsticks, small bowl

Ingredients

4 ounces lemongrass stalk   1 teaspoon salt
2 tablespoons oil   1 tablespoon sugar
1 teaspoon fresh chilies, chopped   1 teaspoon mild sesame oil
$\frac{1}{4}$ cup onions, chopped   1 teaspoon water
1 teaspoon ginger, chopped   2 egg whites
1 cup canned crushed tomatoes   1 tablespoon cilantro, chopped
3 pints chicken or vegetable stock

Method

1. Wash lemongrass, discarding brown leaves, and slice.
2. Cook lemongrass, chilies, onions, and ginger in oil over medium heat for 5 minutes.
3. Add all other ingredients except sesame oil, egg whites, and cilantro.
4. Bring to a boil and simmer 45 minutes. Strain through fine sieve and discard vegetables.
5. Bring soup to a slow boil.
6. Blend sesame oil with water and egg whites. Slowly pour into simmering stock while using chopsticks to pull egg-white mixture into thin strands.
7. Serve at once, sprinkled with cilantro.

B-27. Vegetable Stock for Soup

Garland chrysanthemums, available in Chinese markets, give this soup a unique flavor.

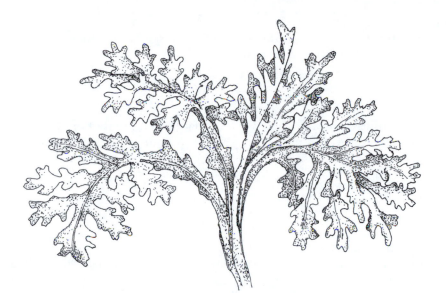

GARLAND CHRYSANTHEMUM

Yield: 1 quart
Equipment needed: Small bowl, cutting board, knife, 3-quart heavy saucepan, wooden spoon, strainer

Ingredients

1 ounce dried Chinese black mushrooms
1 pound napa cabbage
½ pound Chinese garland chrys- anthemums (if available)
½ cup onions, sliced
2 tablespoons oil

1 star anise
1 tablespoon ginger, chopped
1 tablespoon garlic, chopped
2 teaspoons salt
1 teaspoon peppercorns, crushed
1 bay leaf
3 pints water

Method

1. Soak mushrooms in warm water for 1 hour. Carefully remove mush- rooms, leaving sand in bottom of bowl. Discard water.
2. Wash and coarsely chop next three ingredients, but do not peel.
3. Put oil in heavy saucepan and stir-fry chrysanthemums and vegetables over high heat until slightly browned.
4. Add spices and water. Bring to a boil; simmer uncovered for 1 hour.
5. Strain stock, discarding chrysanthemums and vegetables.

B-28. Malaysian Coconut, Tapioca, and Melon Soup

This cold, refreshing soup is much appreciated in hot Thailand. Since it does not contain any meat, the dish can be served to vegetarians.

(continued)

Yield: 8 servings
Equipment needed: 2-quart saucepan, wire whisk, cutting board, knife, paring knife, food processor, large soup bowl

Ingredients

¼ cup minute tapioca	1 tablespoon grated orange peel
4 cups canned coconut milk	1 cup honeydew melon, pureed
1 cup water	1 cup cantaloupe, pureed
½ teaspoon salt	Mint leaves for garnish
¼ cup sugar	

Method

1. Combine tapioca with coconut milk, salt, and water.
2. Bring to a boil and simmer 5 minutes, stirring constantly while mixture thickens.
3. Add sugar and grated orange peel.
4. Stir to cool; refrigerate.
5. Add pureed melons to cold soup. Stir to blend.
6. Serve sprinkled with mint leaves.

Hanamatsuri (April 8)

This Shinto-Buddhist festival, commemorating the birth of Gautama Buddha, means "flower festival" in Japanese. During the celebration, sweet tea is poured over a statue of the infant Buddha symbolizing the sweet rain that is said to have fallen from heaven when Buddha was born. In the United States, where Hanamatsuri has been observed since first-generation immigrants arrived from Japan, a special service may be followed by a community meal.

B-29. Beef Sukiyaki

Beginning in the seventh century CE, eating beef was prohibited in Japan. The custom did not return until 1873 when Japan opened up to Western influences and beef-eating was officially approved by the emperor. One of the most popular dishes of the day was sukiyaki.
Yield: 4 servings
Equipment needed: Cutting board, French knife or Chinese cleaver, wok, wok stirrer, slotted spoon, small bowl, serving dish

Ingredients

3 ounces spinach leaves, washed and drained	8 ounces frozen beef tenderloin
4 ounces fresh shiitake mushrooms	8 ounces tofu (bean curd), cut into 1-inch cubes

1 bunch scallions, trimmed and
   bias-cut into 1-inch slices
2 stalks celery, peeled and bias-
   cut into $1/2$-inch slices
1 cup canned bean sprouts,
   drained

1 tablespoon oil
1 tablespoon sugar
$1/4$ cup water
3 tablespoons soy sauce

Method

1. Wash spinach, drain well, and tear leaves into small pieces. Wash and slice mushrooms.
2. Thinly slice frozen beef tenderloin.
3. Heat oil in wok. Stir-fry beef, adding sugar, soy sauce, and water after meat is cooked.
4. Remove beef with slotted spoon and set aside.
5. Add all other ingredients to wok. Cook quickly at high heat while stirring and tossing with spatula.
6. Return beef to wok, blending all ingredients together.
7. Serve with steamed rice.

Vesak (May)

This most holy Buddhist holiday, commemorating the birth, enlightenment, and death of Buddha, is known throughout Asia by many names, including Visakah Puja or Buddha Purnima in India, Visakha Bucha in Thailand, Waisak in Indonesia, and Wesak in Sri Lanka and Malaysia. Temples are decorated with colorful flags and flowers, and the day is marked with prayers, sermons, religious discourses, processions, and other religious observances. Caged birds or animals are released symbolizing generosity. Buddhists take a ritual bath, wear only white clothes and place gold leaves on Buddha statues in temples. They are encouraged to refrain from eating meat and to share frugal meals with the poor.

B-30. Rice Cooked in Milk (*Kheer*)

Containing no expensive ingredients, this simple rice dish emphasizes the value of frugality. White is the color of respect for Buddha.
Yield: 4 to 6 servings
Equipment needed: Heavy 2-quart saucepan, wooden spoon

Ingredients

1 quart milk
2 tablespoons rice
$1/4$ teaspoon salt

4 cardamom
1 tablespoon sugar

(*continued*)

Method

1. Combine milk, rice, salt, and cardamom in saucepan.
2. Simmer about an hour, stirring occasionally, until milk is reduced by about half.
3. Remove cardamom. Add sugar, stirring well.
4. Pour dessert into shallow serving dish.
5. Serve cold or at room temperature.

Thai Raek Na (May)

This plowing ceremony, still celebrated by Buddhists of Thai ancestry, signals the start of the planting season. A pair of sacred oxen is offered a selection of seven foods; what the oxen choose to eat predicts agricultural production prospects for the coming year. The date has also now become a national holiday called Agriculture Day.

B-31. Shrimp with Spices

Jasmine rice usually accompanies this festive dish. Shrimp serve as a main ingredient in order to conserve scarce agricultural staples until the next harvest.
Yield: 6 servings
Equipment needed: Bowl, wok

Ingredients

3 pounds raw shrimp, peeled	1 teaspoon cardamom, ground
2 teaspoons garlic, chopped	1 teaspoon cloves, ground
2 teaspoons ginger, chopped	1 teaspoon black pepper, crushed
1 teaspoon green chilies, sliced	$1/4$ teaspoon turmeric
1 tablespoon lime or lemon juice	2 tablespoons scallions, greens
$1/2$ teaspoon amchoor powder	only, sliced
1 teaspoon salt	$1/4$ cup oil
1 stick cinnamon, 3 inches long	

Method

1. Combine shrimp with spices, blending well.
2. Refrigerate shrimp at least 2 hours to marinate.
3. Heat oil in wok. Add shrimp. Stir fry quickly until shrimp are pink.
4. Remove from heat and serve.

Dragon Boat Celebration (June)

A popular midsummer event, this Chinese festival recalls the life of Chu Yuan (328–298 BCE), a poet and statesman who drowned himself in Tungting Lake as a protest against corruption within the royal court. Today, boats sporting dragon heads compete in races and reenact the search for Chu Yuan. *Zongzi* is a traditional festival food that dates back to the time of Chu Yuan when people cast pieces of bamboo filled with rice into the river to honor him. One day, the soul of Chu Yuan complained that the river dragon was stealing his food. To prevent this, the bamboo tubes were sealed with leaves and tied with silk strings. Today's zongzi are glutinous rice dumplings, steamed and wrapped in bamboo leaves.

B-32. Zongzi

Zongzi are made in different shapes with a variety of fillings, including hard-boiled eggs, bean paste, dates, fruits, sweet potatoes, walnuts, mushrooms, meats, and dried Chinese red dates. The most popular shapes are triangular and pyramidal. Although fresh bamboo leaves are preferred, they are difficult to obtain and aluminum foil can be used as a substitute. However, the zongzi will lack the traditional flavor and aroma.

Yield: 20 pieces
Equipment needed: Mixing bowls, 2-quart pot, cutting board, knife, steamer basket, pot and lid

Ingredients

8 ounces glutinous rice
10 ounces dried Chinese red dates
1 teaspoon soy sauce
1 teaspoon salt
1 teaspoon sesame oil

Bamboo leaves or aluminum foil
  cut into 5-inch squares, as
  needed
Pan spray
Kitchen twine

Method

1. In separate bowls, cover rice and dates with water and soak overnight.
2. Drain. Boil rice in 1 cup water, cover, and remove from heat.
3. When cool, season rice with soy sauce, salt, and sesame oil.

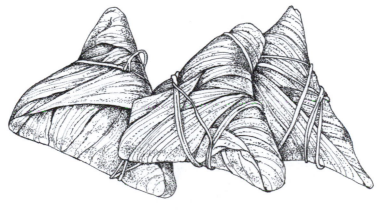

ZONGZI

(continued)

4. Lay bamboo leaves (or foil) on work surface and spray lightly with pan spray.
5. Fill each leaf with 1 tablespoon rice and two or three dates.
6. Shape leaves into bundles and tie loosely with string. (Rice will expand while cooking.)
7. Put bundles in steamer basket and steam for about an hour.

Asalha Puja (July)

This Thai festival commemorates the first teachings Buddha delivered to his early disciples and marks the beginning of the Buddhist religion. During the celebration, many young men in Thailand enter a monastery for a brief stay marked by fasting. Traditionally, a nourishing soup is served beforehand.

B-33. Hot and Sour Shrimp Soup (*Dom Yam Gung*)

This rich, seasoned broth is a delicious combination of lemongrass, lime juice, chilies, and shrimp.
Yield: 6 to 8 servings
Equipment needed: 4-quart saucepan, grater, cutting board, French knife, strainer

Ingredients

2 pounds small shrimp, in shell
1 tablespoon vegetable oil
3 ounces lemongrass, cleaned and cut into chunks
1 teaspoon grated lime peel
1 tablespoon chilies, chopped
2 tablespoons lime juice
8 cups chicken stock or basic vegetable stock (see recipe, p. 22)

2 tablespoons fish sauce
1 teaspoon salt
1 teaspoon sugar
2 tablespoons arrowroot
3 tablespoons cold water
4 tablespoons chopped cilantro
2 scallions, washed and cut into $\frac{1}{2}$-inch inch pieces

Method

1. Peel shrimp, saving shells; set shrimp aside.
2. Sauté shells and oil in saucepan until pink, stirring frequently.
3. Add lemongrass, lime peel, and chilies.
4. Simmer 30 minutes. Strain, discard shrimp shells. Bring soup to a boil again.
5. Blend arrowroot with cold water to make slurry. Add to simmering soup, stirring. (Soup will thicken.)
6. Add shrimp; simmer 5 minutes.
7. Add remaining ingredients. Serve at once.

B-34. Adzuki Beans and Rice with Sesame

These small, reddish-brown beans, popular in Japanese and Thai cooking, are available in health food stores.
Yield: 6 servings
Equipment needed: 2-quart saucepan, frying pan

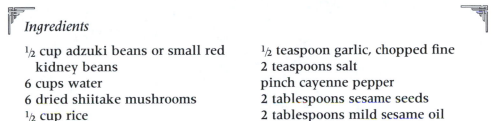

Ingredients

½ cup adzuki beans or small red kidney beans	½ teaspoon garlic, chopped fine
6 cups water	2 teaspoons salt
6 dried shiitake mushrooms	pinch cayenne pepper
½ cup rice	2 tablespoons sesame seeds
	2 tablespoons mild sesame oil

Method

1. Cover beans with 4 cups water, bring to a boil, and simmer one hour.
2. Cover mushrooms with cold water and soak 25 minutes.
3. Discard stems and finely chop mushrooms; add to beans.
4. Add rice, garlic, salt, cayenne pepper, and 2 cups water. Bring to a boil and simmer 25 minutes.
5. Toast sesame seeds in frying pan until light brown.
6. Serve rice and beans sprinkled with toasted sesame seeds and drizzled with sesame oil.

Bodhidharma Day (October)

This day honors the Buddhist philosopher Bodhidharma (470–543 CE), who is considered to be the founder of Zen Buddhism. Born in India, Bodhidharma traveled to China to spread Buddhist teachings and is credited with founding the famous Shaolin system of martial arts. Following are two recipes, one Indian and one Thai.

B-35. Potato Stew with Asafetida

Zen Buddhists are vegetarians. Asafetida, available in Indian stores as a paste or as powder, is a smelly resin that adds a unique flavor to this simple dish.
Yield: 4 servings
Equipment needed: Colander, paring knife, 2-quart pot, 3-quart pot

Ingredients

2 pounds red bliss potatoes, washed, unpeeled, and cut into evenly sized pieces	2 tablespoons ghee or oil
	1 teaspoon asafetida powder
	1 teaspoon cumin, ground

(continued)

ASAFETIDA

½ teaspoon hot pepper, ground	1 teaspoon sugar
1 teaspoon turmeric, ground	2 cups canned tomato juice
1 teaspoon paprika	1 cup water
1 teaspoon salt	

Method

1. Cover potatoes with water and simmer 5 minutes. Drain.
2. Heat ghee or oil, add all spices.
3. Cook over low heat to develop flavor.
4. Add potatoes, tomato juice, and 1 cup water.
5. Simmer 20 minutes.

B-36. Chinese Aromatic Fried Rice

This dish emphasizes the frugal vegetarian lifestyle of Zen Buddhism and offers an ingenious way to use leftover rice. There are many versions, often containing bacon or smoked pork.

Yield: 4 servings

Equipment needed: 2-quart saucepan, small bowl, mixing spoon, colander, wok, small frying pan

Ingredients

4 tablespoons oil	½ cup scallions, greens only,
½ cup onions, chopped	slivered

1 teaspoon ginger, chopped
1 teaspoon garlic, chopped
2 cups long-grain rice, cooked
1 teaspoon chili bean sauce
1/4 teaspoon salt

2 teaspoons oil
3 eggs
1 tablespoon water
2 tablespoons cilantro, chopped

Method

1. Sauté onions, scallions, ginger, and garlic in 4 tablespoons oil over moderate heat until light brown.
2. Add rice, chili bean sauce, and salt. Increase heat; stirring constantly to heat through.
3. Blend eggs with water. Heat 2 teaspoons oil in small pan, add eggs, and scramble. Add scrambled eggs to rice.
4. Serve at once, sprinkled with cilantro.

Bodhi Day (December)

On this day, Buddhists in the Mayahana tradition celebrate Buddha's attainment of enlightenment following years of searching for spiritual truth. Once Buddha understood the nature and causes of suffering and what could be done about it, he formulated the founding principles of Buddhism, known as the Four Noble Truths. Meditation is an important part of the celebration, but many Buddhists may also share a meal.

B-37. Stir-Fried Shrimp with Jasmine Tea Leaves

This dish shows both Southeast Asian and Chinese influences. Tea is a popular flavoring component in Southeast Asia, while adding egg whites to wok-prepared dishes is popular in China.
Yield: 4 servings
Equipment needed: Small pot, tray, wok, wok spatula

Ingredients

1 teaspoon jasmine tea leaves
1/4 cup water
1 pound raw shrimp, peeled and deveined
4 teaspoons cornstarch

4 tablespoons peanut oil
1/4 cup scallions, sliced, including greens
1 tablespoon soy sauce
1 egg white

Method

1. Cover tea leaves with boiling water; set aside.
2. Rinse and drain shrimp; press out excess water.
3. Spread shrimp on tray and evenly dust with cornstarch.

(*continued*)

4. Heat oil in wok or frying pan, add shrimp, and cook for 5 minutes over high heat.
5. Add scallions and cook briefly.
6. Add soy sauce and tea leaves, including soaking water.
7. Bring to a boil. Stir in egg white.
8. Serve with rice.

What Would Buddha Have Eaten?

While the teachings of Buddhism prohibit the taking of life, thereby seeming to support vegetarianism, meat-eating is allowed in certain circumstances. Monks, whose livelihood depends on begging, cannot refuse offerings containing meat. It is likely that even Buddha himself ate meat; some believe he died after consuming tainted pork. However, this recipe is a vegetarian one, based on ingredients available during Buddha's lifetime.

B-38. Spiced Rice with Lotus Root and Mango

Similar in taste to water chestnuts, lotus roots are available fresh or canned in Asian markets.
Yield: 4 main course servings
Equipment needed: Potato peeler, cutting board, paring knife, French knife, small pot, 2-quart heavy saucepan with lid

Ingredients

1 pound raw lotus roots	10 peppercorns, crushed
4 tablespoons ghee or oil	1 teaspoon ginger, chopped
6 black cardamom, crushed	$\frac{1}{2}$ cup scallions, cut in 1-inch
1 cinnamon stick, about 3 inches	pieces
$\frac{1}{4}$ teaspoon mace	1 cup rice
$\frac{1}{4}$ teaspoon turmeric	$2\frac{1}{2}$ cups water
5 whole cloves	1 teaspoon salt
	1 cup mango, not too ripe, sliced

Method

1. Peel lotus root; remove ends (about 12 ounces will remain).
2. Slice, cover with water, and simmer 20 minutes. Set aside.
3. Sauté all dry spices in ghee or oil over moderate heat.
4. Add ginger and scallions, cooking briefly to blend flavors.
5. Add rice and sauté briefly. Add drained lotus root.
6. Add water, bring to a boil. and simmer, covered, 25 minutes.
7. Stir in mango slices.

Note: Spices should not be removed, but should not be eaten.

❦ 2 ❦

CHRISTIANITY

Christianity originated in the Middle East about two thousand years ago in what is now Israel but was then the Roman-occupied province of Judea. The religion is based on the life and teachings of Jesus Christ, who Christians believe was the son of God sent to earth to save humanity from its sins. Jesus encouraged his followers to be less concerned with material possessions and earthly benefits than about spiritual rewards in a future heaven. By mixing freely with the poor and the sick and sharing food with all, he challenged social rules about status and impurity. Jesus preached for only three years, but his ideas and behaviors were seen as a threat by those in power. According to the Bible, the holy book of Christianity, Jesus was put to death by the Romans, but three days later he rose from the dead and ascended into heaven.

Christianity eventually became the official religion of the Roman Empire. In 1054 CE there was a major split between the Western Catholic church centered in Rome and the Eastern Orthodox Church based in Constantinople. In the sixteenth century, the Western church again divided between Catholicism and the many branches of Protestantism. Through the work of missionaries and colonizers, Christianity spread rapidly around the globe. Today, Christianity's more than two billion followers make it the world's most widespread religion. Some 160 million Americans belong to one of the many Christian denominations, making it the largest religion in the U.S. Christian holidays are celebrated by a large percentage of the world's population, even in countries where Christians are a minority.

Food Traditions in the United States

The following is a very brief overview of the cultural origins of Christian sects in the United States that are, in turn, reflected in many of the recipes that follow. It is important to understand that food habits are closely linked to culture, meaning that the typical dishes eaten by members of particular sects when celebrating a religious holiday also reflect cultural food influences.

Catholicism

Maryland was the only settlement in early America that was originally Catholic. However, in the nineteenth and twentieth centuries, immigrants from Catholic Ireland and southern Italy formed a large portion of the U.S. population. Portuguese fishermen and their families established small Catholic communities in New England, while many Catholic Germans, Hungarians, and Poles settled in the industrial areas of the Midwest. Spanish colonial missionaries brought Catholicism to California, Florida, and Texas, while France had similar influences on Louisiana. Devout Catholics observe several feast and fast days during the year. Although few foods are associated with these feasts worldwide, Catholics, including those in the United States, observe local food traditions. The Catholic Church recognizes many saints and martyrs, whose anniversaries may be marked with religious devotions and commemorations. In some countries, more than 160 religious holidays are listed on the church calendar, although many of them are now celebrated only in church or privately. Some examples of these holidays are included in the recipe section.

Protestantism

There are numerous Protestant sects in the United States. The only feast days common to most Protestant religions are Christmas and Easter, but some denominations celebrate specific holidays honoring saints or historic church commemorations. The only denominations with dietary laws fundamental to their faith are Mormons (Church of Jesus Christ of Latter-day Saints) and Seventh-Day Adventists. The largest denominations are listed in alphabetical order below.

- The modern **Baptist** movement originated in England and Holland in the early seventeenth century. The majority of Baptist churches in the United States are located in the South, and their food traditions reflect this heritage.
- The **Episcopal** Church in the United States was officially organized in Philadelphia in 1789. Food traditions are based on local customs or English dishes.
- The first **Lutheran** congregation in North America was founded in 1638 in Wilmington, Delaware. German Lutherans arrived in the country between 1860 and 1920, while Scandinavian Lutherans settled in the prairie states—especially in Minnesota, Nebraska, and North and South Dakota. Lutherans celebrate all Christian holidays; their food traditions reflect their German and Scandinavian heritage.
- **Mennonites** from German-speaking Switzerland, and the **Amish** arrived in Pennsylvania in the early 1700s, where they became known as Pennsylvania Dutch—not because of any connection with Holland, but because they spoke Deutsch (German). Later, a large Mennonite group from the Crimea settled in the prairie states. The Amish and Mennonites celebrate Advent, Christmas, and Easter. Their hearty and simple food has become well known.

- **Methodist** immigrants from England arrived in the American colonies in the 1760s and form the third-largest Protestant group in the United States today. Food traditions are associated with cultural background rather than specific religious occasions.
- The **Moravian** Church originated in eastern Bohemia and Moravia, now part of the Czech Republic. Moravians came to Pennsylvania in 1741 and purchased five hundred acres to create the settlement of Bethlehem. Other congregations were established in New Jersey, Maryland, and North Carolina. Moravian food traditions are based on Czech and Austrian food, and memorial days of special significance to the history and spiritual life of the Moravian Church are celebrated.
- In 1830, Joseph Smith founded the Church of Jesus Christ of Latter-day Saints (abbreviated as LDS), a group generally known as **Mormons**. The headquarters of the church is in Salt Lake City, Utah. Mormons are encouraged to eat mostly grains, to limit meat dishes, and to shun alcohol, tea, and tobacco.
- In 1681 King Charles II of England gave land in what was to become Pennsylvania, to the **Quaker** leader William Penn. The Quakers, also known as the Society of Friends, are peaceful people who worship in silence without structured religious services or clergy. They follow no dietary restrictions. Quaker dishes are robust and often resemble Amish food, but have no significant religious meaning.
- The **Seventh-Day Adventist** church was officially organized in Battle Creek, Michigan, in 1863. Seventh-Day Adventists emphasize healthy eating. About half are lacto-ovo-vegetarians (milk and eggs are eaten but meat is usually avoided). Alcoholic beverages are prohibited, and caffeine-containing drinks are not recommended. Water is consumed before and after meals, and snacking is discouraged. Strong seasonings and condiments, such as pepper and mustard, are avoided.

Orthodoxy

Orthodox Christians in the United States usually belong to ethnic groups that brought their religious affiliations with them when they emigrated. In many cases, their celebrations and food are still anchored in the traditions of their home countries. Major Orthodox denominations in the U.S. are the Greek, Russian, and Serbian Orthodox Churches. Major Greek and Serbian centers are located in New York City's borough of Queens. The Coptic Orthodox Church, which originated in Egypt in the fifth century CE, has U.S. congregations in Jersey City, New Jersey, and Los Angeles. The Orthodox Church in America became established as an independent body in 1970.

Food, Diet, and Cooking

With the few exceptions mentioned above, dietary rules and food taboos are not prominent among modern Christian denominations. Early Christianity was associated with asceticism; this persisted into the eighteenth and nineteenth centuries when frugal eating was part and parcel of religious morality. The Catholic Church had strict rules regarding fasting during Lent: Some religious orders did not serve any meat at all, while many of the faithful observed one or more meatless days each week. In the Middle Ages, doctrine required that people abstain from eating meat on Fridays, in remembrance of the day of the week on which Jesus died. Fish was needed to supply protein on meatless days. Cod, caught in the North Atlantic, then cured and dried in Scandinavia and in Mediterranean countries, became a meat substitute even in countries where fresh seafood was abundant. Since 1966, Catholics have not been required to observe meatless Fridays, though many continue to do so.

Bread is of central symbolic importance in Christianity. In both the Western and Eastern traditions it is part of the sacrament of Holy Communion, in which it is believed to be transformed into the Body of Christ. Eggs also have symbolic value, particularly at Easter when they represent renewed life.

Celebration Recipes

The three religious holidays celebrated by most, if not all, Christians are Christmas, Easter, and Pentecost. Lent and Advent are considered periods of fasting and are observed to varying degrees by all Christian religions. Other holidays and celebrations are exclusive to particular sects or cultural groups. For example, Catholics, some Protestants, and Orthodox churches honor saints on feast days, while a number of other Protestant denominations do not recognize any saints at all. Food is an important part of the celebration of Christian religious holidays, but there are no universal menus; what is eaten is largely influenced by ethnic and cultural background. In many families, new food "traditions" have been invented or ancient religious holiday customs have been successfully blended with secular traditions.

The Orthodox Church year begins on September 1 and includes both movable and fixed celebrations. Fixed festivals are observed thirteen days after those of the Western churches, while movable celebrations are determined by the date of Easter. In the recipe section, movable festivals are listed in the month in which they most commonly occur.

Advent (December)

The four Sundays before the celebration of the birth of Jesus are called Advent and signal the beginning of the Christian church year. Various religious events are observed throughout the world and, for some, this is a time of introspection and partial fasting. Four symbolic candles are placed in an evergreen wreath and one is lit every Sunday as Christians gather to prepare for the coming of Christ.

C-1. Tyrolean Dried Fruit Bread (*Kletzenbrot*)

In many countries it is traditional during the Advent season to make special breads and cookies for Christmas. Tyrolean farmers baked *kletzen*, a bread made with dried Alpine-grown apples and pears that keeps moist for many weeks. Today, a variety of dried fruits and nuts are used in this recipe.

Yield: 2 loaves

Equipment needed: Saucepan, flour sifter, large mixing bowl, mixing spoon, rubber spatula, loaf pan

Ingredients

1 cup buttermilk
1/2 cup brown sugar
1 cup whole-wheat flour
1/2 cup all-purpose flour
1 1/2 teaspoons baking powder
1 teaspoon baking soda
1/4 teaspoon salt
1/2 cup walnuts, chopped

1/2 cup prunes, chopped
1/2 cup dried apricots, chopped
1/2 cup dried apples, chopped
1/2 cup raisins
1/2 cup currants
1/2 cup candied cherry halves
Pan spray
Flour for dusting

Method

1. Warm buttermilk and add brown sugar to dissolve. Cool.
2. Sift the flours, baking powder, baking soda, and salt into a bowl.
3. Add the buttermilk and sugar mixture, blending into a smooth batter.
4. Fold in nuts and dried fruits.
5. Spray loaf pan, dust with flour, and pour in batter.
6. Bake at 350 degrees for about an hour.

C-2. Amish Apple Tarts on Cabbage Leaves

In the eighteenth century, baking in wood-fired hearth ovens was an unreliable process that produced uneven results. Pennsylvania Dutch settlers found that baking pastries on cabbage leaves not only provided some protection from oven hot spots but also added flavor.

Yield: 10 pieces
Equipment: Work table, mixing bowl, rolling pin, 4-inch round cookie cutter, knife

Ingredients

2 cups all-purpose flour
2 tablespoons sugar
8 ounces salted butter at room
   temperature

2 egg yolks
3 tablespoons cold water
1/4 teaspoon mace, ground
1/4 teaspoon pepper, ground

Filling

6 or 7 Red Delicious apples
2 tablespoons flour
3/4 cup brown sugar

1/4 teaspoon cinnamon, ground
10 large Savoy cabbage leaves

Method

1. Sift flour into mixing bowl and make a well in center.
2. Place all remaining dough ingredients in well and blend with fingers until all flour is absorbed.

(continued)

3. Move dough to work surface, knead ingredients together, and shape into ball. Wrap in plastic and refrigerate 1 hour.
4. Peel apples and cut into ½-inch cubes.
5. Combine apples in mixing bowl with flour, brown sugar, and cinnamon.
6. Wash and drain cabbage leaves. Flatten with rolling pin.
7. Roll dough on floured work surface to about ¼-inch thickness.
8. Cut 20 rounds with cookie cutter and place 1 tablespoon of apple filling on 10 rounds.
9. Moisten edges with water and cover with remaining dough rounds. Seal edges by pressing down.
10. Spray cookie sheet, cover with cabbage leaves, and place apple tarts on top.
11. Bake at 375 degrees for 40 minutes, or until tarts are browned. Cabbage leaves will wilt and brown.
12. Eat with cabbage leaves.

C-3. Candy Crisps (*Zuckerstangen*)

A beloved German tradition, the Advent calendar has twenty-four numbered doors that are opened on successive days to reveal a seasonal or religious picture or, today, perhaps a chocolate or small toy. Hot chocolate, accompanied by *zuckerstangen*, may be served as the family opens the calendar. Rice wafer paper is used as a base for this candy's soft dough.

Yield: About 20 pieces

Equipment: Electric mixer with paddle, grater, pastry bag with ½-inch round tip, baking sheets

Ingredients

1 cup sugar	10 sheets rice wafer paper
4 eggs	Pan spray
2 teaspoons grated lemon peel	Sugar for topping
1½ cups flour	

Method

1. Combine sugar, eggs, and lemon peel in bowl of mixer.
2. Blend at medium speed until foamy.
3. Blend in flour; do not overmix.
4. Spray cookie sheets and put rice wafer paper on top.
5. With pastry bag, pipe strips about 3 inches long onto rice paper. Leave space between strips, as dough will spread.
6. Let rest for 30 minutes at room temperature to allow crust to form.
7. Sprinkle with sugar then bake at 350 degrees until light brown.

C-4. German Gingerbread (*Lebkuchen*)

Before sugar was widely available, honey was used to sweeten baked goods. Bakers discovered that natural fermentation caused gas bubbles to form in honeyed dough stored for a few weeks in a cool location. These bubbles made the bread more palatable. *Lebkuchen* dough was started in November, allowed to ferment, and baked in December. Exotic spices were added as a special treat. People loved the honey-spiced breads, and Lebkuchen became a traditional part of German Christmas celebrations.

Yield: About five dozen, depending on shape and size

Equipment needed: Small saucepan, electric mixer with paddle, flour sifter, work surface, dough scraper, plastic wrap, rolling pin, cookie cutter, cookie sheet, pastry brush

Ingredients

$\frac{1}{2}$ cup honey
2 tablespoons corn syrup
1 cup brown sugar
$\frac{1}{4}$ cup water
1 teaspoon vanilla extract
2 eggs
4 cups flour
1 cup confectioners sugar
Juice of one lemon

Water as needed
$\frac{1}{4}$ teaspoon baking soda
$\frac{1}{4}$ teaspoon cinnamon
$\frac{1}{4}$ teaspoon cloves, ground
$\frac{1}{4}$ teaspoon ginger, ground
1 cup almonds, chopped
Flour for dusting
Pan spray

Method

1. Combine honey, corn syrup, brown sugar, and $\frac{1}{4}$ cup water.
2. Bring to a boil and pour into mixing bowl. Add vanilla extract. Cool to room temperature. Add eggs.
3. Sift flour with spices and baking soda and add to mixing bowl.
4. Add almonds.
5. Blend at low speed to combine all ingredients. Dough will be stiff.
6. Move to floured work surface, knead, and shape into ball.
7. Cover with plastic wrap and let dough rest 2 hours.
8. Make icing by blending confectioners sugar with lemon juice. Add water as needed to make thick liquid. If lemon is very large, more sugar may be added.
9. Divide dough and roll $\frac{1}{4}$ inch thick. Cut into shapes. (Favorites are Santa Claus, stars, and hearts.)
10. Place on oiled cookie sheets and bake at 350 degrees until light brown.
11. Cool; brush on icing.

St. Nicholas's Day (December 6th)

''Santa Claus'' comes from the Dutch *Sinterklaas*, or St. Nicholas. St. Nicholas has been venerated as the patron saint of children and sailors since the tenth century.

C-5. Santa Claus Almond Cookies

On St. Nicholas's Eve, Dutch children put a shoe containing bread, hay, or a carrot in front of the fireplace for Sinterklaas's horse. The next morning, the food has been replaced with a cookie!

Yield: 5 dozen

Equipment needed: Flour sifter, work surface, paring knife, cookie sheet, spatula

Ingredients

2 cups flour
2 teaspoons baking powder
10 ounces (2½ sticks) butter or margarine
½ cup brown sugar
1 cup almonds, chopped

1 teaspoon cinnamon
1 teaspoon cardamom, ground
½ teaspoon nutmeg
1 egg
Flour for dusting
Granulated colored sugar

Method

1. Sift flour and baking powder onto work surface. Make a well in center.
2. Cut butter in small pieces and put in well.
3. Add all other ingredients.
4. Knead to form stiff dough.
5. Roll into large ball, cover with plastic wrap, and let rest at room temperature for 30 minutes.
6. Divide dough into walnut-size pieces and roll each piece in granulated sugar.
7. Flatten balls and place on cookie sheet.
8. Bake at 375 degrees until cookies are brown.
9. Remove immediately with spatula while cookies are still hot. (Once cold, cookies are hard to remove.)

C-6. Serbian Beans in Tomato Sauce

In the Orthodox year, St. Nicholas's Day is celebrated on December 19. The red color of this favorite Serbian dish heralds the approach of Christmas.

Yield: 10 servings

Equipment needed: 2-quart heavy saucepan, wooden mixing spoon, slotted spoon, ladle

Ingredients

1½ cups borlotti beans or other dry white beans
1 bay leaf
6 tablespoons lard or oil
½ cup onions, chopped
2 teaspoons garlic, chopped

1½ cups canned crushed tomatoes
2 teaspoons sugar
½ teaspoon hot pepper
2 teaspoons paprika
2 teaspoons salt
1 teaspoon vinegar

Method

1. Soak beans overnight, then rinse, cover generously with water, add bay leaf, and simmer until tender (an hour or longer). Set aside.
2. Cook onions and garlic in fat until light brown. Add tomatoes and spices.
3. Bring to a boil and simmer 20 minutes.
4. Add drained beans and, if necessary, some bean water. Simmer 20 more minutes. Beans should resemble a light porridge when done.
5. Serve hot or cold with wheat bread and Serbian kajmak cheese made from ewe's milk. Feta cheese can be substituted.

Día de Nuestra Señora de Guadalupe (December 12)

In December 1531, the Virgin Mary is said to have appeared three times to Juan Diego, a Mexican Indian woodcutter. Today, Mexicans across North America celebrate Día de Nuestra Señora de Guadalupe. Decorated statues of Mexico's patron saint are displayed, and there are solemn processions, dancing, and gifts of food. Millions of Mexicans make a pilgrimage to Mexico City's Basilica de Guadalupe, on the site where the Virgin reportedly appeared.

C-7. Mexican Chicken and Vegetable Soup (*Caldo Tlalpeño*)

This hearty soup is served with fried tortilla chips.
Yield: 6 servings
Equipment needed: 3-quart soup pot, cutting board, peeler, knife

Ingredients

½ cup chickpeas (garbanzos)
8 cups chicken broth (recipe follows)
1 teaspoon salt
1 teaspoon cumin, ground
1 cup fresh carrots, sliced
8 ounces fresh string beans
1 cup canned crushed tomatoes

1 cup cooked chicken meat, cubed
1 canned medium-size chipotle chili, cut in strips
1 medium-size ripe avocado
1 lime
4 tablespoons cilantro leaves, chopped
Tortilla chips

Method

1. Soak chickpeas overnight. Drain, discard water.
2. Simmer in chicken broth until tender, about an hour.
3. Add salt, cumin, and sliced carrots.
4. Clean string beans and cut into 1-inch pieces. Add to soup with canned tomatoes.

CHIPOTLE CHILI

(*continued*)

5. Simmer until vegetables are tender.
6. Add chicken and chipotle chili.
7. Peel and dice avocado. Cut lime into six slices. Put avocado, lime, and cilantro in large soup tureen or six small soup bowls.
8. Ladle soup on top. Serve with tortilla chips.

C-8. Mexican Chicken Broth (*Caldo de Pollo*)

Yield: 2 quarts
Equipment needed: 4-quart soup pot, knife, strainer

Ingredients

3½- to 4-pound boiling chicken	1 bay leaf
½ cup carrots, diced	½ teaspoon peppercorns
½ cup celery, diced	½ teaspoon coriander seeds, crushed
½ cup onions, diced	
1 teaspoon garlic, chopped	1 teaspoon cumin, ground

Method

1. Wash chicken; remove liver and reserve for other use. Put chicken and giblets in pot, cover with water, bring to a boil, and simmer 1 hour.
2. Add remaining ingredients. Simmer about 40 minutes longer or until chicken is tender.
3. Remove stock from heat and let cool. When cold, remove chicken, strain stock, and refrigerate. Skim accumulated solidified fat from top.
4. Remove chicken meat from bones.

Las Posadas (December 16–24)

Celebrated primarily in Mexico and Central America, this holiday period commemorates Mary and Joseph's journey to Bethlehem and their search for lodgings. *Posada* means lodging house or inn. Each evening, in villages and neighborhoods, the search is reenacted and people gather for house parties. There is plenty of food and drink—including candy for the kids!

C-9. Mexican Pork Soup (*Pozole*)

Dating from pre-Columbian times, this thick soup made from pork and hominy is a favorite in Mexico and the southwestern United States. To make hominy, corn was soaked and cooked in a lime solution to remove the hard hull from the grain. This process provided the added nutritional benefit of making vitamins and protein easier for the body to absorb. Ground hominy is known as *masa harina* and is used in making corn tortillas.

Yield: 10 to 12 servings

Equipment needed: 4-quart soup pot, skimmer, bowl, cutting board, knife

Ingredients

2 pounds pigs' feet, cleaned and split
2 pounds pork; lean leg meat preferred
1 tablespoon salt
1 bay leaf

$\frac{1}{2}$ teaspoon cumin, ground
$\frac{1}{4}$ teaspoon coriander, ground
2 cups hominy, frozen or canned
$\frac{1}{4}$ teaspoon Tabasco sauce
5 limes, halved

Method

1. Place pigs' feet in pot and cover generously with water. Add salt, bay leaf, cumin, and coriander; bring to a boil.
2. Simmer about 1 hour. Add pork and simmer an hour longer, until all meat is tender. Remove meat with skimmer and cool. Save stock.
3. When cool enough to handle, remove bones and cut meat into bite-size pieces.
4. Return meat to stock, adding hominy and enough water to make about 2 quarts of liquid. Bring to a boil; simmer 20 minutes.
5. Season with Tabasco sauce and serve with lime halves.

C-10. Pineapple and Banana Dessert
(*Cajeta de Piña y Plátano*)

Many Mexican families prepare *postres de Posadas,* or holiday desserts. This recipe comes from Veracruz, on Mexico's tropical Atlantic coast, a region where both pineapples and bananas are cultivated.

Yield: 6 cups

Equipment needed: Wide heavy saucepan, cutting board, knife, wooden stirring spoon

Ingredients

1 cup brown sugar
$\frac{1}{2}$ cup water
3 cups canned pineapple, crushed
6 ripe bananas

1 cinnamon stick, about 2 or 3 inches long
2 limes

Method

1. Bring sugar and water to a boil.
2. Simmer until all water is evaporated. Remove from heat immediately. Use caution. The sugar will be very hot.

(continued)

3. Carefully add pineapple. Peel and slice bananas. Add bananas and cinnamon stick to pineapple mixture.
4. Simmer, stirring frequently, until mixture is syrupy, thick, and light brown.
5. Grate lime peel. Add to mixture along with lime juice.
6. Chill.
7. Serve with sour cream.

C-11. Anise Star Cookies

On long winter evenings, the wonderful smell of fresh baking lingers in many homes. These German cookies are sometimes used as Christmas tree decorations, much to the delight of children who try to grab as many as they can reach.

Yield: 25 to 30, depending on size of cookie cutter
Equipment: Work surface, flour sifter, knife, scraper, rolling pin, star cookie cutter, small round cookie cutter for center, baking sheet

Ingredients

2½ cups flour
½ cup sugar
8 ounces (2 sticks) unsalted butter
  or margarine

2 egg yolks
1 tablespoon anise seeds
Flour for dusting
Pan spray

Method

1. Sift flour onto work surface.
2. Make a well in the center and add sugar.
3. Cut butter or margarine into small pieces and add to well along with egg yolks and anise seeds.
4. Blend ingredients together with hands, working from the center of the well outward.

ANISE STAR

5. Begin kneading once flour is incorporated. Continue to knead until firm and dough can be formed into a ball.
6. Wrap in plastic film and refrigerate 1 hour.
7. Dust cleaned work surface with flour. Divide dough into four pieces and roll each piece to a thickness of about $\frac{1}{4}$ inch. Dust with flour to prevent dough from sticking to rolling pin.
8. Dip cookie cutter in flour and cut out stars; place on baking sheet. If using as ornaments, cut out center holes. (Save dough for other use or bake the circles and serves as snacks.)
9. Bake cookies at 375 degrees until light brown.

Christmas Eve (December 24)

Christmas Eve is the final day of Advent, when many Christians avoid eating meat and dairy products, and multicourse fish dinners are commonly served. Traditional European dishes offered before going to Midnight Mass include soups, special breads, and cookies.

C-12. Slovakian Bread Soup (*Velija Lokšy*)

Made with crusty white bread, this traditional dish is from Slovakia, a Central European country that is largely Catholic. Some 750,000 people of Slovakian descent live in the United States.
Yield: 6 servings
Equipment: Large bowl, soup bowl, saucepan, ladle

Ingredients

1 pound fresh, crusty white bread
1 cup poppy seeds, ground
1 quart water

1 cup honey
$\frac{1}{4}$ cup brown sugar
$\frac{1}{4}$ teaspoon salt

Method

1. Break bread, crust and all, into bite-size pieces.
2. Blend with poppy seeds, saving some seeds for garnish.
3. Place bread in soup bowl.
4. Bring water, honey, and sugar to a boil. Cool.
5. When lukewarm, ladle over bread and let soak in. Do not stir.
6. Sprinkle with reserved poppy seeds.

C-13. Ukrainian Dumplings with Sour Cream (*Varenyky*)

On Christmas Eve, Ukrainian Catholics gather for the Holy Supper (*Sviata Vecherya*), a traditional meal of twelve meat- and dairy-free dishes symbolic of the twelve apostles. These might include mushrooms in sauce, baked fish, beans with prunes, and *varenyky*—dumplings served with sour cream that resemble large ravioli filled with cottage cheese. The first dish, *kutya*, is served when the first star is seen in the sky. Made from whole wheat, honey, relish, and poppy seeds, kutya symbolizes family unity, prosperity, and fertility. Traditionally, a spoonful is tossed up to hit the ceiling; if it sticks, the new year will bring good luck!

Yield: 20 dumplings

Equipment needed: Flour sifter, electric mixer with dough hook, work surface, dough scraper, rolling pin, 5-inch round cutter, 4-quart wide saucepan, slotted spoon, 10-inch frying pan

Dough ingredients

2 cups bread flour
1 teaspoon salt
1 egg

½ cup water
Flour for dusting

Filling ingredients

1 cup small-curd cottage cheese
1 egg
1 tablespoon chives, snipped
1 teaspoon salt

1 teaspoon pepper, ground
½ teaspoon nutmeg
4 ounces (1 stick) butter
½ cup bread crumbs

Method

1. Sift flour into bowl of mixer.
2. Add salt and egg. Blend at slow speed, gradually adding water.
3. Mix until stiff dough forms.
4. Dust work surface and knead dough. Shape into large ball. Cover and let dough rest at least an hour.
5. While dough is resting, drain cottage cheese to remove excess moisture. Combine all filling ingredients, except butter and bread crumbs.
6. Divide dough into manageable parts and roll to ⅛-inch thickness. (A pasta machine works well.)
7. Cut dough into 5-inch circles, placing 1 teaspoon filling on each.
8. Fold over to make half-moon shapes. Wet edges and press together to seal.
9. Boil in salted water in large pot until they float. Remove with slotted spoon to serving dish.
10. Add butter to frying pan and heat until light brown.
11. Add bread crumbs and toast over moderate heat, stirring constantly.
12. Top with bread crumbs and serve with sour cream.

C-14. Polish Sweet Sour Carp

Carp cooked in a sweet-and-sour stock thickened with grated gingerbread is a traditional Central and Eastern European dish. A very bony and strongly flavored freshwater fish with red flesh, carp is not always readily available. Catfish or tilapia may be substituted, but the flavor will be milder.

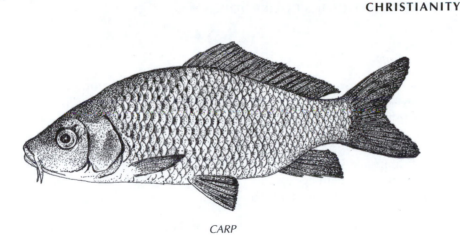

CARP

Yield: 4 servings
Equipment needed: Cutting board, peeler, French knife or grater, saucepan, skimmer or slotted spoon

Ingredients

¹⁄₂ cup carrots, sliced	¹⁄₄ teaspoon salt
¹⁄₂ cup onions, sliced	2 tablespoons grated orange peel
¹⁄₂ cup celery, sliced	¹⁄₄ cup raisins
4 allspice	4 six-ounce fish steaks, with bone
4 peppercorns, crushed	2 tablespoons crushed
3 tablespoons vinegar	gingerbread

Method

1. Put all ingredients except gingerbread and fish in one layer in a wide saucepan.
2. Add 1 cup water and bring to a boil. Cover and simmer 10 minutes.
3. Wash fish and place on top of vegetables.
4. Cover pot and steam over low heat about 10 minutes, checking to be sure there is sufficient water to continue steaming.
5. Transfer fish to serving platter and keep warm.
6. Sprinkle gingerbread on top of vegetables. Blend and cook briefly.
7. Serve fish covered with vegetables.

C-15. Spanish Shortcakes (*Polverones Navideña*)

Served on Christmas Eve as sustenance for those on their way to Midnight Mass, these small almond cookies take their name from the Spanish word for dust, a reference to their powdered-sugar topping.

Yield: 25 pieces
Equipment needed: Flour sifter, electric mixer with paddle, cookie sheet

(continued)

Ingredients

2 cups flour
8 ounces (2 sticks) butter
1 teaspoon vanilla extract

1 cup almonds, ground
1 egg
confectioners sugar for dusting

Method

1. Sift flour and set aside.
2. Cream butter with egg and vanilla extract.
3. Add flour and almonds, blend well.
4. Refrigerate dough.
5. Shape dough into almond-size balls. Place on cookie sheet and bake at 400 degrees until brown.
6. When cool enough to handle, roll balls in confectioners sugar.

Christmas Day (December 25)

Observed today as a commercial and social occasion as much as a religious feast day marking the birth of Jesus, Christmas Day is celebrated around the world on December 25 (January 6 in the Orthodox Church). While there are many ethnic, cultural, and regional adaptations, the traditional American Christmas dinner is modeled after eighteenth-century English colonial customs. The basic formula of turkey or some other roast as a central component, with a dessert such as pumpkin pie, still endures.

C-16. Broiled Oysters

On the East Coast of the United States, oysters are often served at Christmas, either on the half-shell, steamed, or fried.
Yield: 4 to 6 appetizer servings
Equipment needed: Strainer, large bowl, wide cast iron pan or baking dish

Ingredients

1 pint oysters, shucked
1 cup cracker crumbs
1/4 teaspoon cayenne pepper

1/2 cup oil
Lemon wedges

Method

1. Drain oysters and set aside.
2. Blend crumbs with pepper.
3. Toss oysters in crumbs.
4. Place oysters in baking dish and drizzle with oil.
5. Broil at 400 degrees until light brown.
6. Serve at once with lemon wedges.

C-17. Scandinavian Liver Spread (*Leverpastej*)

The Scandinavian Christmas buffet table is loaded with favorite foods like pickled herring, beets, meatballs, sausages, smoked fish, roast meats, potatoes, and desserts. This tasty liver spread is a favorite.

Yield: 10 appetizer servings

Equipment needed: Electric meat grinder with fine blade, large bowl, frying pan, small bowl, food processor, aluminum foil, two loaf pans, large baking pan with 2-inch rim for water bath

Ingredients

1 pound pork liver, washed, skin removed	$\frac{1}{2}$ teaspoon salt
1 pound bacon, cut in 1-inch squares	$\frac{1}{2}$ teaspoon pepper, ground
4 anchovy fillets	3 eggs
$\frac{1}{2}$ tablespoon oil	1 tablespoon cornstarch
1 tablespoon onion, chopped	2 cups heavy cream
	1 teaspoon sugar
	Pan spray

Method

1. Make fine puree of liver, bacon, and anchovy fillets using food processor or fine plate of meat grinder. Set aside.
2. Sauté onions in oil until transparent but not brown. Cool.
3. Blend spices, egg, cornstarch, and heavy cream to form smooth slurry.
4. Combine all ingredients using food processor.
5. Line loaf pans with aluminum foil and fill with liver mixture.
6. Set loaf pans in large baking pan containing an inch of water.
7. Cover large pan with aluminum foil and carefully place in oven.
8. Bake at moderate heat (about 350 degrees) at least 1 hour.
9. Check for doneness. Knife inserted in center should come out clean.
10. Chill. Unmold when cold.

C-18. Dill-Cured Salmon (*Gravad Lax*)

Festive Swedish dinners start with a wide selection of cold appetizers collectively called *Smörgåsbord*. A favorite choice is salt-and-sugar-cured salmon served with mustard sauce. *Note:* This recipe requires several days to marinate.

Yield: 6 appetizer servings

Equipment needed: Small bowl for blending spices, cutting board, fine pliers, French knife, glass or stainless steel pan about 8 × 6 inches and 1 inch high, plastic wrap, slicing knife, china platter

Ingredients

2 tablespoons salt	1 tablespoon sugar

(continued)

1 tablespoon peppercorns, crushed	1 pound boneless salmon center-piece fillet, skin on
½ tablespoon coriander seeds, crushed	1 bunch fresh dill, coarsely chopped, including stems

Method

1. Combine dry spices and blend well.
2. Check salmon for bones by running palm of hand over fish. Using pliers, remove any bones found.
3. Place salmon skin-side-down in glass or stainless steel pan and top with blended spices and chopped dill.
4. Cover with plastic wrap and refrigerate overnight.
5. Turn the fish over and baste with dill mixture. Refrigerate overnight.
6. Turn fish over again and repeat process.
7. Serve very thinly sliced with mustard and dill sauce (see recipe below).

C-19. Mustard and Dill Sauce (*Gravlaxsås*)

Yield: ¾ cup (6 servings)
Equipment needed: Small mixing bowl, wire whisk

Ingredients

6 tablespoons oil	½ tablespoon sugar
2 tablespoons vinegar	1 teaspoon salt
2 tablespoons mustard	1 tablespoon fresh dill, chopped
1 egg yolk	

Method

1. Combine all ingredients except dill in bowl.
2. Stir vigorously with wire whisk until well blended.
3. Add dill just before serving.

C-20. Mexican Cactus Salad (*Ensalada de Nopales*)

Christmas salads are a common addition to the festive table. This one uses cactus paddles that are available fresh (with the spines removed) in the produce section in many supermarkets. Canned nopales may also be substituted.
Yield: 6 appetizer servings
Equipment needed: 2-quart saucepan, colander, cutting board, knife

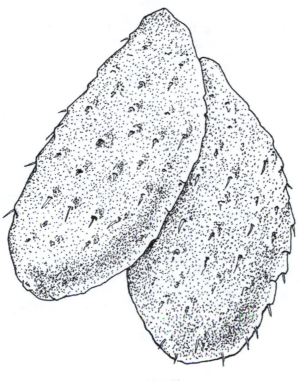

NOPALES

Ingredients

2 pounds fresh cactus
1 small jalapeño chili
4 ounces red peppers, cut in strips
½ cup oil
1 tablespoon mild sesame oil

1 teaspoon salt
1 teaspoon dried oregano
¼ cup vinegar
¼ cup onions, chopped
¼ cup cilantro leaves, chopped

Method

1. Cut cactus paddles in ½-inch strips.
2. Boil cactus in water until tender, about 6 to 10 minutes.
3. Drain and rinse under cold water. Place in large mixing bowl.
4. Cut chili in half; remove and discard seeds. Cut chili halves into small slivers and add to nopales with all other ingredients.
5. Blend well. Allow to marinate in refrigerator for at least 2 hours to let flavors develop.

C-21. Italian Christmas Salad (*Insalata di Rinforzo*)

Neapolitans eat this pretty and nutritious salad daily from Christmas Eve to Epiphany, adding more ingredients each day to "reinforce" the salad.

(continued)

Yield: 10 servings
Equipment needed: Cutting board, knife, large mixing bowl, wire whisk, 3-quart saucepan, colander, mixing spoon

Ingredients

6 anchovy fillets
¼ cup olive oil
¼ cup white wine vinegar
1 teaspoon salt
1 large cauliflower, divided into florets
¾ cup green olives, pitted and cut in half

¾ cup black olives, pitted and cut in half
¾ cup red peppers, diced
2 tablespoons capers
¼ cup fennel, diced
2 tablespoons parmesan cheese, grated

Method

1. Mash and chop anchovy fillets; put in large bowl.
2. Add oil and vinegar, stir well.
3. Boil cauliflower in salted water until cooked but still firm. Drain and add to dressing mixture.
4. Add remaining ingredients while cauliflower is still hot. Carefully blend and refrigerate until ready to serve.

C-22. Christmas Sauerkraut Soup (*Kapustnica*)

Usually prepared a few days before Christmas, the taste of this Slovakian sauerkraut soup improves with each reheating.
Yield: 10 servings
Equipment needed: 3-quart stockpot, strainer, 2-quart saucepan, ladle, strainer, wire whisk, cutting board, French knife

Ingredients

1 ounce dried mushrooms; porcini preferred
8 ounces smoked pork sausage
6 ounces sauerkraut (1 cup drained)
1½ quarts water

1 tablespoon lard or oil
1 teaspoon garlic
1 tablespoon onion, chopped
2 tablespoons flour
½ teaspoon hot pepper
½ cup heavy cream

Method

1. Combine mushrooms, sausage, sauerkraut, and water in 3-quart stockpot and simmer 45 minutes.
2. Remove sausage from stock and cut into bite-size pieces.
3. In 2-quart saucepan, sauté garlic and onions in lard or oil until transparent. Add flour and cook briefly over moderate heat. Set aside.

4. Add about 4 cups sauerkraut stock. Stir with wire whisk and bring to simmer. Add thickened soup to sauerkraut in stockpot. Stir carefully to combine.
5. Bring soup to a boil and add cream. Simmer briefly. Serve with rye or sourdough bread.

C-23. French Hearty Soup (*Pot au Feu*)

After Midnight Mass in France and parts of Canada, families may eat a special meal called *réveillon*. Originally a simple snack of biscuits or a slice of meat pie with a hot drink, over time it became more lavish and substantial. This hearty soup from northern France is made with beef, pork, chicken, and vegetables.
Yield: 8 servings
Equipment needed: 4-quart soup pot, cutting board, knife, spatula, ladle, serving platter, large soup tureen

Ingredients

2 pounds beef brisket, unsalted
1 pound lean pork shoulder
1 chicken, about 3 pounds
1 bay leaf
10 peppercorns
1 sprig marjoram
1/2 tablespoon salt
1 medium onion

1/2 pound parsnips
1 pound carrots
1/2 pound leeks
2 celery stalks
1/2 pound green cabbage
1 tablespoon chives, snipped
16 slices French bread

Method

1. Place beef and pork in soup pot. Divide chicken into quarters and add to pot with giblets (except liver). Rinse with cold water and drain.
2. Fill pot with hot water. Add all spices. Bring to a boil and simmer 1 1/2 hours.
3. Leaving skin on, cut onion in half and cook cut-side-down in heavy pan until dark; add to soup. (The caramelized sugar will color the soup.)
4. Clean vegetables, cut into 1-inch pieces, and add to soup. Simmer until meats are tender.
5. Transfer meats to serving platter and keep hot.
6. Toast bread slices.
7. Use ladle to skim any fat floating on top of soup.
8. Slice meats. Remove vegetables with slotted spoon and arrange them around meats. Sprinkle with chives.
9. Serve meats, vegetables, and soup together with toasted French bread.

C-24. Louisiana Gumbo with Sassafras

Popular as a Christmas dinner starter in the southern United States, this spicy stew is flavored with okra and sassafras and can be made with a variety of meats
(continued)

SASSAFRAS

or seafood. Ground sassafras leaves are sold as filé powder in the spice section of most grocery stores. This recipe is from Acadia, the section of southwestern Louisiana settled by French Canadians.

Yield: 8 to 10 generous servings

Equipment needed: 3-quart soup pot, cutting board, French knife, 3-quart heavy-bottomed soup pot, stirring spoon

Ingredients

1 chicken, 3 to 4 pounds	1 pound okra, fresh or frozen
8 ounces smoked ham, diced	1 teaspoon red pepper flakes
2 tablespoons oil	½ teaspoon garlic, chopped
1 cup onions, diced	1 tablespoon filé powder
½ cup celery, diced	(sassafras)
½ cup canned crushed tomatoes	½ pint oysters, shucked
(with liquid)	Salt to taste

Method

1. Wash chicken, put in soup pot, cover with water, and bring to a boil.
2. Simmer until tender, about 2 hours. Set aside to cool. Save stock.
3. Sauté ham in oil until light brown.
4. Add onions, celery, and 2 quarts of stock. Bring to a boil; simmer 30 minutes.
5. Remove skin and bones from chicken and cube meat.
6. If fresh, wash okra and remove stems; cut into ¼-inch slices. Add to stew with tomatoes, pepper flakes, garlic, and chicken.

7. Blend filé powder with leftover oyster liquid, if available, or with ½ cup chicken stock.
8. Add oysters and filé powder to stew. Heat just to the boiling point, but do not boil. Season with salt, and serve immediately.

C-25. French-Canadian Pork Pie (*Tourtière*)

A traditional French-Canadian Christmas dish, this substantial pie may be served hot or cold.
Yield: 6 servings
Equipment needed: Dutch oven, cutting board, French knife, mixing bowl, work surface, rolling pin

Ingredients

2 pounds lean pork shoulder, diced
½ cup onions, diced
½ cup carrots, diced
½ cup celery, diced
½ teaspoon dried thyme leaves
1 teaspoon salt
½ teaspoon crushed pepper

1 russet potato, about 8 ounces, peeled
1 McIntosh apple, about 6 ounces
3 eggs, hard-boiled
Pan spray
Biscuit mix (7.75-ounce size)
Flour for dusting

Method

1. Combine pork, onions, carrots, celery, and spices in Dutch oven.
2. Bake, covered, at 350 degrees for about 45 minutes.
3. Dice potato and apple; add to pork with 1 cup hot water.
4. Continue baking, covered, at 375 degrees for 20 minutes.
5. Remove from oven and carefully remove lid.
6. Peel eggs and cut in half.
7. Pan-spray shallow baking dish and fill with meat mixture and eggs.
8. Prepare biscuit mix according to directions; knead briefly, roll out, and cover pie.
9. Bake 25 minutes, or until brown.

C-26. Baked Virginia Ham

Genuine Virginia hams, produced from the lean and flavorful leg meat of razorback hogs, are first rubbed with salt and pepper, then air-dried and lightly smoked. Much dryer than other hams, they must first be soaked in cold water to remove their salt-and-pepper crust. Size can be a problem, and some households have even resorted to soaking hams in the bathtub! For the typical meal, the ideal Virginia ham should weigh between 8 and 10 pounds, bone-in.

(continued)

Yield: 12 to 14 servings
Equipment needed: Large pot, roasting pan with rack

Ingredients

8–10 pound genuine Virginia ham	1 teaspoon cinnamon, ground
1 cup light molasses	1 teaspoon allspice, ground
1 teaspoon cloves, ground	1 cup bread crumbs

Method

1. Soak ham overnight; discard water.
2. Put ham in large pot, cover with water, and bring to a boil. Simmer about 3 hours; refill with hot water as needed.
3. Let ham cool, then discard stock.
4. Trim any excess fat and brush with molasses.
5. Blend dry ingredients and sprinkle evenly over ham.
6. Bake at 300 degrees for about 1 hour.
7. Serve with cranberry sauce or stewed fruits, and sweet potato patties.

C-27. Elizabethan Venison with Fennel

Due to the importance of the spice trade, the use of spices was a sign of wealth and prestige in Elizabethan times. Forks were not common, and meats were cooked until spoon-soft. Winter is game season in England, and braised venison makes a festive Christmas dinner.

Yield: 7 servings
Equipment needed: Cutting board, French knife, 2-quart non–stainless steel or glass bowl, Dutch oven with lid

Ingredients

3 pounds venison leg, boneless	$\frac{1}{2}$ teaspoon allspice, ground
2 tablespoons oil	$\frac{1}{2}$ teaspoon mace, ground
1 cup onions, diced	1 fennel bulb with greens, about
$\frac{1}{2}$ cup carrots, finely diced	12 to 14 ounces
1 teaspoon fennel seeds	1 teaspoon salt
$\frac{1}{2}$ teaspoon juniper berries, crushed	8 ounces dried apricots
	4 ounces raisins
1 teaspoon peppercorns, crushed	2 ounces almonds, shredded
1 cup red wine vinegar	1 tablespoon cornstarch
1 sprig fresh thyme	

Method

1. Trim meat, removing all fat. Cut into 2-inch cubes.
2. Marinate overnight in refrigerator with oil, onions, carrots, fennel seeds, juniper berries, peppercorns, red wine vinegar, thyme, allspice, and mace.

3. Put meat, vegetables, marinating liquid, and 1 cup water in Dutch oven and bake, covered, at 350 degrees for 1 hour.
4. Remove greens from fennel; save for garnish. Cut fennel in thin slices and add to meat with salt, apricots, and raisins.
5. Continue cooking at least another hour, adding hot water as necessary to keep meat moist.
6. Once meat is very soft, remove stew from oven and place, uncovered, on stovetop to simmer.
7. Make slurry with cornstarch and 2 tablespoons cold water; add to stew to thicken. Add a little more hot water if necessary.
8. Serve sprinkled with fennel greens.

C-28. Czech Bread Dumplings (*Knedliki*)

Roman Catholicism is the main religion of the formerly Communist country that is now the Czech Republic. Traditional Christmas dishes such as baked carp and roast goose or duckling are accompanied by these bread dumplings.
Yield: 10 dumplings
Equipment needed: Cutting board, French knife, large bowl, frying pan, mixing spoon, large wide saucepan, slotted spoon

Ingredients

10 stale hard rolls (or French bread); about 10 cups bread cubes	1 egg
	1 cup milk
2 tablespoons oil	½ cup flour
½ cup onions, chopped	Salt
¼ cup parsley, chopped	Nutmeg

Method

1. Put bread cubes in large mixing bowl.
2. Sauté onions in oil until cooked but not browned.
3. Add onions and parsley to bread cubes.
4. Blend egg with ½ cup milk. Add to bread.
5. Season with salt and nutmeg and mix together. Bread should be moist, but not soggy. (Add more milk if necessary.)
6. Sprinkle with flour and blend. Press small amount of bread mixture together to form a "test" dumpling.
7. Fill saucepan with water and bring to a slow rolling boil. Drop test dumpling in water. If it falls apart, add a little flour to the bread mixture.
8. Wet hands and shape larger dumplings; carefully lower them into the boiling water and simmer about 10 minutes until they float.
9. Remove with slotted spoon and serve with roast or stew.

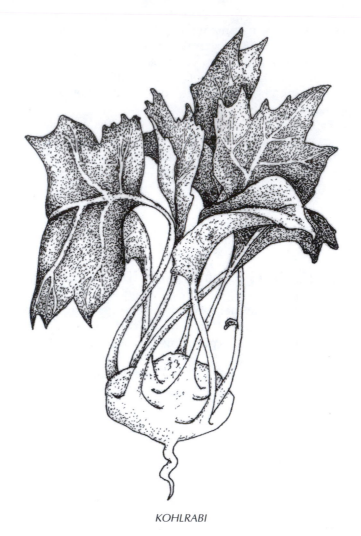

KOHLRABI

C-29. Hungarian Stuffed Kohlrabi (*Töltött Kalarábá*)

Hungarians love stuffed vegetables, and recipes for stuffed peppers, cabbage, and squash abound. Kohlrabi is the enlarged stem from a plant in the cabbage family. Its bulb grows above ground and is usually light green or red in color. Stuffed kohlrabies are typically served on Christmas Day. Medium-size bulbs are preferred, as large ones may be woody inside.

Yield: 12 servings, 2 per serving

Equipment needed: Cutting board, paring knife, French knife, peeler, melon scoop, 1-quart heavy saucepan, wooden spoon, baking dish, soup spoon

Ingredients

24 medium-size kohlrabies, leaves
   and stems removed
2 tablespoons butter
1 pound pork, diced

¼ cup onions, chopped
1 teaspoon garlic, chopped
½ teaspoon dried marjoram
   leaves, crushed

¹/₂ teaspoon caraway seeds
1 teaspoon salt
1 tablespoon paprika

1 cup canned chicken broth
¹/₄ cup bread crumbs
1 tablespoon oil

Method

1. Peel kohlrabies. Cut off tops and even out bottoms so they will stand flat. Save tops.
2. With melon scoop, remove as much pulp as possible from inside kohlrabies, making sure not to puncture walls.
3. Coarsely chop pulp.
4. Cook in butter over moderate heat. Add remaining ingredients except chicken broth, bread crumbs, and oil.
5. Continue to cook over moderate heat until rather dry, stirring frequently to break up lumps. Remove from heat.
6. Fill kohlrabies and place in baking dish. Replace tops.
7. Sprinkle with bread crumbs and oil. Add chicken stock to baking dish.
8. Bake at 275 degrees until kohlrabies are tender, about an hour.

C-30. Scandinavian Poached Preserved Cod (*Lutfisk*)

Lutfisk, a type of dried cod treated with lye, is a traditional Christmas dinner for Swedes and Norwegians. The fish, hard as cardboard when purchased, requires lengthy advance preparation, including repeated soakings and frequent water changes. A common joke is that lutfisk must be soaked on St. Lucia's Day (December 13) to be edible by Christmas.

Yield: 6 servings

Equipment needed: Nonreactive bowl for soaking fish, peeler, paring knife, pot, small saucepan, cutting board, 1-quart heavy-bottomed saucepan, wire whisk, cheesecloth, wide saucepan or Dutch oven

Ingredients

1 pound dried lutfisk
1 tablespoon black pepper, ground
1¹/₂ teaspoons allspice, ground
Parsley for garnish
2 pounds red bliss or Maine
  potatoes
2 tablespoons lye

3 teaspoons salt
3 eggs
1 pint milk
2 ounces (¹/₂ stick) butter
2 ounces flour
1 teaspoon white pepper, ground

Method

1. Soak fish in plenty of water for three days, changing water every day. Fish will eventually rehydrate.

(continued)

2. Tie fish in cheesecloth and place in wide pot or Dutch oven; cover with water. Simmer about 20 minutes. Place fish on large platter and carefully remove cheesecloth.

3. Remove any obvious bones and fins. Sprinkle with 1 teaspoon allspice and black pepper. Garnish with parsley sprigs. Serve with potatoes and sauce (directions follow).

4. Peel potatoes; cut in half if too large. Cover with water and add 1 teaspoon salt. Bring to a boil and simmer slowly, about 20 minutes. When cooked, drain and keep warm.

5. To make sauce, cover eggs with water, bring to a boil, and simmer 10 minutes. Drain and immediately cover eggs with cold water. When cool, crack shells underwater and peel.

6. Heat milk.

7. Cook butter and flour over low heat until slightly yellow.

8. Stir in warmed milk with wire whisk. Bring to a boil; simmer 5 minutes.

9. Season sauce with salt, allspice, and white pepper.

10. Chop eggs coarsely and add to sauce. Cover sauce to prevent skin from forming and keep warm until ready to serve.

C-31. French Christmas Log (*Bûche de Noël*)

Ancient Goths and Saxons celebrated the winter solstice with bonfires and a festival called *Juul*. Today, a large piece of freshly cut wood burned at Christmas is still called a yule log. In French it is known as Bûche de Noël and has given its name to a dessert consisting of a log-shaped, chocolate-cream-filled sponge cake roll "overgrown" with meringue mushrooms.

Sponge Cake Roll

Yield: 10 slices
Equipment needed: Electric mixer with whisk, small bowl, flour sifter, small saucepan, cookie sheet, spatula, parchment paper, work surface

Ingredients

1 ounce (¼ stick) butter	1 cup flour
8 eggs, separated	1 teaspoon grated lemon peel
1¼ cups sugar	Pan spray

Method

1. Melt butter and set aside.
2. Beat egg whites until stiff. Add 1 cup sugar and continue to mix at slow speed until combined.
3. Add remaining sugar, lemon peel, and melted butter to egg yolks and blend.
4. Sift flour.
5. Carefully fold egg mixture and flour into beaten egg whites (do not stir).

6. Line cookie sheet with parchment paper and pan-spray.
7. Spread batter onto paper in rectangle about 10 inches long and ¼ inch thick.
8. Bake at 350 degrees for about 15 minutes, or until light brown on top. Make sure cake does not dry out.
9. Slide cake and paper onto work surface lightly dusted with sugar.
10. Flip cake over when cool enough to handle. Peel off paper.

Chocolate Icing (Ganache)

This icing is very rich, and will stiffen when refrigerated.

Ingredients

8 ounces Baker's chocolate   1 cup heavy cream

Method

1. Using knife, carefully break and chop chocolate into small pieces.
2. Combine with cream in heavy saucepan.
3. Heat, stirring frequently, until chocolate is completely dissolved.
4. Cool, stirring occasionally.
5. Once cool, put chocolate in electric mixer and whip at medium speed until thick. Use immediately.

Log Assembly

Method

1. Spread cake with half of chocolate icing. Roll up, then refrigerate until icing stiffens.
2. Warm remaining chocolate icing in mixing bowl, stirring until spreadable. When filled cake roll is cold and stiff, cover sides and top with icing. Refrigerate.

Meringue Mushrooms

Ingredients

½ cup egg whites (about 3 large   1 cup sugar
  eggs)   Powdered cocoa for decoration
Pinch of cream of tartar

Method

1. Put egg whites and cream of tartar in clean mixing bowl.
2. Whip at medium speed until soft peaks form; gradually add sugar. Continue whipping until stiff meringue.
3. Heat oven to 200 degrees. Using pastry bag, form equal numbers of mushroom caps and short stems on cookie sheet.

(continued)

4. Place cookie sheet in oven and turn off heat. Leave in oven overnight to dry.
5. Store in warm, but not humid, location.
6. Assemble by fastening legs to caps with a little chocolate icing. Sprinkle with cocoa.
7. Decorate log with mushrooms.

C-32. English Steamed Date and Fig Pudding

Once traditionally made with beer instead of milk, "figgy pudding" is featured in the song "We Wish You a Merry Christmas" sung by English carolers as they go door to door. Pecans work well in this recipe, but almonds or walnuts may be substituted.
Yield: 8 servings
Equipment needed: Cutting board, French knife, mixing bowl, stirring spoon, ceramic pudding dish, aluminum foil, water bath

Ingredients

4 ounces dates, pitted	3 tablespoons flour
4 ounces dried figs	3 tablespoons milk
1 cup nuts, coarsely chopped	1 teaspoon baking powder
³/₄ cup sugar	Pan spray
1 egg	1 tablespoon sugar

Method

1. Dice dates and figs and mix well with pecans, ³/₄ cup sugar, egg, flour, milk, and baking powder.
2. Pan-spray ceramic pudding dish and dust with 1 tablespoon of additional sugar.
3. Fill with pudding mixture and cover with aluminum foil.
4. Place dish in shallow pan of water and bake at 350 degrees for 1 hour.
5. Carefully remove from oven. When slightly cooled, remove foil and serve warm with custard sauce or lemon curd (see recipe on page 63).

C-33. Gingerbread Pudding

This dessert from the southern United States was originally made with sorghum molasses, a product that has disappeared from the shelves of many supermarkets. Dark molasses can be substituted. Although called "pudding," the dish actually resembles a cake.
Yield: 10 to 16 servings
Equipment needed: Flour sifter, electric mixer with paddle, ¹/₂-quart pot, plastic scraper, baking pan

Ingredients

2 cups all-purpose flour
1 teaspoon baking soda
1 teaspoon baking powder
1 cup water
4 ounces (1 stick) butter
1 teaspoon cinnamon

1 teaspoon powdered cloves
1 tablespoon powdered ginger
½ teaspoon salt
2 eggs
1 cup molasses
Pan spray

Method

1. Sift flour, baking soda, and baking powder together into mixing bowl.
2. Heat water, add butter to dissolve, and set aside.
3. Add spices to flour and blend at slow speed.
4. Add all other ingredients and mix to form smooth batter.
5. Pan-spray baking pan. Scrape batter into pan and bake at 350 degrees for about 40 minutes.
6. Serve warm with lemon curd (recipe follows).

C-34. Lemon Curd

Yield: 8 servings
Equipment needed: Grater, juicer, fine strainer, large bowl, wire whisk, 2-quart saucepan, spatula, small glass bowls or pots for storing

Ingredients

2 large lemons
4 ounces (1 stick) butter

1 cup sugar
4 egg yolks

Method

1. Grate lemon peel and squeeze juice from lemons. Put lemon peel and strained juice in bowl and add all other ingredients.
2. Place bowl over saucepan half-filled with water. Stir with wire whisk over moderate heat to warm evenly. Do not allow water to boil.
3. Continue to heat mixture until thick and creamy.
4. Remove from heat; keep stirring until cool.
5. Put cooled mixture in glass bowl, cover, and refrigerate until thickened. Serve cold.

C-35. German Baked Apples Filled with Almonds
(*Bratäpfel mit Mandeln*)

At Christmas, Germans love to serve apples, the only locally grown fruit that keeps until winter. Rome Beauties are best for this dish.

(continued)

Yield: 8 servings
Equipment needed: Electric blender, cutting board, peeler, melon scoop, baking pan, teaspoon, pastry brush

Ingredients

¼ cup sugar
½ cup cake or bread crumbs
1 cup slivered almonds
½ teaspoon cinnamon
½ teaspoon ginger, ground

1 egg white
1 cup water
1 tablespoon red currant jelly
8 medium apples
¼ cup butter or margarine, melted

Method

1. Combine first six ingredients with ½ cup water and jelly in blender.
2. Pulse-process to smooth paste.
3. Peel apples horizontally about halfway; the lower, unpeeled part will keep the apples together during baking. Remove center core with melon scoop.
4. Put apples in baking pan. Fill center cavities with sugar paste. Brush with melted butter.
5. Pour remaining water around apples and bake at 350 degrees for about an hour, or until light brown on top.
6. Serve warm.

C-36. Norwegian Christmas Cake (*Julakaka*)

Scandinavians are great bakers. This rich yeast cake is traditionally served on Christmas Day.
Yield: 12 to 16 slices
Equipment needed: Small pot, electric mixer with dough hook, scraper, work surface, 2-quart ring mold, cake rack, small mixing bowl, wooden spoon, pastry brush

Ingredients

½ cup milk
4 ounces (1 stick) butter
½ cup water
1 package dry yeast
3½ cups flour
¼ cup sugar
1 teaspoon salt
1 egg, slightly beaten
1 tablespoon cardamom, ground

1 cup raisins
½ cup candied fruits
¼ cup almonds, coarsely chopped
Flour for dusting
Pan spray
1 egg white
Juice of ½ lemon
Confectioners sugar as needed

Method

1. Warm milk, add butter and melt. Set aside.
2. Warm water to around body temperature and put in mixing bowl.

3. Sprinkle yeast on top; let dissolve.
4. Sift flour and set aside.
5. Add warm milk, salt, egg, sugar, and cardamom to yeast.
6. Using dough hook, blend in sifted flour at slow speed until dough forms. (If too dry, add a little warm milk.)
7. Add raisins, candied fruits, and almonds, blending at slow speed, scraping sides of bowl.
8. Remove dough hook and cover bowl with kitchen towel. Place in warm location and let ferment for about an hour.
9. Flour work surface. Knead dough until silky and smooth.
10. Spray 2-quart ring mold. Shape dough into roll and place in mold. Cover and let rise for about an hour.
11. Bake at 375 degrees for about 45 minutes.
12. Invert on rack to cool.
13. Make icing by combining egg white and lemon juice. Using wooden spoon, stir in sugar until opaque and rather thick.
14. Apply icing to cake with brush.

C-37. Moravian Christmas Cookies

Moravian customs and celebrations are Germanic in origin. In the Moravian center of Bethlehem, Pennsylvania, Christmas is celebrated with a large craft fair called *Christkindlmarkt*, where signs are written in German, an orchestra plays German Christmas carols, and stalls sell traditional Christmas cookies such as these.

Yield: Varies, depending upon size of cookies
Equipment: Food processor, flour sifter, work surface, rolling pin, cookie cutter, cookie sheet

Ingredients

$^{1}/_{2}$ cup shortening
1 cup brown sugar
1 cup molasses
1 egg
4 cups cake flour

1 teaspoon cinnamon, ground
1 teaspoon cloves, ground
$^{1}/_{2}$ teaspoon nutmeg, ground
1 teaspoon baking soda

Method

1. In food processor, blend shortening, sugar, molasses, and egg.
2. Sift dry ingredients and add to egg mixture.
3. Pulse to blend; do not overmix.
4. Roll out dough $^{1}/_{4}$-inch thick on a floured work surface.
5. Cut out fancy shapes, such as stars, using cookie cutters.
6. Place on cookie sheet sprayed with pan spray.
7. Bake at 375 degrees about 10 minutes.

Note: Cookies will be rather dry and will soften during storage after the sugar has absorbed moisture.

St. Basil's Day (January 1)

A fourth-century bishop of Caesarea, Basil was one of the founders of the Greek Orthodox Church. His feast day is also the "name day" celebrated by people christened Vassilios and Vassaliki.

C-38. Greek Christmas Cake (*Vassilopitta*)

Despite its name, this cake is made especially for New Year's Day when pieces are symbolically presented first to St. Basil, then to the house, then to the oldest person present, on down to the youngest household member. The coin hidden within promises the recipient good luck in the New Year.

Yield: 25 slices

Equipment: Small saucepan, strainer, small bowl, flour sifter, electric mixer with dough hook, dough scraper, large round cake pan, paring knife, small cup, table fork, pastry brush

Ingredients

2 tablespoons anise seeds	2 cups sugar
1 cup water	$\frac{1}{2}$ teaspoon salt
5 cups flour	Pan spray
1 cup milk	Flour for dusting mold
2 packages dry yeast	1 cup slivered almonds, for
9 eggs	garnish
10 ounces ($2\frac{1}{2}$ sticks) butter,	$\frac{1}{2}$ cup sesame seeds, for garnish
room temperature	Coin wrapped in aluminum foil

Method

1. Bring anise seeds and water to a boil; simmer 5 minutes. Strain and cool. Discard anise seeds.
2. Sift flour; set 1 cup aside.
3. Warm milk to body temperature, add yeast and 1 teaspoon of the sugar, and stir in reserved cup of flour.
4. Cover with kitchen towel; let stand in warm place.
5. Cream butter, eight of the eggs, salt, and sugar in mixing bowl.
6. Add yeast blend, remaining flour, and anise-flavored water. Blend with dough hook until smooth.
7. Remove dough hook and cover bowl with kitchen towel, letting dough proof (ferment) until about double in size.
8. Pan-spray cake pan; dust with flour.
9. Scrape dough into pan, leveling top, then insert coin.
10. With paring knife, make irregular crisscross slashes on top.
11. Beat remaining egg in small bowl with fork.
12. Brush cake surface with egg; sprinkle with almonds and sesame seeds.
13. Bake at 375 degrees about 1 hour.
14. Unmold and place on wire rack with seeded side up.

Epiphany (January 6)

One of the oldest of Christian celebrations and an important holiday in both the Western and Eastern churches, the Feast of the Epiphany commemorates the arrival of three kings, or magi, who brought gifts to the baby Jesus. In Hispanic neighborhoods, processions take place on the eve of Epiphany with actors dressed in magnificent robes playing the three kings. People in Spain and Mexico exchange presents recalling the magi's gifts to Jesus, whom Christians believe was the son of God.

C-39. Three Kings Sweet Bread (*Roscón de Reyes*)

Baked in the shape of a king's crown, this special Spanish cake always contains a surprise baked inside, such as a dried bean or small coin.
Yield: 16 to 18 slices
Equipment needed: Two small bowls, small pot, strainer, flour sifter, electric mixer with paddle, kitchen towel, baking sheet, pastry brush

Ingredients

1 package dry yeast	¹⁄₂ teaspoon salt
³⁄₄ cup water	5 cups flour
¹⁄₂ teaspoon grated lemon rind	¹⁄₂ cup milk
6 cloves	¹⁄₂ cup candied fruits, diced
1 tablespoon orange flower water	Flour for dusting
3 eggs	Candied fruit slices for decoration
6 ounces (1¹⁄₂ sticks) butter	2 tablespoons coarse sugar
¹⁄₂ cup sugar	

Method

1. Dissolve yeast in ¹⁄₄ cup lukewarm water.
2. Combine ¹⁄₂ cup water with lemon rind and cloves. Bring to a boil; steep for 10 minutes. Strain, and set aside. Discard cloves. Add orange flower water.
3. Cream two eggs with butter, sugar, and salt.
4. Sift flour. Add dissolved yeast to creamed eggs, then at slow speed, gradually add flour, spice-flavored water, and milk to form smooth dough.
5. Blend candied fruits into dough and knead until smooth.
6. Shape dough into a ball. Cover with kitchen towel and let stand in warm place about 2 hours.
7. Shape dough into large ring and place on baking sheet. Pinch ends together.
8. Insert coin or other suitable object that is heat-proof.
9. Blend third egg with 1 tablespoon of water. Paint ring with egg mixture and decorate with candied fruit slices, alternating colors if available.
10. Sprinkle with coarse sugar. Let cake stand in warm place for 30 minutes. Bake at 350 degrees for about 40 minutes.

Submersion of the Holy Cross (January 6)

In this ancient Orthodox ceremony, a priest tosses a tethered cross into the ocean. In the Greek communities of New York's Brooklyn and Astoria, young men dive into the freezing water to retrieve the submerged cross. The person who recovers it is blessed and feted at the ensuing festivities, which include dancing, singing, and lavish food.

C-40. Greek Pork in Lemon and Vinegar Jelly (*Zalatina*)

Around Christmastime in Greece, pigs were slaughtered and all parts used in the preparation of a variety of dishes. The pig's head and feet were made into zalatina, a dish resembling head cheese. Although it may be difficult to purchase a pig's head in a supermarket, ethnic butcher shops do sell the pig's feet, skins, and tongue used in this recipe.

Yield: 20 appetizer servings

Equipment needed: Large saucepan, large slotted spoon, large tray, fine strainer, ladle, small saucepan, nonreactive metal mold, grater, cutting board, French knife

Ingredients

3 pounds assorted pig's feet, skins, and tongue	1 tablespoon salt
1 tablespoon peppercorns	1 tablespoon garlic, crushed
1 large onion	1 teaspoon hot pepper flakes
1 bay leaf	2 lemons
1/2 cup white wine vinegar	Plain gelatin, as needed
	Mint leaves, for garnish

Method

1. Wash all pork parts in hot water and drain.
2. Put all ingredients except lemons and gelatin in large saucepan. Cover with water.
3. Bring to a boil and simmer until all pork is soft, about 3 hours.
4. Carefully transfer all pork to metal tray. Cool.
5. Strain stock into small saucepan.
6. Grate lemon peel and add to stock. Bring to a boil and simmer.
7. Check stock's gelatin strength by dropping spoonful onto cold plate. If stock seems solid, remove from heat. If not, dissolve teaspoon of gelatin into 1/2 cup cold water and add to stock.
8. Squeeze lemon and add juice to simmering stock. Remove all bones and fat from meat while still lukewarm. Cut meat and skins into bite-size pieces and place in mold.
9. Test stock again for gelatin strength. Taste. Stock should be pleasantly acidic, peppery, and a little salty. It will taste milder when blended with meat.
10. Ladle stock over meat and skins; stir and cool. Refrigerate overnight until solid.
11. Unmold on platter, scraping off unwanted pork fat. Garnish with mint leaves. Serve thinly sliced.

Orthodox Christmas (January 7)

Orthodox celebrations of Christmas (also called the Nativity of the Savior) are both colorful and solemn. In the United States, many Orthodox Christians maintain the ethnic traditions of their Eastern European homelands.

C-41. Bulgarian Beef Soup with Meatballs (*Supa Topcheta*)

This hearty beef soup with meatballs is a luxurious dish for the holiday.
Yield: 8 servings
Equipment needed: 3-quart heavy soup pot, stirring spoon, small cast-iron pan, cutting board, knife, fine wire strainer, 2-quart pot, bowl

Ingredients

1 tablespoon oil	2 teaspoons salt
1½ pounds beef stew meat	½ cup rice
1 large onion	8 ounces ground beef
8 ounces parsnips	2 tablespoons onions, chopped
2 stalks celery	1 teaspoon garlic, chopped
8 ounces carrots	2 tablespoons bread crumbs
1 bay leaf	2 tablespoons cold water
1 teaspoon peppercorns	2 tablespoons chives, chopped

Method

1. Put stew meat and oil in heavy soup pot over very low heat until meat browns slightly.
2. Cover with 2 quarts water; simmer 1 hour.
3. Cut unskinned onion in half horizontally. Heat in heavy pan, cut side down, until onion is caramelized. Add to soup.
4. Wash all vegetables, cut into chunks, and add to soup.
5. Simmer 30 minutes longer. Strain broth into another pot. Save meat and vegetables.
6. Cut vegetables into bite-size pieces and set aside.
7. Add rice to broth; bring to slow boil.
8. Combine ground beef with all remaining ingredients except chives. Blend well.
9. With wet hands, shape eight meatballs and add them to simmering soup.
10. Continue to simmer 10 more minutes. Add reserved stew meat and vegetables; bring to a boil.
11. Serve sprinkled with chives.

C-42. Lebanese Meat Turnovers (*Sambousik*)

Lebanon's large Christian population includes Catholic, Orthodox, and Protestant groups. Christmas dinner always starts with little appetizers or *mezzes*, such as these lamb turnovers.

(continued)

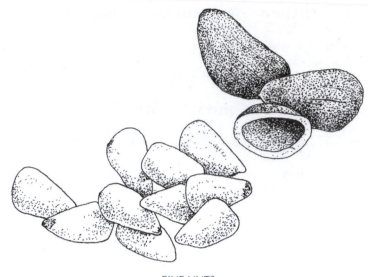

PINE NUTS

Yield: 30 to 40 pieces, depending on size
Equipment needed: Saucepan, mixing spoon

Ingredients

1 pound ground lamb	¹⁄₂ cup pine nuts
1 tablespoon olive oil	1 teaspoon salt
¹⁄₂ cup onions, chopped	1 teaspoon pepper
1 teaspoon garlic, chopped	1 tablespoon flour
1 tablespoon mint leaves, chopped	¹⁄₂ cup yogurt
1 teaspoon coriander, ground	Piecrust as needed (see recipe on page 37)
1 teaspoon grated lemon peel	

Method

1. Cook lamb with olive oil over moderate heat. Stir frequently to break up meat.
2. Add onions and garlic; cook briefly.
3. Add remaining ingredients except flour and yogurt.
4. Cook briefly to blend flavors.
5. Sprinkle with flour and blend in.
6. Add yogurt; bring to a boil. You should have a fairly firm paste.
7. Cool.
8. Make small turnovers using pieces of piecrust and filling. Bake at 375 degrees.

C-43. Rasstegai with Fish

In Russia, Christmas was traditionally celebrated by serving a large variety of hot and cold appetizers called *zazuska*. These usually included caviar, smoked fish, and cold meats, followed by a large roast. The celebration of Christmas was banned after the 1917 revolution, and eighty-five years passed before it was once again celebrated openly. Rasstegai are little boat-shaped yeast breads that can be filled with fish, meat, rice, or eggs.

Yield: 25 to 30 pieces

Equipment needed: Flour sifter, electric mixer with dough hook, work surface, cutting board, knife, small bowl, stirring spoon, rolling pin, 4-inch round pastry cutter, cookie sheet, pan spray, pastry brush

Ingredients

3 cups flour
1 package dry yeast
1 teaspoon sugar
1 teaspoon salt
1½ cups warm water
1 tablespoon oil
Flour for dusting
8 ounces boneless smoked salmon trimmings

8 ounces smoked whitefish, flaked
4 ounces cream cheese
1 tablespoon dill, chopped
1 egg
2 tablespoons milk

Method

1. Sift flour.
2. Combine yeast, sugar, salt, water, and oil in mixing bowl and blend with dough hook.
3. Gradually add flour, blending at slow speed until stiff dough forms.
4. Knead dough briefly on floured work surface; shape into ball. Cover with kitchen towel and let stand at room temperature for an hour.
5. Shred smoked fish, making sure all bones are removed.
6. Blend fish with cream cheese and dill. Keep cool until ready to use.
7. Punch down dough, cover, and let stand again for about 30 minutes.
8. Divide dough into manageable pieces and roll out to thickness of ¼-inch.
9. Cut into circles using 4-inch pastry cutter.
10. Put 1 tablespoon smoked fish filling in center of each circle. Pinch edges of dough together at opposite ends, forming little boats. Leave center open with filling exposed.
11. Pan-spray cookie sheet and put rasstegai on sheet, leaving space in between for pastries to rise.
12. Blend egg with milk and brush on pastries.
13. Let stand in warm place about 15 minutes.
14. Bake at 375 degrees until brown. Serve warm or cold.

C-44. Pork Chops Baked with Apples and Sauerkraut

In the past, suckling pigs graced many a Christmas table. Today's lifestyle makes roasting such large pieces of meat impractical, but pork chops baked with apples and sauerkraut are an acceptable substitute. This dish is usually served with sour cream on the side.

Yield: 6 servings

Equipment needed: Dutch oven, peeler, cutting board, grater

Ingredients

1 tablespoon lard or oil
6 six-ounce pork chops, bone-in
3 large baking potatoes
1 Red Delicious apple
½ cup onions, sliced
1 teaspoon garlic, chopped

1 teaspoon caraway seeds
1 cup canned chicken broth
1 teaspoon black pepper, ground
1 teaspoon juniper berries
2 cups sauerkraut
2 tablespoons bread crumbs

Method

1. Brown pork chops in Dutch oven on both sides and transfer temporarily to platter.
2. Peel and grate potatoes. Set aside, retaining juice. Potatoes will become slightly discolored.
3. Quarter apples, remove core, and cut in thin slices, leaving skin on.
4. Sauté onions and garlic in same fat used for pork. Return pork chops to Dutch oven and distribute all ingredients, except bread crumbs, over meat.
5. Bring to slow simmer and cook, covered, about 25 minutes.
6. Uncover, sprinkle with bread crumbs, and brown in oven set to broil.

C-45. Honey Cakes (*Petruska*)

These Russian honey cakes resemble the German *lebkuchen*, but are made with a blend of rye flour and wheat flour.

Yield: 4 to 5 dozen

Equipment needed: Flour sifter, electric mixer with dough hook, work surface, scraper, rolling pin, cookie cutters, baking sheet

Ingredients

1 cup rye flour
1 cup wheat flour
4 ounces (1 stick) butter
1 cup honey
1 egg
1 teaspoon baking soda

¼ teaspoon salt
½ teaspoon cloves, ground
½ cup dried cherries, chopped
Flour for dusting
Pan spray

Method

1. Sift flours into mixing bowl.
2. Warm honey. Add to butter, egg, baking soda, salt, and cloves and pour into mixing bowl. Blend at low speed until dough is formed.
3. Blend in cherries.
4. Knead dough briefly on floured work surface; form into ball. Dough will be sticky. Cover and let rest about 2 hours.
5. Roll out to about 1/4-inch thickness. Cut into different shapes with cookie cutters.
6. Pan-spray cookie sheet. Bake cookies at 375 degrees for 12 to 15 minutes, or until brown.

Note: Cookies can be glazed, or sprinkled with sugar, before baking.

Death Day of George Fox (January 13)

The birthday of seventeenth-century English Quaker leader George Fox is the most important date recognized by Quakers. After a prayer service, the Friends might gather for a late breakfast featuring home-baked bread.

C-46. Apple Walnut Cake

This delicious moist cake combines sweet apples with a nutty flavor.
Yield: One 8-inch loaf
Equipment needed: Peeler, paring knife, food processor, grater, electric mixer with paddle, flour sifter, scraper, loaf pan

Ingredients

1 pound McIntosh apples	1 teaspoon allspice
1 lemon	1/2 teaspoon cloves, ground
4 ounces (1 stick) butter	1/2 teaspoon cinnamon, ground
1 cup sugar	1/4 cup milk
3 eggs	1 cup walnuts, chopped
1 1/2 cups applesauce	Pan spray
2 cups flour	Flour for dusting
1 tablespoon baking powder	

Method

1. Peel and core apples. Grate lemon peel and set aside.
2. Put apples in food processor. Squeeze lemon juice over apples.
3. Coarsely chop apples. Set aside.
4. Combine and cream butter, sugar, eggs, and lemon peel.
5. Add applesauce.
6. Sift flour with baking powder.
7. Add apples, applesauce, and all remaining ingredients.
8. Blend well with mixer paddle, but do not overmix.

(continued)

9. Pan-spray loaf pan and dust with flour.
10. Scrape batter into pan, smooth top, and bake at 360 degrees for about 45 minutes.

Conversion of St. Paul (January 25)

This saint's day is celebrated by Laotian-Catholic Hmongs. During the Vietnam War, this group helped the U.S. forces, and many were eventually allowed to settle in Minnesota. Three days of festivities in St. Paul, the state capital, include traditional courtship games where young women wear dresses covered with gently clinking coins. Papaya salad is a favorite dish.

C-47. Laotian Papaya Salad

Yield: 8 appetizer servings
Equipment needed: Small frying pan, mixing bowl, mixing spoon

Ingredients

1 tablespoon sesame seeds
½ cup cashews, crushed
4 cups papaya, diced
1 tablespoon hot sesame oil
½ cup celery, diced
2 tablespoons lime juice
2 tablespoons oil

1 teaspoon sugar
1 teaspoon black pepper, ground
1 teaspoon salt
1 teaspoon fish sauce
8 cinnamon sticks, for garnish
8 mint sprigs, for garnish

Method

1. Toast sesame seeds and nuts in frying pan over moderate heat.
2. Combine all ingredients and serve chilled.
3. Garnish with cinnamon stick and mint sprigs.

Moravian Unitas Fratrum (March 1)

This special day marks the anniversary of the founding of the Moravian Church in 1457. Although now included in the Czech Republic, in the fifteenth century Moravia was part of the staunchly Catholic Hapsburg Empire. Fleeing persecution, many Moravians settled in Pennsylvania. Followers' eating habits reflect their Central European heritage.

C-48. Moravian Clear Beef Soup with Cream-of-Wheat Dumplings

Popular on this festive winter holiday, this clear hearty beef soup contains delicious oval-shaped cream-of-wheat dumplings and is served sprinkled with chives.

Yield: 8 servings
Equipment needed: 4-quart soup pot, cutting board, knife, spatula, ladle, serving platter, large soup tureen

Ingredients

2 pounds unsalted beef brisket	½ pound parsnips
1 bay leaf	8 ounces carrots
5 peppercorns	8 ounces leeks
1 sprig marjoram	1 celery stalk
½ tablespoon salt	1 tablespoon chives, snipped
1 medium onion	

Method

1. Place beef in large stockpot with 3 quarts hot water.
2. Add all spices. Bring to a boil; simmer 1½ hours.
3. Cut onion in half, leaving skin on. Cook in heavy pan, cut side down, until onion is caramelized. Add to soup. (The caramelized onion will color the soup.)
4. Clean vegetables, cut into 1-inch pieces, and add to soup. Simmer soup until meat is tender.
5. Remove beef. Discard any fat floating on top of soup.
6. Dice beef and return to soup.

Cream-of-Wheat Soup Dumplings

Yield: About 30 dumplings
Equipment needed: Mixing bowl, whisk, wooden spoon, 2-quart wide casserole, soup spoon, slotted spoon

Ingredients

3 ounces (¾ stick) butter, at room temperature	Pinch of nutmeg
¼ teaspoon salt	2 eggs
	10 ounces cream of wheat

Method

1. Cream butter with spices and eggs until smooth.
2. Add cream of wheat, using wooden spoon. Mixture will become rather heavy.
3. Let rest about 25 minutes.
4. Bring water to simmer in wide casserole.
5. With wet tablespoon, shape oval dumplings and let them glide into the simmering water. Do not crowd, as dumplings will triple in size.
6. Simmer over low heat for about 20 minutes. Remove dumplings to soup plates. Cover with hot soup and serve.

Lent (March to April)

A forty-day period leading up to Easter, Lent is usually marked by observant Christians of all denominations with fasting and abstention. A time of purification, self-reflection, peace-making, and charity to others, Lent encompasses a number of special days celebrated with different Christian traditions. It begins on Ash Wednesday in the Western church, and on Clean Monday in the Orthodox.

C-49. Greek Cheese Pie (*Tiropitta*)

Beginning on the Sunday before Lent, many Orthodox denominations observe "Meatfare Sunday." All meat in the house is consumed, and none is eaten again until Easter. On the following day, "Clean Monday," all cheese, eggs, and butter are eaten before the Lenten fast begins. Although today usually only monks follow these guidelines, the custom of serving dairy dishes on Clean Monday is still practiced in many families. This recipe uses filo (phyllo) dough sheets. Rolled paper-thin, they can be purchased frozen, ready to use, from most supermarkets.

Yield: 10 main course servings

Equipment needed: 1-quart heavy saucepan, wooden spoon, wire whisk, 9 × 13-inch baking dish, pastry brush, paring knife

Ingredients

½ package (8 ounces) filo dough
2 ounces (½ stick) butter
6 tablespoons flour
2 cups milk
½ teaspoon nutmeg
4 eggs

2 tablespoons parsley, chopped
1 pound feta cheese, drained and crumbled
1 cup kefalotori or parmesan cheese, grated
½ cup melted butter

Method

1. Defrost filo dough in refrigerator overnight.
2. Melt 2 ounces butter, add flour, and cook over low heat to blend.
3. Add milk and nutmeg, stirring with whisk; bring to a boil. Simmer 5 minutes, making a thin cream sauce.
4. Remove from heat, add eggs, chopped parsley, and cheeses. Blend to fairly smooth consistency.
5. Butter baking dish and line with two layers filo dough. Let dough hang over the sides.
6. Add cheese filling; fold filo sheets onto cheese.
7. Place remaining filo sheets on top, brushing butter between each sheet.
8. Do not allow any sheets to overhang the pan.
9. Brush top with remaining butter and score top sheets into triangles.
10. Bake at 375 degrees until hot and light brown on top, about 30 minutes.

C-50. Amish Doughnuts (*Fastnacht*)

The day before Lent begins is known as Shrove Tuesday and is celebrated in many countries with carnivals, merry-making, and good food. The Amish celebrate by making yeast doughnuts called *fastnacht*. Before compressed fresh or dry yeast became available, sour-dough starter was saved from day to day for making yeast bread. Preparation began on Monday evening, when the starter was set out to ferment in the warm kitchen overnight. The sourdough was acidic, and the fastnacht were dipped in sweet coffee. Using modern yeast and working in a warm kitchen, these donuts can be made in less than two hours.

Yield: 20 pieces

Equipment needed: Mixing bowls, electric mixer with dough hook, rolling pin, 2½-inch round cookie cutter, kitchen towels, slotted spoon, wire rack, paper towels

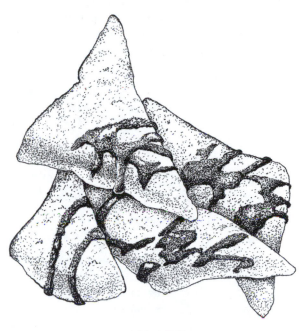

FASTNACHT

Ingredients

1 package (¼ ounce) dry yeast
1 teaspoon plus 2 tablespoons sugar
½ cup warm water
4 cups flour
1 teaspoon salt

1 cup lukewarm milk
2 ounces (½ stick) melted butter
2 egg yolks
Fat for frying
Powdered sugar

Method

1. Dissolve yeast and 1 teaspoon sugar in warm water.
2. Combine flour, remaining sugar, and salt in food processor.
3. Add warm milk, melted butter, egg yolks, and dissolved yeast.
4. Mix with dough hook until smooth.
5. Place in pan-sprayed mixing bowl, cover with kitchen towel, and let dough ferment (proof) in warm place about 45 minutes.
6. When dough has doubled in size, push it down and repeat procedure.
7. Roll out dough on floured work table to thickness of about ¾ inch.
8. Cut rounds with cookie cutter and place on floured sheet pan. Cover with kitchen towel and let stand 20 minutes.
9. Heat oil to 375 degrees.

(continued)

10. Place fritters carefully in oil; they will float.
11. Turn to brown on both sides.
12. Serve dusted with powdered sugar.

C-51. Brazilian Seafood Pie

In the coastal regions of Brazil, a country that is predominantly Catholic, seafood dishes are typical fare during Lent. This seafood pie is served cold.

Yield: 8 to 10 servings

Equipment: Bowl, cutting board, knife, wide saucepan, mixing spoon, large glass baking dish, mixing bowl, wire whisk

Ingredients

8 ounces salted codfish (*bacalhau*)
1/4 cup *dendê* oil
1 cup onions, chopped
1 teaspoon garlic, chopped
2 teaspoons hot pepper seasoning
1/2 teaspoon salt
1/4 teaspoon coriander, ground
1/4 teaspoon cumin, ground
1/2 cup canned crushed tomatoes
1 pound shrimp, cleaned and
  deveined

8 ounces crabmeat
1 cup canned hearts of palm, cut
  into 1/2-inch slices
2 tablespoons parsley, chopped
1 tablespoon lemon juice
6 eggs
1 onion, sliced into 1/4-inch
  rounds

Method

1. Soak salted cod overnight. Change water next morning. Remove all bones and cut fish in 1-inch pieces.
2. Wash again, squeezing out excess water.
3. Sauté onions and garlic in oil until transparent.
4. Add spices, tomatoes, and salted codfish cubes. Bring to a boil and simmer 5 minutes.
5. Add shrimp and simmer 5 more minutes. Fish mixture will be rather dry.
6. Fold in crabmeat, hearts of palm, parsley, and lemon juice.
7. Place in large glass baking dish.
8. Blend eggs with wire whisk and pour over fish. Place onion rings on top.
9. Bake in 375-degree oven until firm and top is browned. Refrigerate before serving.

C-52. Spanish Fried Cheese (*Queso Frito*)

This interesting Lenten dish could be called cheese croquette. It is usually served with dandelion salad, the first wild greens sprouting in spring, although a green salad may be substituted.

Yield: 6 servings
Equipment needed: 1-quart heavy saucepan, wire whisk, wooden spoon, baking sheet, spatula, knife, frying pan

Ingredients

4 ounces (1 stick) butter
1½ cups flour
2 cups milk
¼ teaspoon nutmeg
1 egg plus 4 egg yolks
1 cup grated Manchego or
   parmesan cheese

Pan spray
1 tablespoon cold water
1 cup bread crumbs
Oil for frying

Method

1. Melt butter, add 1 cup flour, and cook over moderate heat to blend.
2. Add milk and nutmeg, stirring with whisk until sauce thickens and starts to bubble.
3. Remove from stove. Let cool slightly. Add four egg yolks and cheese. Blend with wooden spoon.
4. Pan-spray baking sheet. Evenly spread mixture on pan about ¾ inch thick.
5. Refrigerate until cold and solid, preferably overnight.
6. Cut cold mixture into 12 slices. Blend whole egg and water.
7. Dredge slices first in flour, then in egg wash, and then in bread crumbs.
8. Carefully fry each slice on both sides in about ½ inch of oil.

C-53. Emperor's Shredded Pancake (*Kaiserschmarren*)

Named for the Hapsburg Emperor Franz Joseph, this dish is popular in Austria during Lent. Served either as a dessert or light main course for lunch, these tasty pancakes are enriched with beaten egg whites and raisins.
Yield: 4 servings
Equipment needed: Two mixing bowls, two wire whisks, Teflon-coated 8-inch frying pan, spatula

Ingredients

4 eggs
1 cup milk
4 tablespoons light cream
1 cup cake flour
¼ teaspoon salt
2 tablespoons sugar

4 ounces (1 stick) butter
2 ounces raisins
Confectioners sugar for dusting
Raspberry or maple syrup, or
   stewed fruits

(*continued*)

Method

1. Carefully separate eggs.
2. In mixing bowl, combine yolks, milk, cream, flour, and salt, making thick batter.
3. Whisk egg whites until stiff, adding sugar until dissolved.
4. Fold into batter.
5. Melt butter in pan and heat until golden brown.
6. Ladle in half of the batter and sprinkle with raisins.
7. Cook over low heat until dough settles.
8. Carefully turn over pancake. Start breaking it up into smaller pieces with spatula while frying over low heat.
9. Dump shredded pancake on heated plate and keep warm.
10. Repeat process. Sprinkle shredded pancakes with sugar and serve with syrup or stewed fruits.

C-54. Potato Fritters (*Draniki*)

Served as a main course during Lent, this traditional Russian dish resembles Jewish potato latkes, but does not use matzo meal or eggs.
Yield: About 16 fritters
Equipment needed: Grater or food processor with grater attachment, strainer, bowl, wire whisk, tablespoon, frying pan, slotted spoon

Ingredients

2 pounds russet potatoes (about 4 or 5)	1 tablespoon chives, snipped
½ cup flour	1 teaspoon black pepper, ground
1 teaspoon salt	Oil for frying
1 teaspoon baking powder	Sour cream for garnish

Method

1. Peel and grate potatoes, squeeze out liquid. (Peeled potatoes will discolor slightly.)
2. Blend with salt, pepper, baking powder, flour, and chives.
3. With tablespoon, drop small fritters into hot oil. Fry on both sides until brown and crisp. If batter does not hold together, add more flour.
4. Serve with sour cream.

Easter Sunday (March or April)

Easter, the holiest day of the Christian calendar, celebrates the belief that Jesus arose from the dead three days after his crucifixion. Many Easter traditions, however, can be traced back to pre-Christian roots. Eggs, long viewed as symbolic of fertility and new life, became Christian symbols of the resurrection.

The ancient Egyptian custom of placing dyed eggs in temples evolved into the Christian tradition of decorating eggs. In many families, dyed eggs are hidden for the children to find or brought to church to be blessed.

C-55. Ukrainian Easter Eggs

Pysanky, the hand-decoration of Easter eggs, is an ancient art form in Ukraine. A beeswax stylus is used to write or draw on the eggs, and dye colors will not adhere to the wax-covered areas. The wax can be washed off and more designs applied. Originally left intact, the raw eggs were said to represent the tomb of Jesus. As moisture evaporated from inside the eggs, a parallel was made to the resurrection. Today, the contents are usually blown out via tiny holes on either end. Some families decorate hard-boiled eggs with less elaborate designs and eat them during the Easter holidays.

Hard-Boiled Eggs

Vinegar and salt are not necessary when boiling eggs for eating, but are added here to clean the eggs so the wax will adhere better.
Yield: 12 eggs
Equipment needed: 1-quart soup pot

Ingredients

12 eggs   1 teaspoon salt
1 tablespoon vinegar

Method

1. Cover eggs, vinegar, and salt with hot water and bring to a boil.
2. Simmer 12 minutes.
3. Run cold water over eggs until completely cooled.
4. Dry eggs before decorating. You can buy a kit that has all the materials you need, including a special marking tool called a *kistka;* or you can use candle wax, food coloring, and a pencil or modeling tool. Cover the egg with wax, then scrape off the wax wherever you want a color other than white. Dip the egg in yellow dye; the dye will color the portion of the egg that is not covered in wax. Repeat the procedure with darker dyes until you are satisfied with your design. Use the side of a candle flame to melt away the wax when you have finished. If you have used edible dyes, you can peel the eggs and eat them.

C-56. Mexican Squash Flower Soup
(*Sopa de Flor de Calabacita*)

In Mexico, Easter breakfast is called *almuerzo* and often consists of a hearty soup such as this one, which features zucchini blossoms with tortilla chips as an accompaniment.

(continued)

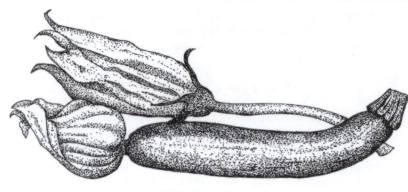

ZUCCHINI BLOSSOMS

Yield: 4 servings
Equipment needed: Colander, paring knife, 2-quart heavy saucepan with lid, whisk, electric blender

Ingredients

20 zucchini blossoms
4 tablespoons (1 stick) butter
½ cup onions, chopped
¼ teaspoon cayenne pepper
1 teaspoon garlic, chopped
1 tablespoon flour
½ teaspoon salt

2 cups canned chicken stock
1 cup heavy cream
1 teaspoon lemon juice
2 tablespoons cilantro leaves, chopped
2 ounces tortilla chips

Method

1. Save four blossoms for garnish; wash the rest and trim off small green leaves.
2. Cook onions, pepper, and garlic in butter until soft. Add washed and drained blossoms.
3. Cover and simmer over low heat until flowers are wilted.
4. Add flour and salt. Cook briefly and set aside to cool.
5. Process flower blend to medium fine puree in blender and return to pot.
6. Add chicken stock and cream; bring to a rolling boil.
7. Remove from heat, add lemon juice, and serve soup sprinkled with cilantro.
8. Place one blossom next to each bowl, with tortilla chips on the side.

C-57. Venetian Rice and Peas (*Risi e Bisi*)

Falling somewhere between a soup and a risotto, this dish is usually served when peas are at the peak of their growing season. An appetizer, it is especially popular on April 25, the feast day of St. Mark, the patron saint of Venice.

Yield: 6 to 8 appetizer servings
Equipment needed: Large pot with heavy bottom, small pot, wooden spoon, cutting board

Ingredients

6 cups chicken broth, fresh or canned
3 tablespoons butter
2 tablespoons olive oil
3 ounces pancetta (Italian bacon), finely diced
1/2 cup onions, diced

1 tablespoon Italian parsley, chopped
12 ounces tiny peas, fresh or frozen
1 1/4 cups rice
4 ounces parmesan cheese, grated

Method

1. Simmer chicken broth and set aside.
2. Combine butter and oil in small pot; sauté pancetta, onions, and parsley.
3. Add peas and 1/2 cup of broth. Bring to a boil and simmer 5 minutes. Set aside.
4. Add rice to remaining broth. Simmer until rice is cooked but still firm in the center (al dente).
5. Combine rice and peas, heating through. Remove from heat, add cheese, and stir to combine.

C-58. Roman-Style Easter Lamb (*Abbacchio alla Romana*)

In Italy, Easter Sunday dinner often features roast lamb. This dish is seasoned with fresh rosemary and chopped anchovy fillets.
Yield: 6 to 8 servings
Equipment needed: Paring knife, roasting pan, spatula, cutting board, knife

Ingredients

1 leg of lamb, boned and tied, about 4 pounds
1 tablespoon fresh rosemary leaves
2 tablespoons olive oil
1 teaspoon garlic, chopped

1 teaspoon black pepper, crushed
1 teaspoon salt
3 canned anchovy fillets, drained
1/4 cup red wine vinegar
1/4 cup water
1 teaspoon cornstarch

Method

1. Unroll meat. Make small slits with paring knife and insert rosemary leaves.
2. Rub with oil, garlic, pepper, and salt; tie again.
3. Roast at 375 degrees for 40 minutes for medium rare. (Temperature should be 160 degrees on meat thermometer.). Roast longer if well-done is desired.
4. Set lamb aside and keep warm.

(continued)

5. Chop anchovy fillets to fine paste. Add to residue in roasting pan along with vinegar and water.
6. Bring to a boil and loosen all pan drippings with spatula.
7. Pour pan gravy into smaller pot and skim fat from top.
8. Reduce to about half. Make slurry with cornstarch and 1 teaspoon water.
9. Add to sauce and bring to a boil; serve with lamb.

C-59. Chicken Chili (*Aji de Gallina*)

The traditional cooking style of Peru, a predominantly Catholic country, uses ground nuts and bread to thicken sauces.
Yield: 6 servings
Equipment needed: Large soup pot, cutting board, knife, 2-quart heavy saucepan, wooden spoon

Ingredients

1 chicken, about $4\frac{1}{2}$ pounds	2 teaspoons garlic, chopped
$\frac{1}{2}$ tablespoon salt	6 slices white bread
1 bay leaf	$\frac{1}{2}$ pound walnuts, finely, chopped
4 green jalapeño chilies	$\frac{1}{2}$ cup parmesan cheese, grated
$\frac{1}{2}$ cup oil	1 cup evaporated milk
1 cup onions, chopped	

Method

1. Cover chicken with water, add salt and bay leaf; simmer until cooked, about $1\frac{1}{2}$ to 2 hours. Cool chicken in its stock.
2. Remove skin and bones; cut into 1-inch cubes. Save 4 cups stock.
3. Split chilies, discard seeds, and cut into small slivers. (*Caution:* Wear gloves when working with hot chilies.)
4. Sauté in oil over moderate heat with onions and garlic. Remove crust from bread and cut into 1-inch cubes.
5. Combine onions and garlic, bread pieces, and reserved chicken stock in large saucepan. Bring to a boil, stirring well, and simmer 20 minutes.
6. Add nuts. Boil until sauce thickens and is reduced by half. Add chicken pieces, cheese, and evaporated milk. Bring to a boil before serving.

C-60. French Alsatian Easter Cake (*Gâteau de Paque*)

Predominantly Catholic, the French province of Alsace borders Germany to the east. Here, Easter breakfast is celebrated with a rich yeast cake. Stirred rather than kneaded, this dough is baked in a ribbed bundt cake mold.
Yield: 15 slices
Equipment needed: Sifter, electric mixer with paddle, small bowl, grater, bundt cake mold, plastic dough scraper

Ingredients

2 packages yeast	2$^1/_2$ cups flour
7 ounces milk	$^1/_4$ teaspoon salt
5 ounces sugar	1 grated lemon peel
6 ounces (1$^1/_2$ sticks) butter, room temperature	4 ounces raisins
1 egg	Pan spray
3 egg yolks	Confectioners sugar

Method

1. Dissolve yeast in 2 ounces warm milk and 1 ounce sugar.
2. Combine butter, remaining sugar, and whole egg in mixing bowl. Stir with paddle at low speed until well blended and sugar is dissolved.
3. Sift in flour; add yeast and all remaining ingredients except raisins.
4. Blend at slow speed until smooth dough is formed.
5. Stir in raisins. Remove paddle, cover bowl with kitchen towel, and let dough ferment in warm place until doubled in size.
6. Pan-spray bundt cake mold; dust with flour.
7. Fill mold evenly with dough.
8. Cover with kitchen towel and let ferment in warm place about 20 minutes.
9. Bake at 375 degrees for 45 minutes. Use cake tester to make sure done.
10. Unmold and dust with sugar.

C-61. Russian Easter Cheese Bread (*Syrnyk*)

Because Eastern Orthodox churches celebrate Easter according to the Julian calendar, the date sometimes falls later than in the Western church. On Easter Sunday, food baskets decorated with candles are brought to the service to be blessed. The contents are then eaten at breakfast that morning. Dishes might include cooked eggs, ham, sausages, headcheese, salads, relishes, and this famous Easter bread.

Yield: 20 slices

Equipment needed: Electric mixer with paddle, flour sifter, cake pan, small bowl, mixing spoon, pastry brush

Ingredients

12 ounces (3 sticks) butter, room temperature	1 teaspoon grated lemon peel
1$^1/_2$ cups sugar	2 cups flour
8 ounces fine-curd cottage cheese	$^1/_2$ teaspoon salt
4 ounces cream cheese	1 teaspoon cinnamon
4 eggs	2 teaspoons baking powder
2 tablespoons honey	$^1/_4$ cup heavy cream
	$^1/_2$ cup walnuts, chopped

(continued)

¹/₂ cup slivered almonds
¹/₂ cup candied orange peel
Pan-spray
Flour for dusting pan

1 egg white
1 tablespoon lemon juice
1¹/₂ cups confectioners sugar

Method

1. Cream together butter, sugar, cottage cheese, cream cheese, eggs, honey, and lemon peel.
2. Sift flour with salt, cinnamon, and baking powder.
3. Mix flour and heavy cream with creamed butter blend at slow speed.
4. Fold in nuts and orange peel.
5. Pan-spray cake pan; dust with flour. Scrape dough into pan and smooth top.
6. Bake at 375 degrees about 40 minutes. Unmold on wire rack.
7. Stir egg white, lemon juice, and enough confectioners sugar together to make a spreadable icing.
8. Brush icing on cake while still hot.

C-62. Greek Roast Leg of Lamb in Paper
(*Arni Psito Sto Hart*)

A traditional Greek Easter meal, roast lamb is often stuffed with fresh herbs such as lemon balm and poppy leaves, or something more substantial like sweet rice cooked with cinnamon and almonds. Spit-roasting is preferred, but oven-roasting the lamb in a paper bag is a substitute method. The meat will not be crisp, but the flavor will compensate.

Ingredients

1 leg of lamb, 4 to 6 pounds
2 garlic cloves, slivered
2 lemons
1 tablespoon fresh oregano

1 tablespoon fresh rosemary
2 teaspoons salt
2 teaspoons black pepper, ground
2 sprigs marjoram

Method

1. Remove aitchbone from lamb if still attached. Trim excess fat and clean shank bone.
2. Peel garlic. Make small incisions in lamb and insert garlic cloves. The amount is up to you.
3. Squeeze lemon over lamb; combine oregano, rosemary, salt, and pepper and evenly season meat.
4. Place on parchment paper and top with marjoram sprigs.
5. Wrap lamb securely using butcher's twine to make a solid parcel. The meat will shrink during cooking.
6. Place in deep roasting pan and bake at 350 degrees for 2¹/₂ hours.

Pentecost (May or June)

Pentecost, called Whitsunday in England, falls forty-nine days after Easter. A traditional Confirmation Day, when teenagers are officially admitted into the Christian church, Pentecost celebrates the descent of the Holy Spirit upon the disciples of Jesus.

C-63. Mormon Baptism Buns

Following Mormon tradition, most children are baptized on the Pentecost Sunday following their eighth birthday. After the ceremony, a reception or open house is held, with fare offered such as sandwiches, cold meats, cheeses, vegetable salads, cookies, brownies, and punch. Mormons consider wheat to be God's special gift to humans, as all other grains were intended for both man and beast.
Yield: 18 to 20 buns
Equipment needed: Small saucepan, electric mixer with paddle, flour sifter, scraper, pastry brush, baking sheet

Ingredients

3/4 cup milk
1/3 cup sugar
1 teaspoon salt
2 ounces (1/2 stick) butter
3 cups flour
1 package dry yeast

1/2 cup warm water
2 eggs
1/4 cup seedless raisins
1/2 cup almonds, chopped coarsely
1/4 cup sugar
Flour for dusting

Method

1. Warm milk and blend with 1/3 cup sugar, salt, and butter.
2. Sift flour into mixing bowl. Make a well in center and add yeast and warm water. Set aside in warm spot until yeast dissolves.
3. Add one egg and one yolk; set remaining egg white aside.
4. Add milk mixture at low speed until all ingredients are combined. Increase speed slightly to form smooth dough.
5. Remove to floured work surface and dust top with flour. Cover with kitchen towel and let proof (ferment) about an hour; dough should increase considerably in volume.
6. Divide into 20 pieces and roll into fingerlike shapes on flour-dusted work surface.
7. Double-back each piece and twist. Tuck under ends and place each bun on pastry sheet.
8. Insert raisins between dough folds.
9. Slightly beat reserved egg white and brush on buns.
10. Sprinkle with almonds and 1/4 cup sugar. (Sweep excess almonds and sugar from baking sheet, as they will burn.)
11. Bake at 375 degrees until brown, about 30 minutes.

C-64. Holy Spirit Soup (*Sopa do Espírito Santo*)

Pentecost is the quintessential festival of the Azores. Those Azoreans who have settled in the United States, particularly in New England, have brought with them their religious celebrations and food traditions.

Yield: 6 to 8 servings

Equipment needed: 4-quart saucepan, cutting board, knife, strainer, 2-quart soup pot, serving platter, ladle

Ingredients

½ cup onions, chopped
2 quarts water
1 chicken, about 4 pounds
8 ounces slab bacon, unsliced
1 pound beef chuck
1 teaspoon peppercorns, crushed
½ tablespoon salt
¼ teaspoon allspice, ground
1 bay leaf
5 garlic cloves, peeled and left whole

1 pound red bliss potatoes
1 pound kale
1 pound savoy cabbage
½ pound Portuguese or Italian sausage
3 mint sprigs
8 slices Portuguese or Italian bread

Method

1. Bring onions, water, chicken, bacon, and beef to a boil, then simmer.
2. Add seasonings, and simmer for about 1½ hours.
3. Scrub potatoes and cut into ¾-inch cubes. Set aside.
4. Remove stems from kale and wash leaves thoroughly, filling sink with water and lifting leaves to filter out sand.
5. Cut kale and cabbage into 1-inch pieces.
6. Check meats. As they become tender, remove to serving platter and keep warm.
7. When all meats are cooked, strain stock into smaller pot. Add potatoes and all vegetables, including garlic cloves.
8. Bring to a boil; simmer 20 minutes. Add sausage; simmer 10 minutes more.
9. Slice meats and sausage. Remove skin from chicken; break into pieces.
10. Put one slice of bread in each bowl. Ladle soup on top, adding mint leaves. Serve meat on side.

Corpus Christi

The Feast of Corpus Christi commemorates the body and blood of Jesus Christ and emphasizes the redemptive action of the sacrament. Established as a universal Catholic celebration by Pope Urban IV in 1264, this feast day takes place on the Thursday after the first Sunday of Pentecost.

C-65. Spanish Honey Cakes (*Galletas de Miel*)

This festive day is celebrated in many Spanish parishes with outdoor processions. Participants stop to pray at three altars decorated with spring flowers. Wheat and honey are mentioned in the liturgy and, traditionally, small honey cakes are eaten.

Yield: 25 pieces

Equipment needed: Flour sifter, electric mixer with paddle, work surface, cookie sheets, rolling pin, 3-inch round cookie cutter

Ingredients

1 cup flour
1 teaspoon baking powder
1/2 teaspoon baking soda
1/4 teaspoon salt
1/2 teaspoon cinnamon
4 ounces (1 stick) butter
1 teaspoon vanilla extract

1/2 cup brown sugar
1/4 cup honey
2 cups whole-wheat flour
1/2 cup milk
Flour for dusting
Pan spray

Method

1. Sift flour together with next four ingredients.
2. Cream butter with vanilla extract, brown sugar, and honey.
3. Gradually add whole-wheat flour, sifted flour, and milk, mixing with paddle at slow speed.
4. Knead dough on floured work surface until smooth. Cover and let stand 30 minutes.
5. Roll out to about 1/4-inch thickness. Pan-spray cookie sheets. Cut dough in rounds; place on cookie sheets and prick with fork to prevent blisters.
6. Bake at 375 degrees 15 to 20 minutes, until brown.
7. Remove with spatula as soon as slightly cooled.

St. James Day (July 25)

One of the original apostles of Jesus, St. James converted Spain to Christianity. An ancient pilgrim trail winds from the French Pyrenees mountains to the Spanish province of Galicia and the apostle's tomb at Santiago de Compostela. Monasteries built along this route offered pilgrims food and shelter.

C-66. Scallops with Anise and Oranges

The city of Santiago de Compostela is located not far from the cold Atlantic coast and its excellent seafood. By tradition, travelers arriving in the city first ate scallops, saving the shells as proof of their successful pilgrimage. Still worn today, these symbolic emblems guarantee pilgrims hospitality on their journey.

(*continued*)

Yield: 4 servings
Equipment: Colander, stainless steel bowl, cutting board, knife, grater, juicer

Ingredients

1 pound bay scallops, rinsed and
  drained
1 lime
1 large orange
1 teaspoon salt

1 teaspoon coarse black pepper
1 anise (fennel), about 10 to
  12 ounces
1 tablespoon olive oil

Method

1. Grate lime and orange peel, add to scallops with lime juice, salt, and pepper. Refrigerate 2 hours.
2. Clean anise, saving some of the feathery top as garnish. Cut anise into strips. There should be about a cup. Add to scallops with oil.
3. Cut orange into sections, removing all pips. Blend into scallop salad. Serve on lettuce leaves.

St. Stephen's Day (August 20)

This holiday commemorates Stephen I, the patron saint of Hungary, its first Christian king, and a symbol of Hungarian independence. When Soviet troops occupied Hungary in 1944, patriots spirited away St. Stephen's crown to a small Austrian village for safekeeping with the U.S. Army until conditions warranted its safe return.

C-67. Day of the New Bread (*Kalács*)

The Hungarian plains are famous for their wheat. Bread is baked from the new harvest on this national holiday.
Yield: 1 loaf
Equipment needed: Small bowl, electric mixer with dough hook, flour sifter, work surface, dough scraper, paring knife, cookie sheet, pastry brush

Ingredients

3/4 cup milk
1 package yeast
1 pinch saffron
3 cups flour
1 teaspoon salt
4 ounces (1 stick) butter

1/4 cup sugar
2 egg yolks
1 egg
Flour for dusting
Poppy seeds

Method

1. Warm ¼ cup of milk to about 90 degrees, add yeast and saffron and place in warm spot.
2. Sift flour into bowl. Add salt.
3. Warm remaining milk and butter. Add sugar and two egg yolks.
4. Separate last egg and save egg white. Add yolk to milk and butter. Blend well.
5. Combine all ingredients except egg white at slow speed with dough hook, forming smooth, rather heavy dough.
6. Knead on flour-dusted work surface; shape into round loaf.
7. Place dough on cookie sheet, cover with kitchen towel, and let rise until doubled in size.
8. With paring knife, make criss-cross slashes for decoration.
9. Sprinkle with poppy seeds and bake at 375 degrees for about an hour.

Feast of San Gennaro (September 20–26)

At the turn of the twentieth century, many immigrants from southern Italy settled in New York City's "Little Italy." The weeklong feast of San Gennaro, the patron saint of Naples, is still celebrated every September with a street fair and much food.

C-68. Sfingi Fritters

Made from a simple baking-powder batter, sfingi fritters dusted with powdered sugar are sold by many food stalls during the San Gennaro festival.
Yield: 24 fritters
Equipment needed: Two mixing bowls, wire whisk, pot for deep frying, 1-inch-diameter ice cream scoop, slotted spoon, wire rack, sifter

Ingredients

2 cups flour
½ teaspoon salt
1 tablespoon baking powder
½ teaspoon cinnamon, ground
½ teaspoon nutmeg, ground
1 teaspoon grated orange peel
½ teaspoon almond extract

2 eggs
½ cup sugar
1 tablespoon oil
⅓ cup milk
Fat for frying
Confectioners sugar

Method

1. Combine the first six ingredients together in mixing bowl.
2. Mix the next five ingredients together in another bowl.

(continued)

SFINGI FRITTERS

3. Combine the two mixtures. Stir all ingredients with wire whisk, forming thick batter. Let stand about 10 minutes.
4. Heat oil or shortening to 375 degrees in heavy saucepan or deep-fat fryer.
5. Using 1-inch-diameter ice cream scoop, drop small balls of batter into fat. Avoid crowding, carefully moving fritters around with slotted spoon so they fry evenly; this will take about 5 minutes.
6. Remove to paper towels and drain. Dust with confectioners sugar.

All Saints' Day (November 1)

Many Christians, including Roman Catholics, Orthodox Christians, Anglicans, and Lutherans, celebrate All Saints' Day. Festivities vary widely across denominations.

C-69. Mayan Mexican Graveyard Pie (*Bil Pollo*)

In Mexico on All Saints' Day, many people visit graveyards to pay respect to departed family members. This recipe is for the traditional Yucatan Mayan Tamale Pie that was offered to the dead. It was originally steamed in banana leaves.

Yield: 10 servings

Equipment needed: Large pot, small saucepan, electric blender, 2-quart saucepan, large mixing bowl, baking pan about 12 × 8 × 3 inches

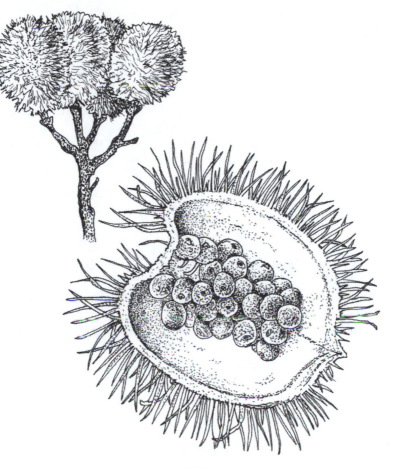

ACHIOTE

Ingredients

1 pound pork stew meat
1 chicken, 2½ pounds
2 tablespoons oil
1 teaspoon achiote
½ cup onions, chopped
1 tablespoon garlic, chopped
¼ teaspoon cumin, ground
¼ teaspoon dried oregano
1 teaspoon cayenne pepper

½ cup green peppers, diced
½ cup canned crushed tomatoes
3 cups masa harina
½ cup lard or vegetable shortening, melted
1 teaspoon salt
1½ cups hot chicken broth or water
Pan spray

Method

1. Cover pork with water and simmer until done, about 30 minutes. Cut chicken in quarters and add to pork. Simmer an additional 30 minutes.
2. Cool pork and chicken in stock. When cold, set pork aside, along with chicken (skin and bones removed). Drain stock and save.
3. Sauté achiote seeds in oil; oil will turn red. Discard seeds. Add onions and garlic to oil and cook briefly. Add spices, green peppers, and tomatoes.

(continued)

4. Simmer over moderate heat until the sauce thickens.
5. Stir in 2 tablespoons of the masa harina and add ½ cup chicken broth. Set aside.
6. Make tamale dough by blending remaining masa harina, melted fat, salt, and saved stock. The amount of liquid needed will vary; the dough should be rather stiff and workable.
7. Pan-spray baking pan. Spread enough dough in pan to form a 1-inch-thick layer on bottom and ½ inch on sides.
8. Place meat and sauce in center and cover with remaining dough.
9. Steam or bake 2 hours in 300-degree oven.
10. Serve hot.

What Would Jesus Have Eaten?

In the time of Jesus, Judea was primarily a subtropical desert. Sheep and goats foraged for meager food. Fishing in the Mediterranean and Lake Galilee provided additional sources of protein. Cultivated crops included wheat, barley, and millet, and honey was used as a sweetener. Dates, figs, and citrus were the principal fruit varieties. Grapes were both eaten as table fruit and made into wine. Olives supplied oil for cooking and illumination. Jesus would have followed Jewish dietary rules and practices.

C-70. Barley Bread

Jesus ate bread, the staple food of the Jews, and referred to himself as the Bread of Life. Food was highly valued and regarded as a gift from God. At the Last Supper, reference was made to wine and bread. The bread was probably made with a combination of barley and wheat flour, although Christian belief stipulates that the bread, or Host, used in the Eucharist must be unleavened and made with pure wheat flour.

Equipment needed: Heavy saucepan, stirring spoon, electric mixer with paddle, 1 quart saucepan, large ice cream scoop, cookie sheet

Ingredients

1¼ cups barley flour   1 teaspoon salt
2 tablespoons olive oil   2 cups water
2 cups whole-wheat flour

Method

1. Toast barley flour in oil over medium heat, stirring constantly, until light yellow and pleasant-smelling.
2. Combine whole-wheat flour and salt in mixing bowl.
3. Add barley flour when it is cool.
4. Bring water to a boil and add to flour mixture.

5. With electric mixer, blend first at lowest speed, increasing to medium, until stiff dough forms.
6. Scoop out balls of dough and flatten with oiled hands into disks about ½-inch thick.
7. Bake on cookie sheet at 400 degrees, about 10 minutes, until brown.
8. Disks will be hard; serve with soup or hot sweetened milk.

C-71. Stuffed Dates

Here is a tasty snack made from simple ingredients.
Yield: 20 pieces
Equipment: Paring knife, 2-quart saucepan, small mixing bowl, grater

Ingredients

20 whole almonds, skin on
20 large dried dates, pitted

1 tablespoon grated orange peel
2 tablespoons honey

Method

1. Cover almonds with water and bring to a boil. Drain carefully. When cool, slip off skins.
2. Add orange peel, blending with honey and almonds.
3. Place one almond inside each date. Serve as snacks.

3

HINDUISM AND SIKHISM

Hinduism

Hinduism is different from many of the other world religions in that it has no single founder, has no one specific religious philosophy, and is not centrally organized. Rather, Hinduism is a "way of life" that guides its followers along the spiritual path of becoming one with the Universal Consciousness. The origin of the religion is unclear, though it evolved in India around 2000 BCE. The word "Hindu" is derived from the name Sindhu, meaning the people of the Indus River region of northern India. Over the centuries, Hinduism has been heavily influenced by other religions such as Zoroastrianism, Buddhism, Sikhism, and Jainism and has adapted accordingly. Traditionally Hinduism has been very tolerant of all other religions. The religion has many deities, both male and female, though all are aspects of Brahman, the supreme Universal Spirit. The most commonly worshipped are the Trinity of Brahma the Creator, Vishnu the Preserver, and Shiva the Destroyer. Other popular deities include Krishna, Lakshmi, and Ganesha. In even the most modest of homes in India, a special place is set aside for worship of the chosen deity, who may be represented by a statue or picture. For Hindus, life is a cyclical process of renewal through reincarnation or rebirth of the soul in a new body. Each reincarnation reflects one's spiritual progress, or *karma*. Good thoughts, words, and deeds in one life lead to a higher reincarnation in the next.

A notable feature of Hindu society is the ancient caste system, which divides people into a multitude of castes and subcastes originally based on occupation and later on heredity alone. For the sake of simplicity, these are classified into four castes. The highest caste, the Brahmins, traditionally were priests and teachers and now are those prominent in the professions and in business. The Kshatriyas were the warrior class, charged with protecting the Brahmins and the community. The Vaishyas, who were farmers and merchants, supported the community economically while the Sudras (peasants, servants, and workers) supported the other three castes through manual labor. In addition, a fifth group is known as the Untouchables (Dalits); traditionally they performed unpleasant and menial tasks and were shunned by other castes. Untouchability has been abolished by law and, particularly in more cosmopolitan cities, caste barriers have largely disappeared. Traditionally upper castes regarded lower castes as ritually unclean and would not eat or intermarry with them.

Today there are about 760 million followers of Hinduism worldwide, mostly in India but also in Nepal, Sri Lanka, and other Southeast Asian countries, as well as in South Africa and the Caribbean. The Hindu population in the United States numbers about one and a half million—concentrated in California and New York, and to a lesser extent in Texas, Illinois, and Florida. Most Hindus in North America are emigrants from India.

Sikhism

In contrast to Hinduism, Sikhism is barely five hundred years old. It was founded in 1469 in India by Shri Guru Nanak Dev who taught the "Oneness of God" and who rejected divisions between people based on religious and social status, proclaiming, "There is no Hindu; there is no Muslim." For Sikhs, all human beings are creatures of God and must be treated equally. Unlike Hindus, Sikhs do not use images in worship. However, like Hindus, Sikhs believe in karma and *samsara* (the Hindu cycle of life and death). Like Muslims, they believe in a single deity and avoid worship of idols. The holy book of the Sikhs, known as the Adi Granth, or Guru Granth Sahib, was completed in 1708 by the last of the Sikh gurus (Shri Guru Gobind Singh Ji), who also gave all males a new surname, "Singh" (Lion), to be added to their first names. Women were to add "Kaur" (Princess) to their names. Guru Singh also created a Sikh community identity known as the *khalsa* that gave male initiates a distinctive dress and appearance. They are known as the Five Ks, based on five words beginning with the letter "k":

- **kesh** uncut hair
- **kanga** a comb to keep hair neat and clean
- **kirpan** a ceremonial sword that is an emblem of courage and adventure to be used for defensive purposes
- **kada** a steel bracelet to remind the wearer of his bond to God
- **kacha** a knee-length undergarment

While Sikh men are easily recognized by their turbans and uncut beards, not all Sikhs today adopt the Five Ks.

There are no central governing bodies in the Sikh religion, and Sikhs have no clergy. A Sikh temple is called a *Gurdwara,* meaning "House of the Guru." All Gurdwaras contain a copy of the holy book and are open to people of all faiths. The Golden Temple situated in Amritsar, Punjab, India, is the most sacred Sikh site. There are about 23 million Sikhs worldwide, the majority living in India's Punjab region. The Sikh population in the United States numbers approximately 250,000. In the U.S., Sikh centers are located in California and New York. A large Sikh community of 100,000 is found in British Columbia, Canada.

Food, Diet, and Cooking

Hindu and Sikh dietary practices are influenced by both spiritual beliefs and social arrangements. The concept of *Ahimsa,* or nonviolence, contained in ancient texts has strongly influenced Indian society. About 30 percent of Hindus are vegetarian, but almost all avoid beef. The cow is a sacred animal, and cows in India are not killed but treated with respect and allowed to wander at will, even in the streets of cities. In the early period of Hinduism the Brahmins, the priestly class, slaughtered cattle on religious holidays and freely shared the meat with all people. As the population grew and agriculture developed, cows were needed as draft animals and for milk. Eventually cows became too valuable to be slaughtered, even when old and sick. Today, many Hindus eat a vegetarian diet, including yogurt and eggs, while some avoid animal products altogether. Except for beef, meat eating is not prohibited; but it is discouraged, especially among the higher castes. Consumption of alcohol is frowned upon. The caste system traditionally affected food consumption because of restrictions on eating with, or even accepting food from, members of a lower caste.

Sikhs share the Hindu reverence for cows and thus avoid beef, and though other meats may be eaten, some Sikhs are vegetarian. Animals must be humanely slaughtered by a single blow known as *jhatka*; thus Jewish kosher and Islamic halal meats are forbidden because they are slaughtered using other techniques. The use of alcohol and tobacco is forbidden. Many Sikhs do not rigidly adhere to dietary laws and readily adapt to the food customs of other cultures.

Many Hindu and Sikh recipes are of Indian origin, so it is useful to understand Indian cooking and ingredients. The country is huge, and the available ingredients vary greatly. The basic staples are rice in the south and wheat in the north. Indian vegetarian dishes are perhaps the best in the world because there is a long tradition and a huge market for vegetarian food. Essential proteins are provided by numerous varieties of legumes (*dal*), yogurt, and milk-based desserts. Lentils, chickpeas, split peas, black-eyed peas, and others are available whole and ground into flour. In the United States, curry, a commercial blend of spices available as a powder or as paste in various degrees of hotness, has been the ubiquitous spice generally associated with Indian cooking. In India, it is almost unknown. Indian cooks generally ignore commercial curry and blend spices to suit the specific dish they are preparing. The most commonly used spices are cardamom, coriander, cloves, cumin, cinnamon, fenugreek, mace, nutmeg, pepper, turmeric, and saffron. These spices may be ground or used whole. Indian cooks usually grind spices as needed, roasting and frying them before use to develop flavor. Ginger, onions, and garlic are used throughout the subcontinent. However, garlic and onions are avoided by orthodox Hindus, who believe they inflame the passions and disturb the mind. Tamarind and amchoor (dried green mango) provide sour taste, and a wide variety of chilies provides varying degrees of hotness. Asafetida is the resin of a tree and smells rather unusual. It is sometimes used as a substitute for garlic by those who avoid that. The most popular fruit is mango, followed by bananas, dates, and papaya.

Ghee, which is rendered butterfat, is most commonly used for cooking. Many Indian meals are accompanied by relishes called *chutney*. The term comes from the Sanskrit word *chatni*, meaning "to lick." Most chutney is made with mango, but many other fruit and vegetable combinations exist. Chutney is normally sweet, sour, and pungent. Breads can be sauteed, deep fried, roasted, baked, or steamed. In North India, they are usually flat breads quickly fried or baked inside a clay oven called a *tandoor*. The oven is heated by charcoal and is used for roasting meats on skewers. Indian desserts are often based on reduced milk, made by slowly boiling milk until thick or even light brown. In South India, many breads are made of ground rice and lentils, including *idlis*, steamed disc-shaped breads, and *dosas*, which resemble thin pancakes.

Celebration Recipes

Hindu religious holidays and celebrations vary among countries and ethnic groups and have different names, meanings, and customs even in different regions of India. Hindu holidays are dated based on a lunisolar calendar (a calendar whose date indicates both the moon phase and the time of the solar year). This means that their Gregorian dates vary somewhat from year to year, but keep in time with the seasons. Dates may also differ slightly between countries. In additional to the numerous religious festivals, Hindus celebrate personal feast days including birthdays, weddings, and funerals.

Sikh holidays and festivals celebrate important dates in the lives of the gurus—the historical spiritual leaders of the Sikh faith—and in the historical development of the religion. Until 1999, Sikhs used a lunar calendar, but since then they have adopted a system based on the solar year, so dates of annual celebrations are now fixed.

Makar Sankranti or Pongal (January)

Makar Sankranti is a time to celebrate the winter solstice and worship the Sun God. Known as Pongal in the Indian state of Tamil Nadu, this ancient festival has additional significance as a harvest festival. Cattle are washed, and their horns are painted and adorned with shining metal caps and multicolored beads; tinkling bells, sheaves of corn, and flower garlands are tied around their necks. In northern regions, bonfires are lit, and offerings of sweets, rice, and popcorn are thrown into the flames. Rice cooked in milk with sugar is a popular dish.

H-1. Saffron Rice Cooked in Milk (*Sarkkarai Pongal*)

The name of this special festival-day dish comes from the word *pongal*, which means "to boil." As genuine saffron threads are very costly, less-expensive powdered saffron is often substituted.

Yield: 10 servings
Equipment needed: 4-quart heavy saucepan, stirring spoon

Ingredients

2$\frac{1}{2}$ quarts milk
1 cup basmati rice
1 cup light brown sugar
2 tablespoons ghee or oil
$\frac{1}{4}$ teaspoon nutmeg
1 teaspoon powdered saffron
1 teaspoon cardamom, ground

2 teaspoons salt
$\frac{1}{2}$ cup almonds, peeled and chopped
$\frac{1}{2}$ cup unsalted cashew nuts, coarsely chopped
$\frac{1}{4}$ cup raisins

Method

1. Simmer milk in heavy saucepan.
2. Wash rice and add to milk.
3. Simmer 1 hour, stirring occasionally.

4. Add brown sugar and ghee.
5. Cook 10 minutes longer to dissolve sugar. Stir in remaining ingredients.
6. Bring to a boil again, and simmer 5 minutes.
7. Serve hot or cold.

H-2. Chickpea Soup (*Karhi*)

This thick soup of North Indian origin is usually served as a Sunday dinner with chickpea fritters or rice. Regional variations may call for ginger and garlic, or hot chili peppers. Buttermilk gives it a pleasantly sour taste, and chopped cilantro makes a pretty garnish.
Yield: 6 servings
Equipment needed: Large bowl, whisk, 4-quart heavy saucepan, mixing spoon, cutting board, French knife

Ingredients

1 cup chickpea flour	1 tablespoon sesame seeds
2½ cups buttermilk	5 cups hot water
2 tablespoons ghee or oil	1 teaspoon turmeric
1 pinch asafetida	2 teaspoons salt
1 teaspoon fennel seeds	½ teaspoon amchoor powder
1 teaspoon cumin seeds	1 tablespoon lime juice
1 teaspoon fenugreek seeds	1 bunch cilantro

Method

1. Whisk chickpea flour and buttermilk together in large bowl, removing lumps.
2. Cook asafetida and all seeds in ghee or oil over medium heat until seeds are lightly toasted.
3. Remove from heat and carefully add water. Return to stove and add chickpea slurry.
4. Stir well and bring to simmer.
5. Add turmeric, salt, and amchoor powder.
6. Simmer 45 minutes, stirring frequently. Add lime juice.
7. Remove cilantro stems. Wash cilantro leaves thoroughly, drain, and coarsely chop. Add leaves to soup.
8. Serve with rice.

H-3. Cauliflower with Ginger and Cilantro (*Dum Gobi*)

Cauliflower, a member of the cabbage family and Mediterranean native, was first developed in the fifteenth century. It reached India in the nineteenth century and was cultivated in the north, where it became a popular vegetable.
Yield: 4 servings

(continued)

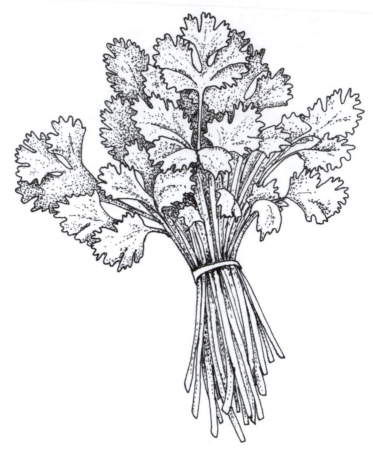

CILANTRO

Equipment needed: Cutting board, paring knife, French knife, wide saucepan with lid, wooden spoon

Ingredients

1 large head cauliflower, about 2 pounds
4 tablespoons ghee or oil
¹/₂ teaspoon turmeric, ground
2 tablespoons gingerroot
1 teaspoon green chilies, seeded and chopped
¹/₂ teaspoon cumin, ground

¹/₂ teaspoon coriander, ground
¹/₂ teaspoon cardamom, ground
1 teaspoon turmeric, ground
¹/₂ teaspoon amchoor powder
1 teaspoon salt
¹/₂ cup cilantro, chopped and loosely packed
1¹/₂ cups water

Method

1. Peel ginger and chop as finely as possible.
2. Remove green leaves from cauliflower and divide into small florets; about 6 cups of florets.
3. Heat ghee or oil in wide saucepan and add next nine ingredients.
4. Cook over low heat to develop flavor, making sure spices do not burn.

5. Remove from heat and carefully add ½ cup water. Bring to a boil and simmer 15 minutes.
6. Add cauliflower and 1 cup water. Stir, cover, and simmer 15 minutes until cauliflower is cooked but not mushy.
7. If necessary, add more water. The cauliflower should steam more than braise.
8. Add chopped cilantro.
9. Serve with Indian bread as main course, or room temperature as appetizer.

H-4. Basmati Rice (*Chawal*)

A staple of India, delicately flavored basmati rice is served as an accompaniment to vegetable and meat dishes.

Yield: 4 cups
Equipment needed: 1-quart heavy saucepan with lid, wooden spoon, fork

Ingredients

2 cups basmati rice
1 ounce (¼ stick) butter

1 teaspoon salt
3 cups hot water

Method

1. Wash rice, soak in cold water 15 minutes, and drain well.
2. Melt butter over medium heat. When it starts to sizzle, add rice and salt, stirring well.
3. Add 3 cups hot water, bring to a boil, cover, and simmer over very low heat for 20 minutes.
4. Fluff with fork.

Vasant Panchami (January or February)

This Hindu festival marks the first day of spring, when the mustard crop is ripe, coloring the fields yellow. Women wear yellow saris, and yellow rice dishes are prepared. Known as Sarasvati Puja in eastern regions of India such as Bengal, the celebration honors the goddess Sarasvati, who represents wisdom, intellect, and knowledge.

H-5. Basmati Rice with Spices and Saffron (*Chawal Pullao*)

This aromatic yellow rice dish is perfect for the festivities, as saffron is an essential ingredient. Powdered saffron has been substituted for the more expensive saffron threads.

Yield: 6 servings

(continued)

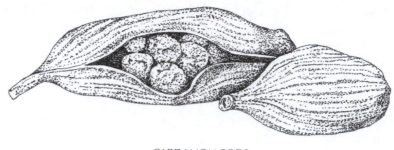

CARDAMOM PODS

Equipment needed: Small bowl, colander, 2-quart heavy saucepan with lid, mixing spoon

Ingredients

2 tablespoons milk
2 teaspoons powdered saffron
1 cup basmati rice
2 tablespoons ghee or oil
1 teaspoon ginger, chopped
1 teaspoon garlic, chopped

1 teaspoon hot pepper flakes
1 teaspoon turmeric, ground
5 cardamom
2 cinnamon sticks
1 teaspoon salt
2¼ cups water

Method

1. Warm milk, add saffron, and set aside.
2. Soak rice 20 minutes, rinse and drain.
3. Sauté all spices in ghee or oil over moderate heat to develop flavor. Do not brown or scorch.
4. Add rice, salt, water, and saffron milk.
5. Bring to a boil, cover, and simmer over low heat 25 minutes.

H-6. Garam-Spiced Chicken Strips

In this recipe, *garam* refers to the relatively hot blend of spices common in many Indian dishes. Garam masala powder can be purchased from any Indian grocery store and many supermarkets, or you can make your own garam masala spice using the recipe on page 119.
Yield: 6 to 8 servings
Equipment needed: Cutting board, knife, blender, nonreactive container, griddle or roasting pan

Ingredients

3 pounds boneless, skinless chicken breasts
5 tablespoons oil

4 tablespoons red wine vinegar
½ cup onions, chopped
2 tablespoons garlic, chopped

1 tablespoon ginger, chopped
1 tablespoon fennel seeds
1 teaspoon cumin, ground
2 teaspoons coriander, ground
1 teaspoon turmeric
1 teaspoon cinnamon, ground

1 teaspoon cloves, ground
1 teaspoon cayenne pepper
1 teaspoon salt
1 teaspoon cardamom, ground
2 tablespoons water

Method

1. Cut chicken breasts into strips, approximately 1-by-2 inches in size.
2. Combine all remaining ingredients and process in blender until smooth.
3. Add blended mixture to chicken strips and refrigerate at least 2 hours.
4. Broil chicken in oven, or cook on griddle, until light brown but not dark.

H-7. Flat Bread (*Paratha*)

Roti is the generic Indian name for bread. Many North Indian breads basically use the same dough made with water and whole-wheat or regular flour. Some call for yeast, others do not. The main difference lies in the cooking process. *Chapattis* are plain, griddle-baked breads. *Parathas* are first brushed with ghee and folded before being griddle-baked. *Poori* is deep fried, and *naan* is yeast-bread baked inside a tandoori oven.

Yield: 8 large pieces
Equipment needed: Electric mixer with dough hook, work surface, rolling pin, griddle, tongs

Ingredients

2½ cups whole-wheat flour
1 teaspoon salt
1 cup water

4 ounces ghee or oil
Flour for dusting

Method

1. Combine flour, salt, and water in mixing bowl.
2. Using dough hook, blend at very slow speed. Dough will be heavy.
3. Knead on floured work surface until smooth, at least 10 minutes. Shape dough into ball and wrap in plastic.
4. Let rest 2 hours at room temperature.
5. Divide dough into 16 pieces and roll each into a thin circle.
6. Brush eight circles with ghee and top with remaining circles. Press to seal.
7. Place circles on floured cookie sheet, cover, and refrigerate 30 minutes.
8. Roll each circle as thinly as possible to about dessert-plate size.
9. Heat griddle to medium heat and brush it lightly with vegetable oil.
10. Turn up heat until griddle smokes. Bake parathas, turning to cook each side. Keep warm until ready to serve.

H-8. Spiced Chickpeas (*Channa Masaledar*)

This traditional dish from the state of Punjab may be served hot as a main course or side dish. To save time, this recipe uses canned chickpeas. If dried peas are used, they should be soaked overnight.
Yield: 6 servings
Equipment needed: 2-quart heavy-bottomed saucepan, wooden stirring spoon

Ingredients

3 tablespoons ghee or oil
1 teaspoon cumin seeds, whole
½ cup onions, chopped
1 tablespoon ginger, chopped
2 teaspoons garlic, chopped
¼ teaspoon cinnamon, ground
¼ teaspoon nutmeg
¼ teaspoon cloves, ground

1 teaspoon coriander, ground
1 teaspoon salt
½ teaspoon hot pepper or cayenne
½ teaspoon amchoor powder
1 tablespoon tomato paste
2 (15½-ounce) cans chickpeas, drained
½ cup water

Method

1. Cook cumin seeds in oil over moderate heat until lightly toasted.
2. Add chopped onions, ginger, and garlic. Cook until onions are transparent.
3. Add remaining spices and stir-fry over moderate heat for 5 to 6 minutes.
4. Add tomato paste, chickpeas, and ½ cup water.
5. Stir to blend, cover, and simmer 10 minutes or until heated through.

Maha Shivaratri (February or March)

Celebrated on the fourteenth day of the Hindu month of Phalguna, this festival is devoted to the worship of Lord Shiva. A day of fasting is followed by a night vigil, after which food is eaten. During the fast, "cooling foods" such as milk, honey, and water are offered to Shiva.

H-9. Spiced Milk Drink (*Thandai*)

Thandai is a popular watery drink made with milk, almonds, and spices that traditionally included hemp seeds.
Yield: 6 servings
Equipment needed: 2-quart soup pot, fine wire strainer, cheesecloth, mixing spoon

Ingredients

1 tablespoon almonds, chopped
1 teaspoon almond extract
1 tablespoon watermelon seeds, peeled

1 tablespoon poppy seeds
1 tablespoon anise seeds
1 teaspoon peppercorns, crushed

½ cup dried rose petals (available in Indian markets)
½ tablespoon rose water (optional)

3 pints water
5 cardamom pods, crushed
1½ cups sugar
1 cup milk

Method

1. Combine all ingredients except sugar and milk. Bring to a boil.
2. Simmer 10 minutes. Add milk and sugar. Cool.
3. Strain through cheesecloth.
4. Chill before serving.

H-10. Cumin Seed Cooler (*Jal Jeera*)

This is a popular thirst-quenching drink in North India during the summer months.
Yield: 5 servings
Equipment needed: Cast-iron pan, food processor, strainer, bowl

Ingredients

2 tablespoons cumin seeds, dry
½ cup mint leaves
¼ cup cilantro
1 tablespoon amchoor powder
½ teaspoon salt

2 tablespoons lemon juice
1 tablespoon sugar
5 cups cold water
2 tablespoons mint leaves, for garnish

Method

1. Toast cumin seeds.
2. Combine all ingredients in food processor, except water and mint leaves used for garnish, and process to fine puree.
3. Strain and add water.
4. Chill and serve sprinkled with mint leaves.

H-11. Sweet Tomato Chutney

Tomatoes were first introduced to India from the Americas by Portuguese traders. They have become staples in moderately hot regions, but not in the tropics where the heat causes them to spoil on the vines. Served as a dip or accompaniment to meat and fish dishes, this chutney recipe uses canned tomatoes to save time.
Yield: 2 cups
Equipment needed: Blender, 2-quart heavy-bottomed nonstick saucepan, wooden spoon

(continued)

Ingredients

1 tablespoon garlic, chopped
1 tablespoon ginger, chopped
³/₄ cup red wine vinegar or mild
   palm wine vinegar
1 cup sugar

1½ teaspoons salt
½ teaspoon cayenne pepper
1 cup canned crushed tomatoes
¼ cup raisins
¼ cup slivered almonds

Method

1. Puree all ingredients except tomatoes, raisins, and almonds in blender.
2. Put blended mixture in saucepan along with tomatoes and raisins, and simmer, stirring frequently, for about 20 minutes.
3. Add almonds and remove from stove.
4. Store refrigerated at least 24 hours, allowing flavors to blend.

H-12. Stewed Lentils (*Masur Dal*)

Available in India in an amazing array of colors, lentils range in size from very tiny to rather large, although to an untrained palate, there is little discernable flavor difference among them. This meatless main course is appreciated after a day of fasting.

Yield: 6 servings
Equipment needed: 6-quart wide heavy-bottomed saucepan, small frying pan

Ingredients

3 tablespoons ghee or oil
1 teaspoon turmeric, ground
1 teaspoon hot pepper flakes
1 teaspoon cumin seeds
1 teaspoon fenugreek seeds
1 tablespoon ginger, chopped
1 tablespoon garlic, chopped

2 cups lentils; red preferred
1 pinch asafetida powder
1 cinnamon stick, about 3 inches
1 bay leaf
2 teaspoons salt
1 tablespoon vinegar
6 cups water

Method

1. Heat ghee or oil in saucepan and cook turmeric, pepper flakes, cumin, and fenugreek briefly over low temperature to develop flavor.
2. Add ginger and garlic. Cook briefly.
3. Add lentils, 6 cups water, and remaining ingredients.
4. Simmer until lentils are soft but not mushy, about 40 minutes. Dish should have the consistency of stew.

Holi (March)

Holi, the spring Festival of Colors, is India's second most important festival (after Diwali). Celebrating the defeat of the child-devouring witch Holika, it also honors the immortal love of Krishna and Radha. The two days of fun, frolic, and partying usually start off with a big bonfire. Powdered colors are dropped from rooftops and people drench each other with colorful water-filled balloons called *abeer*. Huge feasts include mouthwatering delicacies to savor such as *puranpolis*, *malpuas*, and *gunjiyas*. Sikhs also celebrate the Holi festival, which they call Hola Mohalla, on February 21.

H-13. Split Pea–Filled Griddle Breads (*Puranpoli*)

Made with a variety of fillings, these sweet griddle breads are popular throughout India. The name comes from the words for stuffing (*puran*) and flat bread (*poli*).

Yield: 10 pieces

Equipment needed: 2-quart soup pot, strainer, food mill, heavy saucepan, stirring spoon, electric mixer with dough hook, work surface, rolling pin, griddle

Ingredients

½ cup yellow split peas	4 tablespoons ghee or oil
¼ cup brown sugar	¾ cup water
1 teaspoon cardamom, ground	Ghee to grease griddle and to
2 teaspoons salt	serve
2½ cups wheat flour	

Method

1. Cover split peas with plenty of water and simmer until soft but not mushy, about 30 minutes.
2. Drain and discard water.
3. Puree peas in food mill.
4. Cook puree in saucepan over low heat with sugar, cardamom, and 1 teaspoon of the salt, stirring continuously until thick paste is formed.
5. Set aside to cool.
6. Put flour, ghee, water, and remaining salt in mixing bowl and blend at slow speed. Dough will be heavy.
7. Knead on floured work surface for 10 minutes.
8. Shape into ball, wrap in plastic, and let rest 25 minutes.
9. Divide dough into 20 balls.
10. Roll each ball into a 4-inch round.
11. Put about ½ tablespoon each of filling in the center of 10 rounds.
12. Moisten edges with a little water and cover each with second dough round.
13. Carefully roll rounds to about 6 inches across, making sure filling does not ooze out.
14. Oil griddle and fry puranpolis on both sides.
15. Serve hot with melted ghee as an accompaniment to curry dishes.

H-14. Tandoori Baked Chicken
(*Tandoori Murgha*)

Resembling a waist-high pot, the tandoor is a narrow-topped clay oven heated from the bottom by a charcoal fire. It is used for cooking dishes like skewered meat and baking wheat bread called *naan*. For convenience, this recipe uses a gas or electric oven. Although the result is still tasty, it lacks the smoky flavor produced by the traditional tandoor.

Yield: 4 servings

Equipment needed: Cutting board, knife, large mixing bowl, electric blender, large roasting pan with rack

FENUGREEK

Ingredients

1 roasting chicken, 3½ to 4 pounds
1 teaspoon hot pepper
1 tablespoon paprika
1 teaspoon salt
1 teaspoon coriander seeds, ground
1 teaspoon cumin, ground
1 teaspoon cardamom, ground
½ teaspoon cloves, ground

1 tablespoon ginger, chopped
1 tablespoon garlic, chopped
½ cup onions, chopped
½ cup yogurt
2 tablespoons lemon juice
5 drops red food coloring
½ cup fresh fenugreek leaves, loosely packed

Method

1. Cut chicken into eight pieces and place in large mixing bowl.
2. Put all remaining ingredients, except fenugreek leaves, in blender. Puree.
3. Combine spice mixture and chicken pieces, blending evenly to coat all pieces. Cover bowl with foil; refrigerate at least 2 hours or overnight.
4. Heat oven to 375 degrees.
5. Put chicken pieces on roasting rack and roast about 40 minutes.
6. Sprinkle with fenugreek leaves before serving.

H-15. Fried Turnovers (*Gunjiya*)

Indian stores sell special molds for making these appetizers.

Yield: 30 pieces

Equipment needed: Electric mixer with dough hook, work surface, 1-quart heavy saucepan, wooden stirring spoon, rolling pin, deep frying pan, slotted spoon

Ingredients

3 cups wheat flour	1½ cups sugar
4 tablespoons ghee or oil	½ teaspoon green cardamom
1 teaspoon salt	powder
³/₄ cup water	1 ounce almonds, chopped
Flour for dusting	1 ounce dried coconut, shredded
12 ounces khoya (milk solids	1 ounce raisins
available in Indian markets)	Ghee or oil for frying

Method

1. Blend flour, 4 tablespoons ghee, salt, and water at slow speed with dough hook until firm.
2. Knead dough briefly on floured work surface. Form into ball, wrap in plastic, and let rest 30 minutes.
3. Cut khoya into small pieces and cook over low heat, stirring constantly until it melts and is slightly browned.
4. Add sugar, cardamom, almonds, coconuts, and raisins. Cook over low heat until well blended.
5. Set aside to cool. When cooled, mixture will be brittle.
6. Divide dough into 30 pieces and shape into balls on floured work surface.
7. Roll each ball into a 5-inch circle and put ½ tablespoon of filling on each circle.
8. Moisten dough rims, fold over, and seal turnovers tightly.
9. Fry gunjiyas until golden brown on both sides.

H-16. Sweet Fritters (*Malpuas*)

This festive dessert is often decorated with edible sheets of silver called *vark*.
Yield: 16 pieces
Equipment needed: Small frying pan, mixing bowl, whisk, 1-quart saucepan, large frying pan, tablespoon, slotted spoon, serving platter

Ingredients

2 teaspoons fennel seeds	³/₄ cup water
1 cup yogurt	¹/₄ cup lime juice
1 cup flour	1 teaspoon grated lime peel
½ teaspoon baking powder	Oil for frying
1 cup sugar	Vark
10 green cardamom pods, crushed	

Method

1. Toast fennel seeds in dry pan.
2. Mix together with yogurt, flour, and baking powder to form very thick, smooth batter. Set aside.

(*continued*)

3. Make syrup by combining sugar, cardamom pods, and water. Bring to a boil; simmer 10 minutes.
4. Add lime juice and grated lime peel. Set aside.
5. Heat 1½ inches of oil in deep frying pan.
6. Using a moist tablespoon, carefully drop fritters into oil and fry on both sides over low heat.
7. Make sure fritters are fried all the way through.
8. Drain on paper-towel-covered platter, then move malpuas to shallow serving dish and drizzle with syrup.
9. Serve hot or cold, decorated with vark.

H-17. Besan Flour Chapattis (*Papri*)

Indian breads can be made with different flours. These deep-fried snacks use besan (chickpea flour).
Yield: 25 to 30 pieces, depending on size.
Equipment needed: Electric mixer with dough hook, work surface, deep frying pan, tongs

Ingredients

3 cups besan flour	³⁄₄ cup water
1 teaspoon mustard seed oil	1 teaspoon cumin, ground
1 teaspoon salt	Wheat flour for dusting
1 teaspoon red chili powder	Oil for frying

Method

1. Combine all ingredients, except wheat flour and frying oil, and blend at slow speed to form soft dough.
2. Knead briefly on floured work surface, cover with kitchen towel, and let rest for a half-hour.
3. Divide dough into walnut-size pieces and place on floured tray close to stove.
4. Heat about 1½ inches of oil in deep frying pan.
5. Stretch dough pieces and pat thin; place into hot oil one at a time.
6. Deep-fry on both sides until golden brown.
7. Besan bread is best eaten hot.

H-18. Caribbean Lamb Curry with Pecans

Many descendants of Indian laborers live in the Caribbean and celebrate Hindi holidays. Although Caribbean curry dishes are usually made with lamb or chicken, there are also vegetarian recipes.

Yield: 6 servings
Equipment needed: Cutting board, electric blender, heavy-bottomed sauce pot with lid, slotted spoon

Ingredients

1 medium jalapeño chili, seeded and sliced	½ teaspoon nutmeg
¼ cup onions, chopped	½ teaspoon cloves, ground
1 tablespoon garlic, peeled	½ teaspoon cinnamon
1 tablespoon ginger, coarsely chopped	¼ cup oil
1 tablespoon coriander, ground	1 cup onions, thinly sliced
2 teaspoons cumin	3 pounds lamb or goat stew meat
2 teaspoons turmeric, ground	½ tablespoon salt
¼ teaspoon cardamom, ground	¾ cup pecans, shelled
	1 pomegranate
	½ bunch cilantro leaves

Method

1. Remove seeds from chili and discard. Cut chili in slices.
2. Blend chili, chopped onions, garlic, ginger, and all spices with ¼ cup water to make fine slurry.
3. In heavy saucepan, cook sliced onions in oil over medium heat until brown and beginning to crisp.
4. Drain on paper towel and keep warm.
5. Increase heat, add meat, and brown, stirring frequently. As pieces cook, remove with slotted spoon and set aside.
6. Once all meat is browned, return to pot, add spice slurry, and bring to a boil.
7. Add salt, cover with water, and simmer.
8. Puree pecans in blender; add to simmering meat.
9. Cut pomegranate in half. Discard shell; save juice and seeds.
10. When meat is tender, add pomegranate seeds and juice. Bring to a boil once more and serve garnished with chopped cilantro leaves.

Sikh New Year (March 14)

This date marks the beginning of the Sikh Nanakshahi calendar year and also commemorates the accession of Guru Har Rai, the seventh guru in the Sikh line.

H-19. Punjab Fried Wheat Bread (*Poori* or *Puri*)

Bread is the most important staple in a Sikh's diet.
Yield: 15 pieces
Equipment needed: Electric mixer with dough hook, work surface, dough scraper, rolling pin, deep pan for frying

(continued)

Ingredients

2$\frac{1}{2}$ cups whole-wheat flour
1 teaspoon baking powder
1 teaspoon salt
$\frac{1}{2}$ cup lukewarm water
$\frac{1}{4}$ cup yogurt

1 tablespoon anise seeds, chopped
$\frac{1}{2}$ teaspoon cayenne pepper
1 teaspoon coriander, ground
Flour for dusting
Oil for frying

Method

1. Sift flour and baking powder together.
2. Add water, yogurt, salt, and spices. Using dough hook, blend at low speed until firm, heavy dough forms.
3. Knead on floured work surface until smooth.
4. Cover, let rest at least 30 minutes, and briefly knead again.
5. Divide dough into walnut-size balls and place on floured tray.
6. Heat about 1$\frac{1}{2}$ inches of oil in deep pan until a tiny drop of water sizzles.
7. With floured fingers, stretch dough balls into rounds and place, one by one, into hot oil.
8. Fry on both sides until light brown and transfer to paper-towel-covered tray.
9. Serve hot or cold. The bread freezes well.

H-20. Green and Red Lentil Soup (*Dal Shorba*)

This festive red lentil soup is garnished with spinach leaves. The spinach must be added at the last moment so it will remain green.
Yield: 4 servings
Equipment needed: 2-quart soup pot, stirring spoon, cutting board, knife

Ingredients

1 tablespoon oil
1 tablespoon garlic, chopped
$\frac{1}{2}$ teaspoon chili powder
3 teaspoons curry powder

1 cup onions, sliced
1 cup red lentils
4 ounces fresh spinach leaves
Salt and lime juice to taste

Method

1. Gently cook garlic, chili powder, and curry powder in oil to develop flavor.
2. Add onions and cook a few minutes longer.
3. Add red lentils and 2 quarts water. Bring to a boil; simmer 40 minutes, stirring occasionally.
4. Remove from heat. Puree in blender when cool.
5. Wash and drain spinach leaves; coarsely chop.
6. Bring soup to boil again and season with salt and lime juice.
7. Add spinach leaves. Simmer 5 minutes. Add water as needed if soup is too thick.
8. Serve at once.

Vasanta (April)

This holiday honors Rama, the seventh reincarnation of the Hindu god Vishnu. It is one of the most important festivals of the Vaishna Hindu sect.

H-21. Dried Nut Toffee (*Gajjac*)

This Indian toffee contains lots of nuts—beware of potential allergy issues before serving.
Yield: 2 pounds
Equipment needed: Cookie sheet, food processor, heavy saucepan, wooden spoon, rolling pin

Ingredients

2 ounces slivered almonds
2 ounces cashews
2 ounces unsalted peanuts
2 ounces walnut pieces
2 ounces unsalted pistachio nuts
3 cups sugar

1 ounce ghee or oil
$\frac{1}{2}$ cup water
1 tablespoon lime juice
1 teaspoon cardamom, ground
1 teaspoon rose water

Method

1. Carefully toast all nuts on cookie sheet in 375-degree oven.
2. Allow to cool. Coarsely chop in food processor.
3. In heavy saucepan, cook sugar, ghee, and water over medium heat, stirring frequently.
4. When sugar starts to melt, stir continuously until completely melted and light brown.
5. Remove from heat and add all nuts, lime juice, cardamom, and rose water. Stir to blend.
6. Carefully pour hot sugar mixture on large marble slab or oiled cookie sheet.
7. Grease rolling pin with pan spray and carefully flatten sugar mixture to a thickness of about $\frac{1}{2}$ inch.
8. When cool, break into pieces. Store in sealed container.

Vaisakhi (April)

Both a religious and an agricultural festival, Vaisakhi celebrates the end of the harvest and marks the beginning of the lunar new year. At daybreak, devout Hindus throughout India bathe in the holy rivers. Sweets are distributed, old enmities are forgiven, and life is full of joy and merriment. In the state of Kerala the festival is called Vishu and is celebrated with fireworks, the purchase of new clothes, and unusual arrangements of flowers, grains, fruits, cloth, gold, and money called *vishu kani*. Viewed early in the morning, these displays ensure a year of prosperity. Vishu is also a day of feasting, and dishes are prepared using nearly equal proportions of salty, sweet, sour, and bitter items.

H-22. Sour Mango Soup (*Mampazhapachadi*)

The flavor of mangoes varies greatly from sour while green to very sweet when ripe. This recipe requires a green, still sour, mango.
Yield: 6 servings
Equipment needed: Cutting board, French knife, 2-quart heavy soup pot, stirring spoon, 6-inch cast-iron pan

Ingredients

1 pound lean lamb stew meat, trimmed of fat	1 quart water
2 tablespoons ghee or oil	1 teaspoon salt
½ cup onions, diced	½ teaspoon cumin seed
2 teaspoons garlic, chopped	1 teaspoon amchoor powder
2 teaspoons ginger, chopped	3 tablespoons rice flour
1 cup green mango, peeled and diced	1 cup milk
	1 teaspoon vinegar
1 bay leaf, dried	3 tablespoons parsley, chopped

Method

1. Cut lamb into ¼-inch cubes.
2. Add 1 tablespoon of ghee to soup pot and cook lamb over medium heat for about 20 minutes, stirring frequently, until slightly browned.
3. Add onion, garlic, and ginger and continue cooking another 10 minutes.
4. Add mango, bay leaf, water, and salt and bring to a boil; simmer 1 hour.
5. Add cumin seeds to remaining ghee in cast-iron pan. Heat carefully until cumin seeds start to splatter. Remove from heat. When cold, add to soup.
6. Add amchoor powder, rice flour, and milk to soup and bring to a boil.
7. Add vinegar.
8. Serve hot soup sprinkled with parsley.

H-23. Fruit and Mint Chutney (*Podina* Chutney)

Chutney, basic to Indian cooking, comes in many different varieties. This sweet-sour version is best served with meat.
Yield: 5 cups
Equipment needed: Saucepan, strainer, mixing bowl, food processor

Ingredients

8 ounces apricots, dried	½ tablespoon grated orange peel
1 cup water	1 cup orange segments, skinless and seedless (about two large oranges)
3 cups apple, diced and cored (two apples, 6 or 7 ounces each)	

1 teaspoon grated lime peel

1/4 cup lime juice

2 tablespoons sugar

1 tablespoon green chilies, seeded
and chopped

1/2 teaspoon cayenne pepper

1 teaspoon salt

1 cup mint leaves, washed,
chopped, and tightly packed

Method

1. Soak apricots in water for 10 minutes. Bring to a boil, simmer 10 minutes, then drain.
2. Combine all ingredients in food processor and blend to medium-fine puree.
3. Store refrigerated in glass or plastic container. Chutney will taste better after all flavors have blended (about 24 hours).

H-24. Samosas

One of the most popular street foods in India, this savory deep-fried snack is made of pie dough filled with spicy potatoes or meat.

Yield: 22 to 24 pieces

Equipment needed: Sifter, food processor with steel blade, work surface, dough scraper, 2-quart pot, paring knife, ricer, heavy pot, stirring spoon, large mixing bowl, rolling pin

Ingredients

4 cups pastry (soft)
flour

2 teaspoons salt

6 ounces shortening

Cold water, as
needed

Flour for dusting

1 pound russet
(baking)
potatoes

3 tablespoons ghee
or oil

1 teaspoon fennel
seeds

1 teaspoon cumin,
ground

1 teaspoon salt

1/2 teaspoon hot
pepper flakes

1/2 cup onions,
chopped

1 teaspoon garlic,
chopped

1/2 cup chives,
snipped

1 egg

Fat for frying

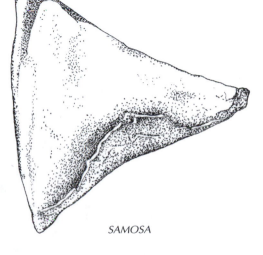

SAMOSA

Method

1. Sift flour into food processor bowl.
2. Add 1 teaspoon of salt and shortening. Pulse until mixture resembles coarse flakes.

(continued)

3. Gradually add cold water in small amounts until stiff dough forms. Do not overmix.
4. Knead 5 minutes on floured work surface. Roll into ball, wrap in plastic, and set aside to rest.
5. Wash potatoes, cover with water, and bring to a boil. Simmer until soft, then drain.
6. When potatoes are cool, press though ricer.
7. Cook all spices in fat over low heat to develop flavors, being careful not to burn.
8. Add onions and garlic and simmer over low heat. Add ½ cup water, continuing to simmer until all water is evaporated, about 10 minutes.
9. Combine cooked onions with potatoes, spices, remaining salt, chives, and egg. Mixture should be rather dry.
10. Divide dough into about two dozen balls. Cover and refrigerate for 15 minutes.
11. Roll each ball into a circle about 5 or 6 inches across.
12. Fill lower half of each circle with 1 tablespoon filling.
13. Moisten rim with water and fold over. Press rim with fork to form decorative seal.
14. Deep-fry until golden brown.

H-25. Sweets (*Pedhas*)

Traditionally made in different colors, these popular sweets are served in small foil cups or on bonbon paper and are beautifully arranged on platters.

Yield: 10 to 15 pieces, depending on size

Equipment needed: Cutting board, knife, wide saucepan, wooden stirring spoon

Ingredients

12 ounces khoya (milk solids available in Indian markets)
1½ cups confectioners sugar
½ teaspoon cardamom, ground
3 to 4 drops red or yellow food coloring

¼ cup unsalted pistachio nuts, shelled
1 tablespoon cardamom seeds, crushed

Method

1. Chop khoya into small pieces.
2. Cook in saucepan with sugar over low heat, stirring continuously, until mixture thickens and melting khoya forms very soft paste.
3. Continue stirring over low heat until paste stiffens.
4. Remove from heat. Add ground cardamom and food coloring.
5. Allow to cool, stirring frequently.
6. When mixture is lukewarm and pliable, shape into small patties with moist hands.

7. Press one pistachio nut into each patty; decorate with crushed cardamom.
8. Chill and serve.

Sikh Vaisakhi (April 13)

Vaisakhi, the New Year festival, is one of the most important days in the Sikh religious calendar. Also on this date in 1669, Guru Gobind Singh established the Sikh community of the Khalsa Panth. Men and women dressed in folk attire dance the *bhangra* and *gidda* to the beat of *dholak* drums. These vigorous dances tell the story of planting and reaping.

H-26. Punjabi Mixed Spice (*Garam Masala*)

This generic spice combination is used in many recipes and was prepared with a mortar and pestle until the invention of electric blenders. Indian stores carry many varieties of ready-made garam masala, both as a dry spice and a paste.
Yield: About $1/2$ cup
Equipment needed: Cast-iron pan, blender

Ingredients

5 tablespoons coriander seeds
3 tablespoons cumin seeds
$2^1/2$ tablespoons black
  peppercorns

2 black cardamom seeds
1 cinnamon stick, about 2 inches
5 cloves
$1/2$ teaspoon nutmeg

Method

1. Toast the coriander and cumin in a cast-iron frying pan over medium heat until lightly roasted.
2. Cool and grind with remaining ingredients. Store in a tightly lidded jar.

H-27. Lamb Masala (*Chaamp Masala*)

This rich, flavorsome dish originates in the fertile state of Punjab, the birthplace of the Sikh religion.
Yield: 8 main-course servings
Equipment needed: Electric blender, heavy-bottomed saucepan with lid, stirring spoon

Ingredients

2 tablespoons ginger, peeled and
  coarsely chopped

2 teaspoons cumin, ground
3 tablespoons garlic, chopped

(continued)

1 cup plus 2 or 3 tablespoons water	1½ cups yogurt
3 lamb shanks, trimmed, all fat removed	1 teaspoon salt
	1½ tablespoons garam masala (see preceding recipe)
1 cup canned crushed tomatoes	3 tablespoons lemon juice
1 cup onions, chopped	2 or 3 tablespoons cilantro leaves, chopped
1 teaspoon cayenne pepper	

Method

1. Puree ginger, cumin, and garlic with 2 or 3 tablespoons water in blender.
2. Combine lamb shanks, tomatoes, onions, cayenne pepper, yogurt, salt, 1 cup water, and ginger-garlic paste into a large, heavy-bottomed saucepan. Stir, and bring to a boil.
3. Reduce heat, cover, and simmer for 50 minutes or until shanks are tender, stirring occasionally. Sauce will thicken; be careful it does not scorch.
4. Remove meat to warmed serving platter.
5. Add garam masala and lemon juice to sauce. Bring to a boil. Sauce should be rather thick. If too thick, add a little water; if too thin, simmer to reduce sauce.
6. Pour over lamb shanks and garnish with chopped cilantro.

H-28. Peas with Farmer Cheese (*Mattar Paneer*)

This Punjabi dish, with some variation in the spices, is eaten all over North India and is considered a vegetarian main course.

Yield: 6 servings

Equipment needed: Electric blender, cutting board, French knife, spatula, large frying pan, 2-quart heavy-bottomed saucepan

Ingredients

¾ cup onion, chopped	¼ teaspoon turmeric, ground
1 tablespoon ginger, copped	1 cup tomatoes, chopped, fresh or canned
12 ounces paneer (Indian cheese)	
¼ cup vegetable oil	1 teaspoon salt
1 teaspoon dried red pepper flakes	½ teaspoon black pepper, ground
	2 cups buttermilk
1 tablespoon coriander, ground	12-ounce package frozen peas

Method

1. Mix chopped onion and ginger with 2 ounces water in blender or food processor to make smooth paste.
2. Cut cheese into 1-inch cubes.
3. Heat oil in frying pan over medium heat.
4. Carefully fry cheese cubes on all sides. Remove cheese to platter and keep warm.

5. Allow pan to cool briefly.
6. Add ground spices and return to heat. Cook briefly, until water has evaporated and paste turns light brown.
7. Add remaining ingredients and bring to a boil.
8. Add fried cheese pieces and defrosted peas. Bring to a boil and simmer 5 minutes.

Pooram (April or May)

In the southwestern Indian state of Kerala, the Hindu celebration of Pooram is the most colorful of the temple festivals. As music plays, elephants carrying umbrellas circle the temples and, at midnight, fireworks are launched into the sky.

H-29. Chickpea Flour Pancakes (*Besan ka Cheela*)

Pancakes are popular the world over. Here is a version from the Gujarat region of West India.

Yield: 10 thin pancakes
Equipment needed: Mixing bowl, wire whisk, 6-inch crepe pan, 4-ounce ladle, spatula

Ingredients

1 cup besan flour
1/4 cup wheat flour
1 teaspoon baking powder
1 1/4 cups milk
2 teaspoons salt
1 teaspoon chili powder
1 teaspoon green chilies, finely chopped
1/2 cup fenugreek leaves, finely chopped
Oil for frying

Method

1. Blend all the ingredients into a thick but pourable batter.
2. Let rest for 15 minutes.
3. Lightly oil crepe pan and place over medium heat.
4. When pan is hot, ladle in a small amount of batter until bottom is evenly covered.
5. Turn pancakes over with spatula to brown both sides.
6. Serve hot with mint chutney.

Arjan Dev (May 2)

This Sikh day of abstinence from meat and dairy products celebrates the birthday of the fifth Guru, Arjan Dev. He is credited with beginning the compilation of the Adi Granth, the sacred scripture of the Sikhs, and building Harimandir, the Holy Temple of the Sikhs at Amritsar.

H-30. Lentil Stew (*Masoor Dal*)

This dish is a typical vegetarian main course. It is perhaps the most famous lentil dish of West Bengal.

Yield: 8 servings

Equipment needed: 2-quart saucepan, heavy-bottomed saucepan, stirring spoon

Ingredients

2 cups masoor dal (orange or red
   split lentils)
2 quarts water
1 teaspoon salt
1½ teaspoons garam masala (see
   recipe on page 119)
1½ teaspoons turmeric
1 cup onions, chopped

⅓ cup ghee
1½ tablespoons garlic, chopped
2 tablespoons ginger, chopped
1 jalapeño chili, seeded and
   chopped
½ cup canned crushed tomatoes
1 bunch cilantro leaves, chopped

Method

1. Rinse lentils thoroughly, until water is clear.
2. Combine with 2 quarts water, bring to a boil, and simmer slowly for 20 minutes.
3. Add salt, garam masala, and turmeric.
4. In about 30 minutes, when lentils are soft and creamy, turn off heat.
5. In heavy-bottomed saucepan, fry onions in ghee until light brown. Add garlic, ginger, and chilies; continue to cook over moderate heat until lightly browned.
6. Add tomatoes, bring to a boil, and simmer 5 minutes.
7. Stir tomato-spice mixture into cooked lentils. Carefully reheat, while stirring to prevent scorching.
8. Garnish with cilantro.
9. Serve as vegetarian main course with bread and salad.

Amavas (June)

During this festival honoring Surya, god of the sun, Hindus fast during the day, engage in ritual bathing, make offerings to a sacred fire, and chant mantras.

H-31. Vegetable Puree (*Avial*)

The vegetables in this flavored puree may be microwaved or cooked in water on the stovetop. This recipe is usually served as a side dish with rice.

Yield: 10 side-dish servings

Equipment needed: Food processor, 2-quart heavy saucepan, wooden spoon

Ingredients

½ cup lima beans, cooked
½ cup carrots, diced and cooked
½ cup plantain, diced and cooked
½ cup cauliflower florets, diced and cooked
2 tablespoons unsweetened coconut flakes
1 tablespoon ghee or oil
2 teaspoons cumin seeds
1 green chili, seeded and chopped

¼ teaspoon mustard seeds, crushed
¼ teaspoon turmeric, ground
1 cup buttermilk
½ teaspoon asafetida powder
Salt to taste
1 tablespoon cilantro leaves, finely chopped
½ teaspoon curry leaves (optional)

Method

1. Puree all vegetables with coconut flakes in food processor.
2. Heat ghee or oil in heavy saucepan and cook cumin, chili, mustard seeds, and turmeric over low heat to develop flavor.
3. Add buttermilk, asafetida powder, and vegetable puree.
4. Season with salt to taste.
5. Warm puree until thick, stirring continuously.
6. Garnish with curry leaves and cilantro.
7. Serve with rice.

Guru Purnima (July or August)

Celebrated on the full moon in July or August, this holiday commemorates the ancient sage Sri Vysa, who edited the Hindu scriptures known as the Vedas. It is also marks the beginning of the eagerly awaited monsoon rains.

H-32. Chicken Curry with Tomatoes (*Murgha Kari*)

Curry powder is available in different degrees of flavor intensity. Medium-hot powder is recommended for this dish.
Yield: 6 servings
Equipment needed: Cutting board, French knife, 8-inch cast-iron frying pan, 2-quart heavy-bottomed saucepan, mixing spoon

Ingredients

6 six- to eight-ounce chicken legs
2 cups onions, chopped
1½ tablespoons curry powder

1 cup canned crushed tomatoes
2 teaspoons salt
1 cup water

Method

1. Remove skin from chicken legs and set aside. Separate legs into drumsticks and thighs at joints. Cut skin into 2-inch squares.

(continued)

2. Cook chicken skins in cast-iron pan in 375-degree oven for 30 minutes, or until skin pieces are crisp and all fat rendered.
3. Remove skins from pan and drain on paper towel.
4. Cook onions and curry powder in rendered chicken fat until onions are transparent.
5. Add chicken legs and cook briefly over moderate heat.
6. Add tomato sauce, salt, and water. Simmer about 20 minutes or until chicken legs are thoroughly cooked.
7. Serve sprinkled with crisp chicken skin.

Janmashtami (August)

Also known as Sri Krishna Jayanti, this is the day Hindus celebrate the birth of Lord Krishna. A day of fasting and devotional readings is followed by joyous celebrations. Krishna is believed to have loved milk products and sweets.

H-33. Almond Milk (*Badam Phirni*)

The smooth, rich, creamy taste of *Badam Phirni* makes it a favorite on party menus.
Yield: 6 servings
Equipment needed: Electric blender, 2-quart soup pot, strainer, 2-quart heavy-bottomed saucepan, wire whisk, ladle, serving dishes

Ingredients

1 cup slivered almonds	$\frac{1}{2}$ teaspoon cloves, ground
1 quart milk	1 teaspoon almond extract
2 tablespoons rice flour	1 tablespoon rose water
$\frac{1}{2}$ teaspoon salt	2 tablespoons pistachio nuts,
$\frac{1}{2}$ cup sugar	chopped

Method

1. Blend almonds with 1 cup water to make slurry.
2. Combine with milk and bring to a boil. Remove from heat and let steep 20 minutes.
3. Strain milk into saucepan. Save almonds.
4. Make slurry with rice flour and 3 tablespoons cold water.
5. Bring milk to boil again. Add rice flour slurry while stirring with wire whisk to thicken milk.
6. Remove from heat. Add almonds and all remaining ingredients except pistachio nuts.
7. Ladle mixture into serving bowls.
8. Serve chilled, sprinkled with pistachio nuts.

H-34. Carrot Halwa

The art of making sweet halwa with nuts was introduced in India during the Moghul period by traders from the Middle East and Asia Minor.
Yield: 8 servings
Equipment needed: Peeler, knife, grater or food processor, 2-quart heavy-bottomed saucepan, wooden stirring spoon

Ingredients

1 pound carrots, peeled and finely grated	1/2 teaspoon cloves, ground
1 cup sugar	1 tablespoon lemon juice
2 cups milk	2 ounces ghee or oil
1/2 teaspoon cardamom, ground	2 ounces raisins
	1/4 cup nuts

Method

1. Combine carrots, sugar, milk, spices, and lemon juice. Bring to a boil.
2. Simmer at low heat, stirring frequently until carrots are fully cooked and most milk is evaporated, about 40 minutes.
3. Add ghee or oil. Continue cooking over low heat until mixture is dry and starts to brown.
4. Add raisins and nuts.
5. Serve cold as dessert.

Onam (August or September)

Onam is the most important Hindu harvest festival in the Indian state of Kerala. Ranging from four to ten days, the festivities encompass worship, music, dancing, sports, boat races, and good food.

H-35. Chicken in Foil

This baked chicken dish is served as an evening meal. Before aluminum foil became available, the chicken was wrapped in banana leaves.
Yield: 4 to 6 servings
Equipment needed: Cutting board, knife, electric blender, pastry brush, heavy-duty aluminum foil, Dutch oven or deep roasting pan

Ingredients

3 1/2 pounds roasting chicken	3 tablespoons garlic, chopped
2 tablespoons jalapeño chilies, chopped	2 tablespoons ginger, chopped
	2 teaspoons salt
1/2 cup lemon juice	2 tablespoons ghee or oil

(continued)

2 teaspoons cumin, ground   1 teaspoon pepper, ground
2 teaspoons coriander, ground

Method

1. Remove skin from chicken and poke holes in breast and thighs.
2. Puree all remaining ingredients.
3. Use pastry brush to spread spice slurry liberally on chicken and in holes.
4. Place chicken on large piece of foil, breast up. Seal foil.
5. Wrap packet in another layer of foil.
6. Place on rack in roasting pan. Bake at 400 degrees for 1 hour.
7. Reduce heat to 375 degrees and cook 30 minutes longer.
8. Remove from oven. Set aside to cool slightly. Open wrapped chicken, being careful of escaping steam.
9. Lift chicken from foil and put on serving platter. Serve pan juices on side as dip.

H-36. Butter-Broiled Bananas

India is the world's leading banana producer, and most of these are for domestic consumption. Not surprisingly, banana recipes are popular.
Yield: 6 servings
Equipment needed: 1-quart heavy saucepan, wooden stirring spoon, paring knife, large baking dish

Ingredients

4 ounces (1 stick) butter
1 tablespoon lemon juice
$1/4$ cup orange juice
2 tablespoons brown sugar
2 tablespoons honey

$1/4$ teaspoon mace
$1/4$ teaspoon cinnamon
6 bananas, ripe but not mushy
4 tablespoons slivered almonds

Method

1. Melt butter and add lemon juice, orange juice, brown sugar, honey, mace, and cinnamon. Bring to a boil; simmer 5 minutes. Set aside.
2. Peel bananas, cut in large wedges on bias, and place in baking dish.
3. Pour syrup over bananas and broil until top is browned.
4. Sprinkle with almonds and put back under broiler very briefly to brown almonds.

Raksha Bandhan (August)

Held during the full moon of the Hindu month of Shravan, this occasion celebrates the love between brothers and sisters. Sisters tie a sacred piece of thread (known as *rakhi* or *raksha-sutra*) on the wrist of their brothers, after which the siblings feed each other delicious sweets.

H-37. Cottage Cheese and Fruit Dessert

This simple dessert needs no cooking, making it a good choice for a hot evening. Other fruits may be substituted.
Yield: 8 servings
Equipment needed: Mixing bowl, wire whisk, peeler, paring knife, stirrer, serving bowl

Ingredients

8 ounces fine-curd cottage cheese	1 cup seedless grapes
8 ounces ricotta cheese	1 small papaya, about 10 ounces
2 tablespoons unsweetened cocoa	$\frac{1}{4}$ cup cashews
1 cup sugar	$\frac{1}{4}$ cup slivered almonds
1 teaspoon grated lemon peel	$\frac{1}{4}$ cup pistachio nuts, coarsely
2 apples	chopped
1 large orange	

Method

1. Using wire whisk, blend together cottage cheese, ricotta cheese, cocoa, sugar, and grated lemon peel, making sure cocoa is evenly distributed.
2. Peel, core, and dice apple. Add to cottage cheese.
3. Peel and section orange. Add to cottage cheese with washed grapes.
4. Peel, remove seeds, and dice papaya. Add to cottage cheese with cashews and almonds.
5. Refrigerate 1 hour; serve sprinkled with pistachio nuts.

Ganesha Chaturti (August or September)

Honoring Ganesha, the elephant-headed gods who removes obstacles and grants success to human endeavors, this Hindu harvest festival is also known as *Haritalika*. Ganesha wears a dainty tiara atop his massive head and has four pudgy hands, each holding a symbolic object joined to his sizeable belly. On this holiday, women wear green bangles, green clothes, and golden jewelry and offer the god fresh fruits and green vegetables in thanks. They also distribute beautifully painted coconuts to their female friends and family. When these rituals are over, green foods and foods made with coconut are eaten.

H-38. Sea Bass in Green Chutney

Featuring green, the favorite festival color, this dish traditionally is prepared using a whole fish baked in banana leaves. For this recipe, the process has been shortened by using fish fillets baked in foil.
Yield: 6 servings
Equipment needed: Strainer, 1-quart saucepan, food processor, baking pan, aluminum foil, brush

(continued)

Ingredients

2 bunches cilantro leaves	¹⁄₂ teaspoon hot pepper flakes
2 tablespoons ghee or oil	¹⁄₂ teaspoon salt
1 teaspoon ginger, chopped	6 bass or snapper fillets, 6 ounces
1 teaspoon mustard seeds	each
1 teaspoon garlic, chopped	2 lemons

Method

1. Wash and trim cilantro, making sure all sand is removed.
2. Briefly cook all spices in 1 tablespoon of oil to develop flavor.
3. Remove from heat and cool.
4. Combine spice mixture and cilantro; puree in food processor or blender to medium-fine consistency.
5. Cut foil into six large pieces; brush each with remaining oil.
6. Place one fillet on each piece; top with green sauce.
7. Fold foil to make pockets, crimp edges.
8. Bake fish packages in baking pan at 400 degrees for 20 minutes.
9. Open packages carefully, allowing steam to escape.
10. Serve fish with lemon wedges.

H-39. Green Mint and Cilantro Chutney
(*Podina Dhania Ki*)

Relishes and chutneys are basic to Indian cooking. This recipe may have served as the inspiration for the traditional British mint sauce served with lamb.
Yield: 1 cup
Equipment needed: Colander, cutting board, knife, food processor

Ingredients

1 cup mint leaves without stems, loosely packed	¹⁄₂ teaspoon amchoor powder
	¹⁄₂ teaspoon cardamom, ground
1 cup cilantro without stems, loosely packed	1 ounce sugar
	1 teaspoon green chilies, chopped
2 scallions	1 tablespoon ginger, chopped
1 pomegranate	2 tablespoons lemon juice
¹⁄₂ teaspoon red pepper flakes	

Method

1. Carefully wash mint and cilantro leaves to remove sand. Drain.
2. Split, wash, and cut whole scallions in 1-inch pieces.
3. Halve pomegranate; save juice and seeds.
4. Combine all ingredients in food processor or blender and process to medium-fine blend.
5. Refrigerate 24 to 36 hours before serving.

H-40. Dessert Dumplings (*Modakas*)

Believed to be Ganesha's favorite sweets, these steamed dumplings are filled with coconut. The freshly grated kind used in this recipe is available in ethnic stores.
Yield: About 30
Equipment needed: 2-quart saucepan, stiff wire whisk, stirring spoon, 2-quart wide heavy saucepan, steamer with lid, wide steamer basket

Ingredients

$2\frac{1}{2}$ cups water
1 teaspoon salt
$\frac{1}{2}$ teaspoon cloves, ground
3 teaspoons oil
$1\frac{1}{2}$ cups rice flour
1 cup sweet coconut, grated

1 cup unsweetened coconuts, grated
1 cup palm or brown sugar
$\frac{1}{2}$ cup milk
$\frac{1}{2}$ cup candied fruits, chopped
Pan spray

Method

1. Combine water, salt, cloves, and oil. Bring to a boil. Remove from heat.
2. Stir rice flour into boiling water, first with wire whisk, then with wooden spoon as dough stiffens. Set aside.
3. Cook coconut and sugar in wide saucepan over low heat, stirring continuously. Mixture will become sticky and light brown. Carefully add milk and continue cooking until all moisture is evaporated.
4. Remove from heat. Blend in candied fruits; set aside.
5. While rice dough is still warm, shape into small balls with wet hands. Poke a hole in center of each ball; fill with 1 teaspoon coconut mixture. Seal holes. Shape dumplings with pointed ends resembling garlic bulbs.
6. Pan-spray steamer basket and steam dumplings for 10 minutes.
7. Serve warm or cold.

H-41. Coconut Rice (*Kheer Ade*)

Coconut milk and spices combine to provide a mouthwatering dish.
Yield: 4 servings
Equipment needed: 2-quart soup pot, colander

Ingredients

$\frac{1}{2}$ cup basmati rice
1 cup water
1 quart milk
5 green cardamom pods, ground
14 ounces coconut milk, canned
$\frac{1}{2}$ teaspoon salt

$\frac{1}{4}$ cup sweetened coconut flakes
$\frac{3}{4}$ cup sugar
$\frac{1}{4}$ teaspoon nutmeg, ground
1 tablespoon rose water
$\frac{1}{4}$ cup slivered almonds, toasted

(*continued*)

Method

1. Bring rice and water to a boil.
2. Simmer 5 minutes; drain.
3. Combine milk, green cardamom, and rice. Simmer 20 minutes, stirring frequently.
4. Add coconut milk, salt, coconut flakes, sugar, and nutmeg. Simmer 10 minutes longer, until kheer ade thickens.
5. Place in serving dish.
6. Serve sprinkled with rose water and topped with slivered almonds.

H-42. Steamed Rice in Banana Leaves (*Potali*)

In South Indian cuisine, banana leaves are often used as plates. Many dishes are also cooked in banana leaves.

Yield: 16 bundles

Equipment needed: Pot, blender, mixing bowl, cutting board, 1-quart heavy saucepan, potato masher, stirring spoon, pastry brush, steamer with insert

Ingredients

1 cup rice
1 cup unsweetened coconut, grated and dry
1/8 teaspoon salt
1/2 cup water
12 ounces paneer (Indian farmer's cheese)

1/2 cup palm sugar
1 tablespoon cardamom powder
2 tablespoons ghee
Fresh banana leaves, or aluminum foil as substitute

Method

1. Soak rice overnight.
2. Drain and mix in blender with coconut flakes, salt, and water.
3. Pulse to break up rice. Set aside.
4. Finely dice paneer and combine with sugar and cardamom in saucepan.
5. Cook over low heat and mash until well-blended paste results.
6. Brush banana leaves or foil with ghee.
7. Put 1 tablespoon each of rice and sweet filling on every leaf.
8. Fold to make a loosely sealed package.
9. Place in steamer basket, folded side down.
10. Steam 25 minutes. Serve hot.

Vara Lakshmi (August or September)

This Hindu festival, popular in South India, includes purification rites and the tying of a sacred thread around the right hand of the worshipper. Offerings of different sweets are made to Lakshmi, the goddess of wealth and prosperity. Married women customarily ask the goddess to bless their husbands with long life and good health.

H-43. Banana Fudge (*Kele Ka Halwa*)

This delicious banana dessert is easy to prepare.
Yield: 4 servings
Equipment needed: Paring knife, heavy wide saucepan, potato masher, stirrer, serving dish

Ingredients

4 ripe bananas
2 tablespoons ghee
1 cup sugar

½ teaspoon nutmeg, ground
1 teaspoon cardamom, ground

Method

1. Peel and mash bananas.
2. Add ghee, sugar, and spices.
3. Cook together over low heat, stirring continuously, until bananas start to brown and sugar starts to caramelize.
4. Spread banana paste in serving dish and cool, but do not refrigerate.
5. Cut into squares and serve.

Installation of the Guru Granth Sahib (September 1)

On this date, Sikhs gather at the Golden Temple at Amritsar to commemorate the consecration of their holy book, the Guru Granth Sahib. Celebrations include processions and readings.

H-44. Potatoes and Rice (*Aloo Pulao*)

Potatoes are cultivated in the north and appear frequently in Indian recipes. This dish is used as vegetarian main course.
Yield: 6 servings
Equipment needed: 2-quart saucepan with lid, stirring spoon

Ingredients

2 tablespoons ghee
½ tablespoons garlic, chopped
2 tablespoons onions, chopped
½ teaspoon turmeric, ground

1 teaspoon cumin seeds
2 cloves
1 cinnamon stick, about 2 inches
2 green cardamom pods

(continued)

2 teaspoons salt
½ teaspoon red chili powder
½ cup rice
1 pound potatoes diced in small
   pieces, about 2 cups

2 cups water
Cilantro leaves to garnish

Method

1. Heat ghee in saucepan.
2. Add spices.
3. Stir to develop flavor. Do not allow spices to burn.
4. Mix in rice and potatoes, add water, and bring to a boil.
5. Cover and let simmer over low heat for about 20 minutes.

Navratri—Nine Nights of Durga (September or October)

All of the many customs attached to Navratri (Nine Nights) relate to the Hindu mother goddess and her various forms. The first three days and nights of the festival are dedicated to Durga, the warrior goddess, who is dressed in red and mounted on a lion; the next three to Lakshmi, goddess of wealth and prosperity, who wears gold and is mounted on an owl; and the last three to Saraswati, goddess of knowledge, who is dressed in milky white and seated on a pure white swan. In Gujarat, farmers sow seeds, thank the goddess for her blessings, and pray for better yields. Sweetmeats are prepared for the celebrations, and children and adults dress up in brightly colored apparel for the evening festivities.

H-45. Sweet Pumpkin Curry (*Kaddu Ki Sabzi*)

In this recipe, the slight sweetness of the pumpkin is offset by the heat of the curry and mustard seeds.
Yield: 6 side-dish servings
Equipment needed: 2-quart heavy saucepan, stirring spoon

Ingredients

3 tablespoons ghee or oil
2 tablespoons mild curry powder
1 teaspoon mustard seeds
1 teaspoon turmeric, ground
2 pounds yellow pumpkin, peeled
   and cubed

2 teaspoons salt
2 tablespoons sugar
1 tablespoon lemon juice
3 cups water

Method

1. Toast spices in oil over low heat to develop flavor.
2. Add pumpkin, salt, sugar, lemon juice, and water.
3. Bring to a boil, cover, and simmer until pumpkin is soft, about 25 minutes.

Dussehra (October or November)

A ten-day festival celebrated in various ways across India, Dussehra is the most important festival of Bengalis. Celebrating Hindu Lord Rama's victory over the evil Ravana (whose effigy is burned), as well as the defeat of the buffalo demon Mahishasura by the warrior goddess Durga, Dussehra is considered an auspicious time to start new ventures. Sweets are prepared, and children and adults dress up in brightly colored new clothes.

H-46. Chicken Dilruba

Although this dish uses the more costly whole saffron threads, less-expensive (and less-flavorful) powdered saffron can be substituted.

Yield: 4 servings

Equipment needed: Small bowl, food processor, deep skillet or heavy saucepan, wooden mixing spoon, cutting board, knife

Ingredients

$\frac{1}{8}$ teaspoon whole saffron
2 tablespoons warm milk
1 cup onions, diced
2 tablespoons ginger, chopped
6 tablespoons ghee or oil
1 chicken, 3–4 pounds, skin removed, cut into pieces
$\frac{1}{4}$ cup almonds, ground
$\frac{1}{4}$ cup walnuts, ground

$\frac{1}{4}$ cup sesame seeds
1 cup plain yogurt
1 cup water
2 tablespoons garam masala (see recipe on page 119)
1 teaspoon turmeric, ground
Salt to taste
$\frac{1}{4}$ cup cashews, for garnish
Fresh cilantro leaves, chopped

Method

1. Soak saffron in warm milk and set aside.
2. Process onions and ginger in blender or food processor to a smooth paste.
3. Heat ghee or oil in a deep, heavy skillet and gently brown the onion-ginger mixture, stirring often.
4. Add the chicken and carefully cook over medium heat until it begins to brown.
5. Add saffron and next eight ingredients.
6. Cook over medium heat, stirring often, until chicken is very tender and sauce is very thick (about 25 minutes).
7. Garnish with cashew nuts and chopped cilantro leaves.

H-47. Bengali Cabbage Curry (*Bandhakopir Dalna*)

In British colonial times, the province of Bengal extended from the warm Indian Ocean to the cool foothills of the Himalayas. This recipe uses cabbage and potatoes, two vegetables usually associated with northern Europe. Potatoes, which originated in the South American Andes, were introduced to India by Portuguese explorers in the seventeenth century.

Yield: 4 servings

Equipment needed: Saucepan, strainer, wide saucepan with lid, slotted spoon, small pan

Ingredients

2 cups potatoes, cut in small cubes	1 tablespoon ginger, chopped
4 tablespoons oil	1 teaspoon sugar
2 tablespoons turmeric	1½ teaspoons coriander seeds, whole
2 teaspoons green chili paste or ¼ teaspoon cayenne pepper	1 pound cabbage, finely sliced
1 tablespoon cumin, ground	2 bay leaves
1 teaspoon coriander, ground	Salt to taste
	Sugar to taste

Method

1. Cover potatoes with water, bring to a boil, and drain immediately.
2. Add oil to heavy saucepan and cook potatoes over medium heat until browned on all sides. Remove with slotted spoon and set aside.
3. Add next seven ingredients to oil; cook briefly to develop flavor.
4. Add shredded cabbage and cook a few minutes over low heat to blend.
5. Add potatoes, bay leaves, and enough water to barely cover cabbage. Cover and simmer 20 minutes.
6. Season with salt and sugar.

H-48. Chickpea Dal (*Chana Masaledar*)

Pious Hindis abstain from meat on all holidays. This vegetarian dish is popular throughout India.

Yield: 4 servings

Equipment needed: 2-quart soup pot, stirring spoon

Ingredients

3 tablespoons vegetable oil	½ teaspoon salt
¼ teaspoon cumin seeds	¼ teaspoon hot pepper
1 cup onions, diced	½ teaspoon amchoor powder
¼ teaspoon cinnamon, ground	¼ cup canned crushed tomatoes
¼ teaspoon nutmeg, ground	1 can (16 ounces) chickpeas
¼ teaspoon cloves, ground	1 cup water
1 teaspoon coriander, ground	1 tablespoon sweetened coconut flakes
1 tablespoon garlic, chopped	
1 tablespoon ginger, chopped	

Method

1. Cook cumin seeds in oil over low heat until they start to sizzle.
2. Add onions and cook until they start to brown.
3. Add spices and tomatoes. Cook briefly.
4. Drain chickpeas and add to mixture.
5. Add water and coconut flakes. Bring to a boil; simmer 10 minutes.

H-49. Frozen Milk (*Kulfi*)

Easy to make, this popular dessert uses reduced milk. In India, the mixture is served frozen in cone-shaped containers.

Yield: 4 servings
Equipment needed: Wide 3-quart heavy-bottomed saucepan, stirring spoon, ladle, serving dishes

Ingredients

6 cups milk
2 tablespoons sugar
½ teaspoon cardamom, ground

2 tablespoons pistachio nuts, chopped

Method

1. Combine milk with 1 tablespoon of sugar. Bring to a boil.
2. Simmer over low heat, stirring occasionally, until milk is reduced to about 2 cups, about an hour or so.
3. Remove from heat and add remaining sugar, cardamom, and pistachios.
4. Stir until cool and thick.
5. Portion into serving dishes and freeze until solid.

Karva Chauth (September or October)

This festival takes place nine days before Diwali, the Festival of Lights, on the fourth day of the waning moon in the Hindu month of Kartikr. It is especially significant for women of North India. Karva Chauth is symbolic of wifely loyalty, and married women pray to the gods for their husbands to live long and prosperous lives. On this date, women begin their fast well before sunrise and do not break it until spotting the rising moon.

H-50. Tamarind Sauce (*Imli Ke* Chutney)

This rather pungent condiment is served with meat or fish.

Yield: 1 cup
Equipment needed: Cutting board, French knife, 1-quart saucepan, stirring spoon

(continued)

TAMARIND

Ingredients

8 ounces dried dates, pitted
½ cup tamarind juice, available
  canned
½ cup water
1 cup brown sugar

1 teaspoon garam masala (see recipe on page 119)
1 teaspoon cumin powder
½ teaspoon cloves, ground
1 teaspoon salt

Method

1. Cut dates into small pieces and finely chop.
2. Combine with all other ingredients in saucepan and bring to a boil.
   Simmer 10 minutes.
3. Serve hot or cold as condiment.

Diwali (October or November)

Celebrated twenty-one days after Dussehra, the Hindu five-day Festival of Lights gets its name from the tradition of lighting thousands of oil lamps and electric lights to welcome the return of Lord Rama after fourteen years of exile. It is as important to Hindus as Christmas is to Christians. New clothes are worn, gifts exchanged, and sweets shared. Often there are fireworks displays. Sikhs also observe this holiday.

H-51. Five-Jewel Creamed Legumes

This vegetarian main course is made with different legumes.
Yield: 8 servings
Equipment needed: Colander, 3-quart soup pot, stirring spoon, deep frying pan, small frying pan

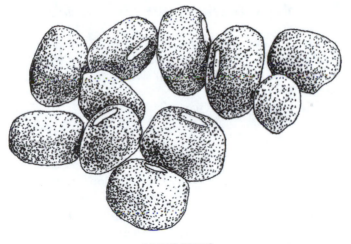

MUNG BEANS

Ingredients

¹/₂ cup dried white kidney beans
¹/₂ cup yellow split peas
¹/₄ cup green mung beans
¹/₄ cup red lentils
¹/₂ teaspoon turmeric, ground
2 teaspoons salt
8 tablespoons vegetable oil
1 cup onions, medium, sliced in thin rings
2 teaspoons garlic, chopped

2 teaspoons ginger, chopped
1 tablespoon green chilies, minced
1 cup canned crushed tomatoes
1¹/₂ teaspoons cumin seed
¹/₂ teaspoon cayenne pepper
1 teaspoon paprika
4 tablespoons cilantro leaves, chopped

Method

1. Wash kidney beans thoroughly in several changes of water.
2. Cover with water and simmer 1 hour.
3. Add split peas, mung beans, and lentils. Add more water to cover, bring to a boil.
4. Simmer over medium heat, partially covered, for about 30 minutes.
5. Add turmeric and salt.
6. Heat 6 tablespoons of oil in a large frying pan. Add onions and cook until light brown, stirring constantly.
7. Add garlic, ginger, chili, and tomatoes. Cook over high heat until most of moisture has evaporated.
8. Combine tomato and spice blend with legumes; continue simmering over low heat.
9. Add cumin, cayenne, and paprika to remaining oil in small frying pan. Lightly toast spices.
10. Add spices to stew.
11. Serve sprinkled with chopped cilantro leaves.

H-52. Caribbean Black-Eyed Peas (*Urhad Dal Sabat*)

A public holiday, Diwali is one of the most important of religious celebrations in Trinidad and Tobago. As a form of personal sacrifice, no meat is prepared, but many tasty vegetarian dishes and traditional sweets are offered.
Yield: 6 to 8 servings
Equipment needed: 2-quart saucepan, stirring spoon

Ingredients

2 cups black-eyed peas
1½ teaspoons salt
1½ teaspoons coriander, ground
1 teaspoon cumin, ground
½ teaspoon turmeric, ground
2 tablespoons vegetable oil

½ cup onion, chopped
2 tablespoons garlic, chopped
1 tablespoon ginger, chopped
½ teaspoon cumin seeds
½ cup canned crushed tomatoes, undrained

Method

1. Soak black-eyed peas overnight.
2. Drain, cover with water. Add salt, coriander, turmeric, and cumin; simmer 1½ hours.
3. Sauté onions in oil until transparent. Add garlic, ginger, and cumin seeds; cook briefly.
4. Add tomatoes and cook 5 minutes. Combine mixture with cooked black-eyed peas. The mixture should be soupy.

H-53. Sesame Halwa

Halwa is a generic name for ancient sweets popular in India, Pakistan, the Middle East, and more recently, the Caribbean. This recipe, made with sesame seeds, is one of many variations.
Yield: 25 pieces
Equipment needed: Small cast-iron pan, 1-quart saucepan, candy thermometer, electric mixer, suitable cake mold, plastic wrap or parchment paper, pan spray

Ingredients

½ cup sesame seeds
15 ounces tahini paste (available in jars or cans)
½ teaspoon cardamom, ground
1 tablespoon ghee (not oil)

1 teaspoon rose water (optional)
Pan spray
2 cups sugar
½ cup water

Method

1. Toast sesame seeds in cast-iron skillet over medium heat; they will brown quickly.

2. Using electric mixer with paddle attachment, blend sesame seeds at low speed with tahini paste, cardamom, ghee, and rose water.
3. Line cake pan or mold with aluminum foil. Pan-spray.
4. Combine sugar and water. Bring to a boil and continue to cook until temperature reaches 275 degrees (hard-ball stage).
5. Carefully add hot sugar syrup to sesame mixture; it will thicken immediately. Blend well at low speed.
6. Scrape hot paste into prepared mold, pressing in as tightly as possible.
7. Cool and serve as snack.

H-54. Almond Rice Dessert (*Badam Phirni*)

Diwali is celebrated in Hindu communities throughout the United States. Indian stores in New York display posters announcing parades, and restaurants serve holiday desserts, such as this special dish.

Yield: 6 servings
Equipment needed: Cutting board, French knife, heavy saucepan, heavy wire whisk, stirring spoon, serving dish

Ingredients

6 ounces almond paste
3 cups milk
5 tablespoons sugar
3 tablespoons rice flour

$^{1}/_{4}$ teaspoon saffron powder
1 teaspoon cardamom, ground
1 tablespoon pistachio nuts, chopped

Method

1. Cut almond paste into small pieces and combine in saucepan with milk, sugar, rice flour, and saffron, using heavy wire whisk to blend ingredients.
2. Bring to a boil over low heat, stirring continuously.
3. Remove from heat and cool, stirring occasionally.
4. When lukewarm, portion into individual dishes. Sprinkle with cardamom and pistachios.

H-55. Ricotta Dessert (*Roshogolla Rasgulla*)

With few exceptions, baked desserts are seldom made in hot climates. Ricotta cheese dumplings are popular not only in India, but also in central Europe, where they are served with brown butter and toasted bread crumbs.

Yield: 6 servings
Equipment needed: Mixing bowl, stirring spoon, 1-quart saucepan, wide saucepan, ice cream scoop, slotted spoon, ladle, deep serving platter

(*continued*)

Ingredients

1 pound ricotta cheese
2 tablespoons flour
2 tablespoons cream of wheat
1 egg yolk
½ teaspoon grated lemon peel
1 cup sugar
2 cups water

1 tablespoon lemon juice
5 drops rose water essence
4 tablespoons walnuts,
  chopped
1 teaspoon cinnamon,
  ground

Method

1. Combine ricotta cheese, flour, cream of wheat, egg yolk, and grated lemon peel. Set aside.
2. Combine sugar, water, and lemon juice in saucepan. Bring to a boil, simmer 10 minutes, add rose water, and set aside to cool.
3. Fill wide saucepan with water and bring to a boil.
4. Shape small ricotta cheese dumplings with ice-cream scoop; drop into simmering water.
5. Cook over low heat about 15 minutes. Dumplings will rise to surface when cooked.
6. Remove with slotted spoon to serving platter. Ladle sugar-lemon syrup over dumplings; sprinkle with walnuts and cinnamon.
7. Serve at room temperature.

H-56. Diwali Ladoos (*Besan Ke Ladoo*)

Ladoo is a generic term for ball-shaped desserts. This dish is made from toasted besan flour blended with ghee, sugar, and spices.
Yield: 25 pieces
Equipment needed: 2-quart heavy saucepan, stirring spoon

Ingredients

1 cup ghee
4 cups besan flour
½ cup cashews, chopped

½ cup almonds, chopped
1 teaspoon cardamom, ground
2 cups powdered sugar

Method

1. Melt ghee in heavy saucepan. Add besan flour and cook over low heat, stirring continuously, until flour smells toasted.
2. Add nuts and cardamom; remove from heat. Cool.
3. Add sugar and blend well.
4. Shape into walnut-size pieces. Refrigerate briefly.

H-57. Mawa Ladoos

These ladoos are made with khoya, a milk solid available in Indian markets.

Ingredients

12 ounces khoya
4 ounces cream cheese
1/2 teaspoon baking powder
1/4 cup flour
Flour for dusting
2 cups sugar

1 cup water
5 cardamom pods, crushed
1 tablespoon grated lemon peel
2 tablespoons lemon juice
Oil for frying

Method

1. Blend khoya and cream cheese together in food processor until soft.
2. Add baking powder and flour to form soft dough.
3. Shape into 16 to 18 balls on floured work surface.
4. Simmer sugar, water, and cardamom pods together for 10 minutes.
5. Add lemon peel and lemon juice and keep warm.
6. Heat oil until a drop of water sizzles. Carefully fry dough balls over medium heat, moving them around for even browning. *Note:* If ladoos begin to split open, oil is too hot.
7. Top with warm lemon syrup.

Guru Nanak Dev (November)

During this celebration of the birth of Guru Nanak the founder of Sikhism, food offerings called *prasad* are made in Sikh temples and then shared among worshippers. Served warm, these sweet-tasting dishes are made from semolina or wheat flour, sugar, and ghee. Traditionally celebrated in November, the date of these festivities will eventually change to April 14, the correct birthdate of Guru Nanak.

H-58. Potatoes with Poppy Seeds (*Aloo Posto*)

Potatoes and poppy seeds are used in many Punjabi recipes. This vegetarian dish is often served on Guru Nanak Dev.
Yield: 6 servings
Equipment needed: 1-quart saucepan, strainer, wide heavy-bottomed frying pan, slotted spoon, roasting pan, small pan, spatula

Ingredients

3 cups potatoes, cut in 1/2-inch
  cubes
1/2 cup oil
4 whole green chilies

1 teaspoon turmeric powder
4 tablespoons poppy seeds
Salt to taste

(continued)

Method

1. Cover potatoes with water. Bring to a boil and simmer 5 minutes; drain.
2. Heat oil in frying pan, adding 3 whole chilies. Fry over medium heat to flavor oil.
3. Discard chilies. Carefully add potatoes to oil; fry until golden brown on all sides. With slotted spoon, remove potatoes to roasting pan.
4. Chop remaining chili and add to oil with turmeric and poppy seeds.
5. Fry over medium heat to develop flavor.
6. Pour flavored oil over potatoes, blending evenly with spatula.
7. Roast in 375-degree oven for 20 minutes.

H-59. Sweetened Semolina (*Kahara Prasad*)

Yield: 6 servings
Equipment needed: 1½-quart pot, strainer, 1½-quart heavy saucepan, wooden spoon, serving bowl

Ingredients

1 pint water	½ cup sugar
1 pint milk	4 ounces ghee
5 cardamom	1 cup cream of wheat
¼ teaspoon saffron, ground	2 ounces raisins
½ teaspoon cloves, ground	1 ounce slivered almonds
1 cinnamon stick, about 2 inches	1 teaspoon cinnamon, ground

Method

1. Combine water, milk, sugar, and spices (except ground cinnamon). Bring to a boil, simmer 15 minutes, and set aside.
2. Melt ghee; add cream of wheat. Cook over moderate heat, stirring constantly, until cream of wheat is golden brown. Set aside.
3. Strain seasoned liquid and add to cream of wheat. Return to heat and bring to a boil, stirring constantly.
4. Lower heat and simmer 5 minutes. Mixture will thicken and may splatter. Stir occasionally. Add raisins.
5. Set aside. When cool enough to handle, scoop into serving dish and sprinkle with almonds and cinnamon.
6. Serve chilled.

What Would Guru Nanak Dev Have Eaten?

In northern India, green, curry (*saag*) is made with spinach, mustard greens, or, as here, with collard greens. A vegetarian dish would have been most suitable for the Sikh founder.

COLLARD GREENS

H-60. Collard Greens (*Haak*)

Yield: 4 servings
Equipment needed: Colander, 2-quart heavy saucepan with lid, cutting board, French knife

Ingredients

2 pounds collard greens
2 tablespoons oil
1/4 cup onions, chopped
1 teaspoon green chilies, minced

1 red chili pod
1 teaspoon salt
2 tablespoons mustard oil
1/2 teaspoon asafetida

Method

1. Break stems off collard greens. Wash leaves repeatedly in water to remove sand.
2. Cut into 1-inch squares.
3. Heat oil until smoking. Cool, then sauté onions and chilies. Add collard greens, salt, mustard oil, and asafetida.
4. Stir, then cover pot.
5. Simmer over moderate heat for 35 minutes. If vegetables become too dry, add small amount of water to prevent scorching.

4

ISLAM

The religion of Islam was founded in the seventh century CE by the Prophet Muhammad, who was born in Mecca in what is now Saudi Arabia. Muhammad preached that all aspects of life should be lived in submission to God; the Arabic word *Islam* literally means "submission." While his ideas attracted many followers, Muhammad was seen as a threat to those in power. As a result he was forced out of Mecca, and in 622 he journeyed with his followers to Medina. This journey, known as the Hijra, marks the beginning of the Muslim calendar. As Muhammad gained more and more support, he was able to return to conquer Mecca, which has since remained the holy center of the Islamic world. Followers of Islam are called Muslims; they believe in the oneness of God—whom they call Allah—and they believe that Muhammad is the last of God's prophets. Islam is based on five pillars of faith:

- **declaration of faith (***shahadah***)** "There is no God but Allah, and Muhammad is His messenger" is the basic statement of the Islamic faith. Reciting this aloud three times in front of witnesses is all that is needed to become a Muslim.
- **prayer (***salat***)** Muslims pray five times a day, always facing in the direction of Mecca.
- **almsgiving (***zakat***)** Zakat is a tax of 2.5 percent on wealth that all Muslims must pay; it is used for charitable purposes and to support the mosque.
- **fasting (***sawm***)** Muslims observe several fasts during the year, of which Ramadan, the ninth month of Muslim year, is the most important.
- **pilgrimage (***hajj***)** All Muslims who are physically able are encouraged to make a hajj or pilgrimage to Mecca at least once in their lifetime. Annually, about two million Muslims gather in Mecca to pray and proclaim their faith in Allah.

The holy book of Muslims is the Qur'an, which in Arabic means "to recite." The word of God as recorded in the Qur'an, together with the words and deeds of Muhammad written down in the *hadith*, guides Muslims in their everyday lives, including their food practices.

Islam is a rapidly growing religion. The world Muslim population is more than 1.2 billion, with the largest populations in Indonesia, followed by Pakistan, Bangladesh, North Africa, and countries of the Middle East. Muslim communities are also growing in many European countries. The U.S. Muslim population, which includes immigrants, converts to Islam, and children born to these groups, is estimated at around five million. Muslim communities are concentrated in large cities on the East and West Coasts, although every state has at least one mosque, and there are approximately 650,000 Muslims living in Canada. The ethnic makeup of the Muslim population in the United States is difficult to ascertain accurately, but about 35 percent are Asian, about 25 percent are Arab, and about 30 percent are African Americans.

There are two main Islamic sects, and a number of smaller groups. The largest by far is the Sunni, representing more than 80 percent of all Muslims. Shiites form the other main group and differ from Sunnis in some beliefs and practices. Both are influenced by the smaller mystical Sufi school of Islam. A significant number of African Americans are black Sunni Muslims. The most prominent Black Muslim group is the Nation of Islam, a religious organization founded in the 1930s.

Food, Diet, and Cooking

Medieval Arabic cuisine was based on simple foods such as sheep, milk, dates, bread, beans, and lentils. Desert nomads ate only food they could carry with them and traveled with animals such as sheep, goats, and camels that provided meat and milk. Historically, as Islam spread and Muslims became active in global trade, urban cuisine was influenced by interactions with foreign courts. In the time of the Abbasid dynasty (eighth–tenth century), banquets at the royal courts of the caliphs of Baghdad were renowned for their variety and lavishness. Meat was plentiful, including sheep (sheep's head was highly prized), goats, gazelle, chickens, ducks, geese, partridges, pigeons, and quail. Dishes were sweetened with sugar or syrup or spiced with saffron, pepper, cinnamon, and cardamom—which earlier had just been trading goods. Favorite vegetables and fruits included eggplants, spinach, melons, pomegranates, dates, apricots, oranges, peaches, grapes, figs, quince, and apples. Sugarcane, unknown in Europe until the eighth century, was cultivated in the river valleys of the Nile and Indus. Marzipan, a paste made with ground almonds and sugar, probably originated in the Middle East. As Islam spread to other parts of the world, so did the cuisine, which influenced and blended with local traditions to create distinctive new dishes.

The Qur'an mentions food frequently, praising it as one of God's gifts to humanity. Islamic dietary restrictions resemble the Jewish kosher rules. They are based on respect for animals and sensible hygienic precautions. There are three terms to remember. *Halal* means lawful, permitted, or acceptable in the sight of God. *Haram* means unlawful, prohibited, or forbidden. *Mushbooh* means doubtful or suspect. All foods are placed in one of these categories, and eating halal is obligatory to all Muslims. Halal products are:

- Milk
- Fish—which must be alive when taken from the water

- Most vegetables and grains
- Legumes such as beans, lentils, and peas
- Nuts
- Cows, sheep, goats, chickens, and camels (To be halal they must be ritually slaughtered by a Muslim butcher, who prays to Allah while cutting the jugular vein of the animal. This is intended to spare the animal unnecessary suffering.)

Haram, or forbidden, foods are:

- Pork products
- Most carnivorous animals, birds of prey, and land animals without external ears (such as insects and reptiles)
- Shellfish and eels
- Animals not slaughtered according to Islamic law, or already dead before slaughtering is due to take place
- Animals killed in the name of anyone other than Allah
- Blood and blood products
- Alcohol or other intoxicating substances (Some devout Muslims will not drink coffee, though others consider it a symbol of hospitality.)

Mushbooh food is of uncertain status and should be avoided. Processed foods may fall into this category, as the ingredients are often of unknown origin. However, Islamic authorities do produce guides to help people select halal and avoid haram foods in the marketplace.

While Muslims around the world are obliged to observe these dietary restrictions, actual foods eaten differ widely between countries according to availability and custom. Consequently, there is a wide range of traditional festive dishes to be found among Muslim communities. Islamic families in North America, therefore, celebrate religious holidays with foods from many parts of the Muslim world. Some American Muslim families emulate Middle Eastern customs and serve food buffet-style on the table or on a cloth laid on the floor. Often a short prayer is said before the meal, and all are required to wash their hands before and after eating. Only the right hand is used to touch and pass food, as the left hand is considered unclean. Usually everyone sits together and eats, but in some families the custom of men and women eating separately is observed.

Celebration Recipes

The Muslim calendar (Hijra) began in 622 CE, the year Muhammad fled from Mecca to Medina, and is signified by AH, meaning "After Hijra." It is based on lunar months of twenty-eight or twenty-nine days and is ten to eleven days shorter than the Gregorian calendar used in the West. So while holiday dates are fixed on the Muslim calendar, they move around on the Gregorian calendar. The sighting of the new moon determines the date when many holidays are celebrated and so varies by location. Holiday dates are now commonly posted on Internet sites, along with applications to easily convert between the two calendars. The Muslim calendar dates are used here.

Eid-al-Adha (10 Dhu-al Hijja)

Celebrated at the end of the annual pilgrimage to Mecca, this four-day festival commemorates the prophet Abraham's offering of his son Ishmael as a sacrifice in obedience to God's command, and God's mercy in allowing Abraham to substitute an animal sacrifice instead. At the Feast of Sacrifice (*Bakr Eid* in India), Muslims recall their own vows of submission to God. Those who can afford to do so make their own animal sacrifice—usually a sheep. The meat is divided in thirds and shared with family, friends, and the poor. During Eid-al-Adha, people visit and exchange gifts.

IS-1. Baked Goat and Rice (*Gosht Biryani*)

Goat and lamb are traditional dishes served on this holiday. Either may be used in this Indian recipe featuring delicate basmati rice. Meat cooked with spices and baked with rice is popular in both India and North America. Although India is often thought of as being a Hindu country, it has one of the largest Muslim populations in the world.

Yield: 4 main-course servings

Equipment needed: Large mixing bowl, wire whisk, 3-quart saucepan, soup pot, colander, cutting board, French knife, small bowl, 3-quart Dutch oven, aluminum foil

Ingredients

1 cup yogurt	1 cup canned stewed tomatoes
1 teaspoon red chili powder	2 sticks cinnamon, about 2 inches
½ teaspoon turmeric powder	3 black cardamom pods
½ teaspoon coriander powder	1 teaspoon black peppercorns
1 teaspoon garam masala powder	2 bay leaves
1 teaspoon ginger, finely chopped	1 cup basmati rice
1 teaspoon garlic, finely chopped	Salt to taste
Pinch of saffron strands	4 tablespoons cilantro, chopped
1 pound goat or lamb stew meat	½ cup canned fried onion rings

Method

1. Combine yogurt with chili powder, turmeric, coriander, garam masala, ginger, garlic, and saffron in mixing bowl.
2. Add meat; blend evenly. Cover bowl with foil and refrigerate overnight.
3. Put meat with marinade and crushed tomatoes in saucepan. Add 1 cup water.
4. Bring to a boil, cover, and simmer over low heat 40 minutes. Add water if stew gets too dry; it should have a soupy consistency.
5. Fill soup pot three-quarters full with water. Add cinnamon sticks, cardamom, peppercorns, and bay leaves. Bring to a boil and simmer 20 minutes.
6. Add rice, bring to a boil again, and boil 10 minutes. Drain rice in colander. (Do not worry about spices in rice.) Set rice aside.
7. Spread meat evenly in Dutch oven and place precooked rice on top. Do not blend.
8. Cover pot with aluminum foil, bring to a boil on stove first and then bake at 350 degrees about 30 minutes.

9. Carefully remove pot from oven. Wait 5 minutes before removing foil.
10. Sprinkle with cilantro and onion rings.

IS-2. Sweet Lamb Stew (*Mrouzia Tajine*)

In Morocco, the Feast of Sacrifice is known as *Aïd el-kebir* and is celebrated with a pungent yet sweet lamb stew. The predominant flavor comes from *ras al-hanout*, a subtle curry-like blend of some twenty spices, available at Moroccan specialty stores. In this recipe, more commonly available spices are used as a substitute.
Yield: 6 servings
Equipment needed: Saucepan, frying pan or cookie sheet, mixing bowl, stirring spoon

Ingredients

2 pounds lean lamb stew meat
1 cup onions, chopped
1 tablespoon ginger, chopped
1 teaspoon cinnamon, ground
½ teaspoon cardamom, ground
½ teaspoon pepper, ground
½ teaspoon cumin, ground

½ teaspoon turmeric
½ teaspoon hot pepper
2 teaspoons salt
½ cup almonds, skins removed
4 tablespoons honey
1 cup raisins
3 tablespoons cornstarch

Method

1. Combine all ingredients except almonds, honey, raisins, and cornstarch in saucepan.
2. Blend well and let marinate overnight.
3. Cover with water, bring to a boil, and simmer over low heat until meat is tender. Add water occasionally to keep meat barely covered.
4. Quickly toast almonds until light brown.
5. Add raisins and honey to stew. Return to a boil.
6. Make slurry with cornstarch and 2 tablespoons cold water. Add to stew. Return to boil.
7. Sprinkle with almonds.
8. Serve with rice, bread, or other starch.

IS-3. Smoked Eggplant Puree (*Baba Ghannooj*)

Well-known in Tunisia and throughout the Middle East, this dip's smoky flavor comes from burning off the outer skin of the eggplant—which can be a messy project! Serve sprinkled with parsley and garnished with black olives.
Yield: 6 servings
Equipment needed: Roasting pan, cutting board, knife, food processor

(continued)

Ingredients

1 large eggplant (about 2 pounds)
½ cup olive oil
¼ cup onions, finely chopped
1 teaspoon garlic, very finely chopped and mashed
2 tablespoons lemon juice

2 teaspoons salt
2 teaspoons pepper, ground
½ cup tahini (sesame paste)
2 tablespoons parsley, chopped
2 tablespoons black olives, pitted

Method

1. Puncture eggplants and rub with oil.
2. Place eggplants in roasting pan and set directly under oven broiler.
3. Cook until skins start to blister, then rotate eggplants to char on all sides.
4. Carefully remove from oven and place eggplant in large bowl with cold water.
5. When cooled, remove as much charred skin as possible. (Use caution as eggplant may still be steaming hot inside.)
6. On cutting board, split eggplant lengthwise and remove seeds.
7. Put in food processor with onions, garlic, lemon juice, salt, pepper, and tahini. (Canned tahini paste often separates into oil and solid paste. Make sure to stir the contents of the can to get equal amount of oil and solids.)
8. Process to puree while adding oil in steady stream.
9. Garnish with parsley and olives.

IS-4. Fish Roe Dip (*Tarama*)

Called *tarama* in Turkey, cured red mullet roe is the base for this salty Middle Eastern spread.

Yield: 4 servings

Equipment needed: Cutting board, knife, electric mixer with paddle

Ingredients

6 slices white bread
4 ounces fish roe (tarama)
¼ cup onions, chopped

¾ cup olive oil
1 tablespoon lemon juice

Method

1. Remove crusts from bread.
2. Soak bread slices in cold water for about 10 minutes.
3. Remove and squeeze out all water.
4. Add to mixing bowl with roe and onions, blend at slow speed.
5. Add lemon juice.
6. Slowly add oil to achieve a smooth consistency.

IS-5. Lamb with Figs, Grapes, and Almonds

Albania, a small country in the Balkans, became Muslim when the Ottoman Empire occupied the area in the nineteenth century. Many Albanian immigrants to the United States in the twentieth century went into the restaurant business.

Yield: 4 servings

Equipment needed: Heavy saucepan, slotted spoon, small bowl, wooden mixing spoon, cutting board, knife

Ingredients

4 ounces shallots, peeled and left whole	1/2 teaspoon pepper, ground
2 tablespoons olive oil	1 bay leaf
1/2 cup whole almonds, peeled	1 tablespoon honey
1 pound lean lamb stew meat	1/2 cup almonds, finely ground
1 tablespoon shallots, chopped	8 dried figs
1/2 tablespoon flour	1/2 cup seedless grapes
1 teaspoon salt	1 tablespoon lemon juice

Method

1. Roast whole shallots and whole almonds in oil until light brown. Remove with slotted spoon; set aside.
2. Add lamb, cooking over high heat until lamb starts to brown. Stir frequently. Add chopped shallots.
3. Sprinkle meat with flour; stir to blend. Add spices, honey, and ground almonds. Add water to cover meat.
4. Simmer 45 minutes. Add a little more water if stew gets too dry.
5. Cut figs in half and add to stew. Simmer 10 minutes longer or until lamb meat is tender.
6. Add grapes and lemon juice. Bring to a boil and serve at once.

IS-6. Stuffed Lamb Shoulder (*Kabourga*)

Not everyone can afford a whole lamb for the sacrificial meal. This festive Egyptian dish is an economical alternative.

Yield: 6 to 8 servings

Equipment needed: 1-quart saucepan with lid, mixing spoon, paring knife, butcher's twine, roasting pan

Ingredients

2 tablespoons oil	1/2 cup rice
1/2 cup pine nuts	1/2 cup onions, chopped

(continued)

1 cup water

2 teaspoons salt

1 teaspoon pepper

½ cup bulgur

1 tablespoon parsley, chopped

1 tablespoon mint, chopped

3 pounds lamb shoulder, boned

1 tablespoon garlic

1 teaspoon salt

Method

1. Toast pine nuts in oil until light brown. Add rice and onions, toast briefly, then add water, salt, and pepper.
2. Bring to a boil, cover, and simmer 20 minutes.
3. Add bulgur, parsley, and mint. Blend and cool until completely chilled.
4. Trim excess fat from meat. Cut and open meat to large square shape.
5. Add cold stuffing. Roll up, then tie with butcher's twine. Leave room for stuffing to expand.
6. Rub with garlic and salt and place in roasting pan with 1 cup water.
7. Roast at 375 degrees until meat is brown and internal temperature is 160 degrees.
8. Remove from oven and let rest 20 minutes before slicing.

IS-7. Lamb Curry (Lamb *Korma*)

Korma is a mild curry from India. If this recipe is made with purchased curry powder, eliminate all other spices in the recipe, cook the curry powder in oil over low heat, add the chopped almonds, and then follow the recipe from the step where the lamb is added.

Yield: 4 servings

Equipment needed: Electric blender, heavy-bottomed saucepan, cutting board, heavy French knife

Ingredients

1 tablespoon coriander seeds

¼ teaspoon cumin

2 teaspoons turmeric

2 teaspoons ginger, chopped

¼ teaspoon cloves, ground

½ tablespoon cinnamon

2 cardamom pods

¼ teaspoon mace

1 teaspoon cayenne pepper

½ tablespoon salt

¼ cup sliced almonds

1 tablespoon oil

2 pounds shoulder lamb chops

1 cup onions, chopped

1 tablespoon garlic, chopped

1 tablespoon brown sugar

1 can (12 ounces) coconut milk

2 tablespoons lemon juice

Method

1. Combine all spices and almonds in blender.
2. Add 2 tablespoons water and puree into fine paste.
3. Cook spice blend and oil in saucepan over low heat to develop flavor. Make sure spices do not burn.
4. Add meat, onions, and garlic. Cook over low heat without scorching.

5. Add sugar and coconut milk. Braise over low heat until meat is tender, adding water if necessary.

6. When meat is tender, remove from heat and add lemon juice. Serve with rice.

IS-8. Barbecued Lamb Breast

Many Muslims living in Caribbean countries celebrate traditional Islamic holidays. The marinade in this recipe contains bitter orange juice, a common ingredient in the Caribbean. If bitter orange juice is not available, use equal amounts of orange juice and lime juice.

Yield: 4 servings
Equipment needed: Plastic container, brush, smoker or barbecue grill

Ingredients

1 teaspoon cumin
1 teaspoon garlic, chopped
1/4 cup bitter orange juice
1/2 teaspoon cayenne pepper
1 teaspoon salt

1/2 cup tomato ketchup
1 teaspoon curry powder
4 Denver ribs (trimmed lamb ribs)

Method

1. Combine first seven ingredients and brush on lamb. Refrigerate 24 hours.
2. Cook over slow heat in smoker or on barbecue grill. Sugar content in ketchup will cause meat to brown easily.
3. Ribs may also be cooked on oven rack at low temperature.

IS-9. Sweet Vermicelli Pudding (*Seviyan/Savia/Sewian*)

This dessert is a typical Eid dish of Arabian origin.
Yield: 4 servings
Equipment needed: 4-quart heavy saucepan, wooden stirrer

Ingredients

3 ounces vermicelli
4 ounces (1 stick) butter
8 cups (2 quarts) milk
1/2 teaspoon cardamom, ground
1 teaspoon cinnamon

1 teaspoon salt
1/2 cup sugar
2 tablespoons raisins
2 tablespoons pistachio nuts, coarsely chopped

(*continued*)

Method

1. Break vermicelli into small pieces and sauté in butter until light brown.
2. Add milk and spices. Bring to a boil. Cook over low heat about 45 minutes, stirring frequently. Mixture will thicken.
3. Add sugar and raisins. Pour pudding into shallow bowl; serve cold, sprinkled with pistachios.

IS-10. Almond Ice Cream

Almond desserts are well known throughout the Middle East. While traditional recipes use reduced milk, modern ones feature sweetened condensed milk instead.
Yield: 8 servings
Equipment needed: Electric blender, 1-quart heavy-bottomed saucepan, wire whisk, mixing bowl, ice cube trays

Ingredients

1 pound almonds, peeled
2 tablespoons sugar
1 pint milk
2 (6-ounce) cans condensed milk

1 cup heavy cream
4 tablespoons rose water
$\frac{1}{2}$ cup pistachio nuts, coarsely
    chopped

Method

1. Combine almonds and sugar in blender or food processor; chop to fairly smooth paste.
2. Combine paste with milk. Stir with wire whisk and bring to a simmer.
3. Simmer 20 minutes, stirring occasionally. Remove from stove and cool completely.
4. Put heavy cream in bowl; whip until thick but not stiff.
5. Add remaining ingredients and blend well.
6. Place mixture in ice cube trays or other suitable flat containers.
7. Freeze until solid.

IS-11. Cherry Bread Pudding

Bosnia, located in the Balkans, has a large Muslim population, but the cooking is more European than Middle Eastern. The area is well known for cultivating cherries and apricots. In Bosnia, sour cherries are popular, but they are difficult to purchase in the United States. If sour cherries are not available, canned Bing cherries can be substituted, but the sugar amount should be reduced slightly.
Yield: 6 servings
Equipment needed: Baking sheet, 8 × 12-inch glass baking dish, small bowl, wire whisk, ladle

Ingredients

6 slices Italian bread, about 3
    inches wide and ½ inch thick
4 tablespoons butter, room
    temperature
1 can (15 ounces) cherries

1½ cups milk
3 eggs
¼ cup sugar
1 teaspoon cinnamon

Method

1. Butter bread and place on baking sheet.
2. Set under broiler briefly, until brown. Set aside.
3. Drain cherries; save juice.
4. Combine cherry juice with milk, egg, sugar, and cinnamon. Blend well.
5. Put toasted bread slices in baking dish. Ladle half of milk mixture over bread. Bake in 325-degree oven for 10 minutes to set custard.
6. Sprinkle cherries on top, add remaining milk mixture, and bake 20 minutes longer.

Al Hijra (1 Muharram)

The first day of the month of Muharram is the start of the Islamic year. It marks the historic journey of Muhammad from Mecca to Medina in 622 CE and the founding of the Islamic state. Although there are no specific religious rituals, some Muslims see Al Hijra as a time to make resolutions for the new year and to think about how to lead a better life. Greeting cards may be exchanged, and meals are shared with family and friends.

IS-12. Millet Porridge

Drought-resistant millet grain is widely cultivated in North African desert countries. This rather austere dish is eaten with honey.
Yield: About 4 cups
Equipment needed: 2-quart saucepan with lid, stirring spoon

Ingredients

1 cup whole millet grains
1 teaspoon salt
1 teaspoon cardamom, ground

1 teaspoon cinnamon
3½ cups water
1 tablespoon olive oil

Method

1. Stir together millet, salt, spices, and water in saucepan.
2. Bring to a boil, cover, and lower heat.
3. Simmer 25 minutes.
4. Remove from heat and let rest 20 minutes.
5. Stir in olive oil.

IS-13. Tunisian Terabilesi Bread

During the second and third centuries BCE, Carthage struggled against and eventually fell to Rome in the Punic Wars. The wheat fields around Carthage became the bread basket of the Roman Empire. Olives, popular throughout North Africa, give this bread a unique taste. Those used in this recipe are genuine oil-cured olives, not canned California olives.

Yield: 2 loaves

Equipment needed: Electric mixer with dough hook, saucepan, small wire whisk, baking sheet, knife

Ingredients

2 cups whole-wheat flour
2 cups plus 1 tablespoon
   all-purpose flour
1 package dry yeast
1½ teaspoons salt

2 cups lukewarm water
1 cup pitted black olives, coarsely
   chopped and drained
Flour for dusting
Sesame seeds

Method

1. Combine whole-wheat flour, 2 cups all-purpose flour, and next four ingredients at slow speed until dough is blended.
2. Knead on floured work surface until smooth.
3. Wrap dough in plastic, and let rest 1 hour at room temperature.
4. To make glaze, combine water and remaining tablespoon of flour in saucepan and bring to a boil, stirring continuously. Set aside to cool.
5. Knead dough again on flour-dusted work surface.
6. Divide into two pieces and roll into tight balls. Set on baking sheet and let rest 30 minutes.
7. With knife, make four cuts on top of each loaf and brush with cooled glaze. Sprinkle with sesame seeds.
8. Bake at 400 degrees for 50 minutes.

IS-14. Malaysian Roast Lamb

The Malaysian Peninsula, surrounded by Hindu and Buddhist lands, is a predominantly Muslim area. Halal meats—lamb, beef, and chicken—feature in many dishes.

Yield: 8 servings

Equipment needed: Cutting board, knife, plastic or stainless steel container to marinate meat, roasting pan, meat thermometer, strainer, small sauce boat

Ingredients

2 lemongrass stalks, cleaned and
   cut into slivers
½ tablespoon garlic, chopped
1 tablespoon mustard powder

2 tablespoons oil
1 teaspoon cumin powder
1 teaspoon anise powder
1 teaspoon sugar

$^1/_2$ cup mint leaves, coarsely
 chopped
1 teaspoon hot pepper
1 cup water

$^1/_2$ cup vinegar
3-pound leg of lamb, boned and
 rolled

Method

1. Combine all ingredients, except lamb, to make marinade.
2. Add lamb and refrigerate overnight.
3. Roast lamb at 375 degrees, basting frequently with marinade, until internal temperature is 160 degrees.
4. Remove from oven and let rest 20 minutes before slicing.
5. Bring marinade to boil and reduce to $^3/_4$ cup. Strain.
6. Serve sliced lamb with reduced marinade.

IS-15. Indonesian Spiced Shrimp
(*Sambal Goreng Undang*)

Indonesia has the largest Muslim population in the world. In this archipelago of more than 17,000 islands, of which 600 are inhabited, it is not surprising that seafood is an important staple. This spicy shrimp dish is served with rice.
Yield: 3 main-dish servings, with rice
Equipment needed: Electric blender, wok, spatula

Ingredients

2 dried red chilies in pod
$^1/_2$ cup onions, chopped
1 tablespoon garlic, chopped
1 tablespoon ginger, chopped
1 teaspoon salt
$^1/_4$ teaspoon tamarind paste

3 tablespoons oil
5 green cardamom pods
1 pound shrimp, peeled and
 deveined
1 cup canned coconut milk

Method

1. Put all ingredients, except shrimp and coconut milk, in blender and process to paste.
2. Rinse blender with 2 tablespoons water to remove all remnants of paste and add liquid to wok with paste.
3. Stir-fry over moderate heat until paste starts to brown slightly.
4. Add shrimp. When shrimp turns pink, add coconut milk. Cook briefly and remove from heat.

IS-16. Lemon Chicken

This recipe comes from Saudi Arabia, where lemons are commonly used in cooking.
Yield: 4 servings
Equipment needed: Grater, cutting board, knife, stainless steel bowl, roasting pan

(continued)

Ingredients

1 large lemon
1 tablespoon garlic, chopped
4 tablespoons olive oil
½ teaspoon hot pepper

1 teaspoon salt
1 teaspoon fennel seeds
1 chicken, 2½ to 3 pounds

Method

1. Grate lemon rind and squeeze juice.
2. Combine all spices in stainless steel bowl.
3. Cut chicken into four pieces and place in marinade. Refrigerate for 2 hours, turning chicken frequently to spread spices.
4. Place chicken and marinade in roasting pan; cook in 350-degree oven for 45 minutes, basting frequently. (After 45 minutes, most of the marinade should be absorbed by the chicken.)

IS-17. Honey-Baked Shredded Dough (*Tel Kadayif*)

The Turks get credit for inventing *yufka*, a paper-thin dough made with only bread flour, water, and a tiny amount of oil. The concept of using dough without yeast or any other leavening spread throughout the Middle East, Greece, and even north into Austria and Hungary. Shredded yufka is called *kadayif* and is available in many supermarkets under the Greek name *kataïfi*.

Yield: 20 servings
Equipment needed: Small pot to melt butter, 2-inch-high baking dish about 8 × 12 inches, 1-quart pot, ladle, knife

Ingredients

8 ounces (2 sticks) butter
1½ pounds kataïfi, frozen
8 ounces hazelnuts, coarsely ground
1 teaspoon cinnamon

2 cups sugar
1 cup honey
2 tablespoons lemon juice
2 tablespoons rose water

Method

1. Pour 4 ounces melted butter into baking dish. Put half of frozen kataïfi dough on top.
2. Sprinkle with nuts and cinnamon, then put remaining kataïfi dough on top.
3. Cover with remaining butter. Bake at 350 degrees until top is brown.
4. Combine sugar and honey with 3 cups water. Bring to a boil; simmer 20 minutes. Add lemon juice and rose water.
5. Ladle hot syrup evenly over baked kataïfi dough. Cut in squares with sharp knife and serve chilled.

Ashura (10 Muharram)

Ashura, a day of fasting for all Muslims, commemorates two Biblical events—the day Noah left the Ark, and the day Moses was saved from the Egyptians by God. It is also the day on which the Prophet Abraham (Ibrahim) was born and the Ka'ba was built in Mecca. For Shiites, Ashura also has a special significance, as it commemorates the ancient battle of Kerbala, at which Hussein, grandson of Muhammad, was slain. This is a day of mourning for Shiites, who prepare a simple Ashura meal and serve it to the community in remembrance of the last meal of Hussein and his companions.

IS-18. Pomegranate Mint Tea

Once the new moon appears, black-clad Shiites assemble and recite plaintive verses in memory of Imam Hussein over a sweetened cold drink. The cool drink is meant to remind people of the terrible thirst Hussein and his family had to suffer.
Yield: 1 quart
Equipment needed: 2-quart nonreactive pot, wooden spoon, cutting board, French knife, strainer, bowl, pitcher

Ingredients

4 tablespoons dried pomegranate
   seeds
2 tablespoons honey

2 bunches fresh mint
$\frac{1}{2}$ cup sugar
5 cups water

Method

1. Combine pomegranate seeds and honey with 5 cups water.
2. Bring to a boil; steep 20 minutes; strain.
3. Thoroughly wash mint to remove sand.
4. Chop coarsely, including stems.
5. Combine mint with sugar in bowl. With wooden spoon, stir and press down, squashing leaves and stems to extract flavor.
6. Pour pomegranate water over mint. Refrigerate overnight.
7. Strain into pitcher and serve ice cold.

IS-19. Millet Pancakes

Millet flour made from drought-resistant millet grain is used in this breakfast dish from North Africa. Millet flour has a unique flavor, and its grayish color is not very attractive. To make the pancakes more palatable, replace 1 cup millet flour with 1 cup pancake mix.
Yield: 20 pancakes
Equipment needed: Mixing bowl, wire whisk, griddle, ladle, spatula

(continued)

Ingredients

2 cups millet flour
1¼ cups lukewarm water

1 teaspoon salt
Margarine or butter for frying

Method

1. Blend flour, water, and salt with wire whisk to make smooth batter.
2. Set aside for 4 hours at room temperature, or refrigerate overnight. Batter will ferment slightly.
3. Fry pancakes in butter on medium-hot griddle.
4. Serve with honey.

IS-20. Lentils with Rice (*Moujadara*)

This dish is a favorite in Iraq and in Middle Eastern delis in the United States.
Yield: 6 to 8 main-course servings
Equipment needed: 3-quart saucepan, stirring spoon

Ingredients

½ cup vegetable oil
1 cup onions, diced
1 cup lentils
½ cup long-grain rice

1½ teaspoons salt
¼ teaspoon black pepper, ground
1 tablespoon sesame oil
½ cup cilantro leaves, chopped

Method

1. Combine oil and onion in heavy saucepan and sauté over low heat until onions are glossy.
2. Add lentils and 3 cups water.
3. Bring to a boil; simmer 40 minutes, stirring occasionally.
4. Add rice and spices. Simmer 25 minutes.
5. Add enough water to keep the mixture barely covered.
6. Serve sprinkled with sesame oil and cilantro.

IS-21. Persian Lamb Stew

This stew is seasoned with parsley; its beautiful green color is like the Islamic flag.
Yield: 6 to 8 servings
Equipment needed: Dutch oven, cutting board, French knife, small saucepan, wooden mixing spoon

Ingredients

3 pounds lean lamb stew meat
2 tablespoons olive oil

½ tablespoon salt
1 teaspoon turmeric

½ teaspoon cayenne pepper
1 cup crushed tomatoes
2 cups canned chickpeas, drained
3 bunches Italian (flat leaf) parsley

1 bunch scallions
1 lemon
2 tablespoons butter
¼ cup water

Method

1. Combine meat, oil, and spices in Dutch oven and roast in 400-degree oven, uncovered, for 45 minutes. Stir occasionally.
2. Add crushed tomatoes and chickpeas. Place back in oven with lid on.
3. Lower heat to 375 degrees; simmer 1 hour.
4. Wash parsley, discard stems. Chop leaves and set aside.
5. Wash scallions. Cut across in fine slices, including green tops. Set aside.
6. Grate lemon and add to scallions.
7. Squeeze lemon, set juice aside.
8. Melt butter and add sliced scallions and lemon peel.
9. Add water and braise over low heat about 10 minutes until scallions are wilted.
10. Remove lamb stew from oven.
11. Add lemon juice and parsley just before serving.

IS-22. Persian Sweet Rice (*Shekar Polo*)

Sweet rice is a popular accompaniment to meat dishes. The authentic way to cook the rice is to use a cast-iron pot and let the rice bake to the bottom. The slightly browned and crisp rice is considered a delicacy. If dried sour cherries are not available, replace with dried cranberries.

Yield: 6 side-dish servings
Equipment needed: 2-quart heavy saucepan with lid, wooden spoon

Ingredients

½ cup dried sour cherries
2 tablespoons oil
2 tablespoons slivered almonds
½ cup onions, chopped
½ cup celery, thinly sliced

1 cup rice
2 cups canned chicken broth
1 teaspoon cinnamon
1 teaspoon black pepper, ground
1 cup water

Method

1. Cover dried cherries with 1 cup water and set aside.
2. Cook almonds in oil over moderate heat, stirring continuously until light brown.
3. Add onions and celery; continue cooking over low heat until onions turn glossy.
4. Add rice, chicken broth, cherries and soaking water, cinnamon, and pepper.
5. Bring to a boil, cover pot, and simmer 20 minutes.
6. On low heat, cook 5 minutes more to allow crust to form.

Shab-E-Barat (13–14 Shaban)

Held on either the thirteenth or fourteenth day of the eighth month of the Muslim year, this feast begins fifteen days before the beginning of Ramadan. *Shab-E-Barat* means "Night of Forgiveness"; people pray to God for forgiveness of their sins, for it is believed that on this night a person's fate is decided for the coming year. Streets are illuminated with lanterns and candles, and fireworks light up the sky. Blessings known as *fatiha* are recited over meals in the name of the Prophet, his daughter Fatima, and her husband Ali. Sweets are prepared and given to friends and relatives.

IS-23. Fritters in Syrup (*Gulab Jamin*)

American Muslim families often serve this famous South Asian dessert of rose-scented small dumplings in sweet syrup.

Yield: 25 fritters

Equipment needed: Mixing bowl, 1-quart saucepan, deep frying pan, slotted spoon or skimmer

Ingredients

4 ounces powdered milk	3 cardamom pods
4 ounces pancake mix	2 tablespoons lemon juice
4 ounces heavy cream	4 drops rose water (optional)
4 cups water	Ground cinnamon
2½ cups sugar	Oil for frying

Method

1. Combine powdered milk, pancake mix, and cream to make stiff dough.
2. Refrigerate 1 hour.
3. Combine water, sugar, and cardamom pods. Bring to a boil; simmer 1 hour.
4. Add lemon juice and rose water. Set aside to cool.
5. With moist hands, shape dough into 25 balls.
6. Deep-fry fritters at medium heat until browned. Remove with slotted spoon and drain on paper towels. Make sure fritters are cooked through.
7. Put in syrup. Sprinkle with cinnamon.

Mawlid-al-Nabi (12 Rabi al-Awwal)

Mawlid is a celebration of the birthday of the Prophet Muhammad, founder of Islam. Though not all Muslims observe this, those who do, participate in prayers and listen to stories about the Prophet's life. Mosques are decorated and illuminated. Families and friends gather to share meals and give food to the poor.

IS-24. Chard and Lentil Soup

Lentils have long been an important part of human diets and are a valuable source of protein. While this recipe uses inexpensive meat for flavor, it may also be made as a meatless dish.

Yield: 6 to 8 servings

Equipment needed: 2-quart soup pot, cutting board, knife, colander, 2-quart pot with lid, strainer, 2-quart soup pot, ladle

Ingredients

1 pound lamb neck
1 quart water
2 pounds green chard
2 tablespoons olive oil
1 cup lentils
1 teaspoon cumin

1 cup onions, chopped
1 teaspoon vinegar
2 teaspoons salt
1 teaspoon garlic
1 teaspoon hot pepper

Method

1. Rinse lamb neck, add water, and bring to a boil. Simmer 1½ hours.
2. Discard chard stems and wash leaves carefully to remove all sand.
3. Cut washed chard leaves into pieces about 1-inch square.
4. Heat chard with oil in 2-quart pot to wilt leaves. Cover; lower heat to steam leaves for 5 minutes. Set aside.
5. Strain lamb stock, discard bones, and add lentils remaining ingredients. Bring to a boil and simmer 35 minutes.
6. Carefully ladle lentil soup over chard. Bring to a boil and continue to simmer until lentils are soft, about 20 minutes. Add more water if necessary to obtain about 2 quarts soup.

IS-25. Semolina Cooked in Water (*Lââssida*)

Plain cream of wheat is the basis of this Moroccan breakfast dish, usually served with honey.

Yield: 8 servings

Equipment needed: 6-quart saucepan, stirring spoon

Ingredients

8 ounces semolina (coarse cream of wheat)
2 quarts water
4 ounces (1 stick) butter

1 teaspoon salt
1 tablespoon cinnamon, ground
Honey to taste

(continued)

Method

1. Bring semolina and water to a boil, stirring continuously.
2. Add butter and salt. Simmer 10 minutes over low heat. Be careful, mixture will splatter.
3. Serve hot, sprinkled with cinnamon and honey.

IS-26. Stewed Fish over Rice and Noodles

Though it has its roots in Egyptian cooking, this colorful dish is of African-American origin.

Yield: 4 servings

Equipment needed: Cutting board, knife, wide saucepan, spatula or mixing spoon, 2-quart heavy saucepan

Ingredients

1½ pounds whiting fish fillets or any other solid fish
3 tablespoons oil
1 cup red peppers, diced
1 cup yellow peppers, diced
1 cup green peppers, diced
1 cup broccoli florets
1 cup cauliflower florets

1 cup canned crushed tomatoes, with juice
1 teaspoon dried oregano leaves
1 teaspoon dried sage leaves
½ teaspoon cumin, ground
Salt and pepper to taste
8 ounces vermicelli noodles

Method

1. Cut fish into 1-inch cubes and set aside.
2. Heat oil in saucepan. Add garlic and all vegetables.
3. Sauté over high heat about 10 minutes, stirring frequently. Vegetables should brown slightly.
4. Add tomatoes and spices. Bring to a boil.
5. Add fish, bring to a boil again, and simmer 5 minutes. Do not stir or break up fish pieces.
6. Boil noodles according to package instructions. Serve fish over noodles.

IS-27. Yam Patties

Grown in the tropics and many parts of Africa, yams are the tuberous roots of a vine that probably originated in Asia. What Americans commonly call a yam, though, actually is a sweet potato. The confusion may have started when slaves in the New World, upon first tasting the sweet potato, called the yam-like vegetable *nyam*. These patties, served on holidays, are delicious as a side dish with meat.

Yield: 8 servings

Equipment needed: Baking sheet, knife, ricer, mixing bowl, griddle, ice cream scoop, spatula

Ingredients

2 pounds yams	2 eggs
1 teaspoon oil	2 tablespoons breadcrumbs
1 teaspoon salt	Pan spray
1 teaspoon pepper	

Method

1. Wash yams and rub with oil.
2. Bake at 375 degrees for about 45 minutes. Test yams to ensure they are fully cooked.
3. Cool, peel, and put through ricer while still warm.
4. Blend with next four ingredients; let sit 20 minutes.
5. Warm griddle and pan-spray.
6. Using ice cream scoop, portion yam paste onto griddle. Flatten lightly with spatula.
7. Brown on each side.

IS-28. Algerian Roast Chicken with Sweet Stuffing

Flavored with lemon, this dish uses a typical North African mix of spices, nuts, and raisins.

Yield: 4 servings

Equipment needed: Small pan, spoon, cutting board, knife, colander, food processor, mixing bowl, roasting pan, brush

Ingredients

4 tablespoons oil	1 teaspoon salt
2 tablespoons onions, chopped	½ cup pistachio nuts
8 ounces chicken livers	½ cup raisins
6 slices white bread	1 lemon
1 teaspoon cinnamon	1 chicken, about 3 pounds
1 teaspoon pepper	

Method

1. Sauté onions in 2 tablespoons of oil; set aside to cool.
2. Clean chicken livers, removing all skin and fat. Remove crust and cut bread into cubes.
3. Combine livers, spices, and onions in food processor to make coarse paste.
4. Blend in nuts and raisins.
5. Halve lemon and rub over chicken inside and out.
6. Fill chicken cavity with liver paste. Close opening with toothpicks or small skewer.
7. Place chicken upright in roasting pan, brush with remaining oil, and roast at 350 degrees for 1½ hours.

IS-29. Iranian Fruit Rice with Fish

Rice is a staple food in Iran. Any firm-fleshed fish fillet with skin can be used in this recipe. Bass or snapper works well.

Yield: 4 servings

Equipment needed: Heavy skillet, cutting board, French knife, spatula, 1-quart soup pot, colander, Dutch oven

Ingredients

2 pounds firm fish fillets	4 ounces dried apricots, halved
½ cup flour	½ cup raisins
¼ cup oil	½ cup slivered almonds
½ cup onions, chopped	1 teaspoon cinnamon
1 cup rice	1 teaspoon pepper, ground
1 cup canned sweet cherries, pitted	1 teaspoon salt
1 tablespoon lemon juice	1 teaspoon turmeric
	2 cups canned chicken stock

Method

1. Cut fish fillets in 1-inch squares.
2. Dry with paper towel and coat in flour, shaking off excess.
3. Heat oil in frying pan. Carefully add fish fillets a few at a time and cook over medium heat until brown on both sides.
4. Remove fish with spatula to Dutch oven. Set pan with oil aside.
5. Boil rice in water for 10 minutes. Drain and sprinkle over fish.
6. Sauté onions briefly in pan with oil. Add onions and oil to fish and rice in Dutch oven.
7. Drain cherries, discarding juice.
8. Sprinkle cherries, lemon juice, dried fruits, almonds, and spices over fish and rice.
9. Add spices to chicken stock. Pour seasoned stock over rice and fish. Do not stir.
10. Place Dutch oven on stove and bring contents to a boil.
11. Cover and simmer 20 minutes.

IS-30. Malaysian Chicken in Coconut Cream
(*Rendan Santan*)

Coconut is a common ingredient in Malaysian cooking. The inclusion of hoisin sauce in this recipe shows the influence of Chinese cuisine, while the shredded coconut gives the sauce a crunchy texture.

Yield: 4 servings

Equipment needed: 2-quart saucepan, wooden spoon, French knife, cutting board

Ingredients

4 ounces frozen grated coconut,
  unsweetened (available in
  ethnic stores)
½ cup onions, chopped
1 tablespoon green chilies,
  chopped
2 tablespoons butter
1 teaspoon coriander, ground
1 teaspoon anise, ground
1 teaspoon ginger, ground

2 tablespoons grated lemon rind
½ teaspoon hot pepper
1 lemongrass stalk
2 tablespoons lemon juice
1 tablespoon hoisin sauce
1 teaspoon brown sugar
2 teaspoons salt
1½ cups coconut milk
4 chicken breasts, skinless,
  6 ounces each

Method

1. Sauté coconut, onions, and chilies in butter until light brown.
2. Add dry spices and sauté briefly.
3. Clean lemongrass, cut in 6-inch sections, and then slice horizontally.
4. Add 1 cup water and all other ingredients except chicken, blend, and bring to a boil.
5. Simmer 25 minutes.
6. Cut chicken breasts into two pieces each. Add to sauce and cook over moderate heat about 10 minutes.

Ramadan

Ramadan, the ninth month of the Islamic calendar, is the holiest period of the Islamic year. The much-anticipated start of the month is based on a combination of physical sightings of the moon and astronomical calculations. One of the last five odd-numbered days of the month is called the Laylat al-Qadr (Night of Power), marking the date of the revelations of the first verses of the Qur'an to the Prophet Muhammad. Through a carefully observed fast, Ramadan is a time to demonstrate devotion to God and to practice self-discipline and fellowship. The daily period of fasting starts at dawn and ends at sunset. The usual practice is to have a pre-fast meal (*suhoor*) before dawn and a post-fast meal (*iftar*) after sunset. Larger meals, served later in the evening, feature some of the many Ramadan food specialties.

Suhoor: Early Morning Meal

Since eating is forbidden during the day, the early morning meal is consumed just before dawn. Traditional Islamic foods for suhoor are porridge, bread, or fruit. It is believed that the Prophet Muhammad recommended including dates as part of the suhoor meal.

IS-31. Date Sweetmeat (*Holwar Tamar*)

Yield: 40 pieces
Equipment needed: Small cast-iron pan, food processor, cutting board, French knife, 1-quart heavy-bottomed saucepan, wooden spoon, cookie sheet

(*continued*)

Ingredients

½ cup white sesame seeds
2 cups walnuts, coarsely chopped
  (about 12 ounces)
1 pound dry dates, pitted

¼ cup ghee or vegetable
  shortening (not oil)
¼ cup sugar
Pan spray

Method

1. Toast sesame seeds over medium heat until light brown. Set aside.
2. Chop walnuts in food processor until medium-fine consistency.
3. Cut dates into small pieces and place in heavy saucepan with ghee.
4. Heat over moderate heat, stirring continuously.
5. Keep cooking until well combined and dates start to caramelize on bottom of pan.
6. Add sugar. When melted, add walnut pieces and sesame seeds; blend well.
7. Pan-spray cookie sheet. Put hot mixture on top and flatten with spatula to about ½-inch thick.
8. Place in refrigerator briefly to harden.
9. Cut into small pieces.

IS-32. Benne Cookies

Benne is a West African name for sesame seeds. Benne cookies, also known as Benne cakes, are well known in the southern United States and should be kept in an airtight container.
Yield: About 50 cookies
Equipment needed: Cast-iron frying pan, stirring spoon, electric mixer with paddles, flour sifter, cookie sheet, teaspoon, metal spatula

Ingredients

1 cup sesame seeds
8 ounces (2 sticks) butter, room
  temperature
8 ounces light brown sugar
½ cup sugar
2 eggs

1 teaspoon salt
½ teaspoon cinnamon, ground
½ teaspoon cardamom, ground
1½ cups flour
½ teaspoon baking powder
Pan spray

Method

1. Toast sesame seeds in dry, cast-iron frying pan over moderate heat until light yellow; stirring continuously. Cool seeds.
2. Combine butter with brown sugar, eggs, salt, and spices. Blend with electric mixer at low speed until creamy.
3. Sift flour and baking powder together. Add flour and sesame seeds to creamed eggs; blend at low speed.
4. Pan-spray cookie sheet. With teaspoon, drop small cookies on sheet.
5. Leave space between cookies, as they will spread.
6. Bake at 350 degrees for about 15 minutes, or until brown around the edges.

7. Remove immediately with metal spatula.

8. Cookies will harden rapidly and turn brittle when cool.

IS-33. Fig and Date Bread

This Egyptian cake consists essentially of dried fruits held together with a small amount of flour and eggs. It keeps well, but should sit at least a day before slicing.

Yield: 12 slices

Equipment needed: Large mixing bowl, mixing spoon

Ingredients

1 cup orange juice

2 tablespoons lemon juice

2 eggs

8 ounces dried dates, pitted and coarsely chopped

8 ounces dried figs, stems removed and coarsely chopped

$\frac{1}{2}$ cup flour

1 teaspoon baking powder

$\frac{1}{8}$ teaspoon allspice, ground

$\frac{1}{8}$ teaspoon cloves, ground

Method

1. Combine orange juice, lemon juice, and eggs. Blend well.

2. Add all other ingredients.

3. Place mixture in baking pan, cover with aluminum foil, and bake at 350 degrees for about an hour.

4. Refrigerate until completely cold before slicing.

IS-34. Syrian Flat Bread

Flat breads, prepared in various ways, are common throughout South Asia and the Middle East. This one is from Syria.

Yield: 30 pieces

Equipment needed: Electric mixer with paddle, rolling pin, baking sheets

Ingredients

$1\frac{1}{2}$ cups whole-wheat flour

2 cups flour

1 teaspoon salt

1 package dry yeast

1 cup warm water

1 tablespoon cumin seeds

Flour for dusting

Method

1. Sift flours and salt into mixing bowl.

2. Make a well in center; add yeast and water.

(continued)

3. Blend at low speed until soft dough forms.
4. Knead on floured work surface and shape into ball.
5. Cover with plastic wrap. Let rest 3 hours.
6. Divide dough into 30 pieces.
7. Roll pieces into small rounds as thin as possible; they should be almost translucent.
8. Sprinkle with cumin seeds.
9. Place on baking sheets and bake at 475 degrees about $1\frac{1}{2}$ minutes. Bread should be crisp and light brown.

IS-35. Agras

Agras is a sweet, nonalcoholic beverage made with grape juice, sugar, mint, and almonds that is popular among Tunisian Muslims.

Yield: 3 pints

Equipment needed: Electric blender, 2-quart pot, strainer with cheesecloth, $1\frac{1}{2}$-quart glass or plastic juice container

Ingredients

1 cup mint leaves, loosely packed	3 cloves
1 cup slivered almonds	$1\frac{1}{2}$ cups water
1 tablespoon lemon juice	$\frac{1}{2}$ cup sugar
2 cardamom pods	1 quart grape juice, red or white

Method

1. Puree mint leaves and almonds in food processor.
2. Put in pot and add lemon juice, spices, and water. Bring to a boil; steep for 20 minutes.
3. Add sugar and grape juice. Return to a boil, then cool. When cold, strain through cheesecloth. Refrigerate. Serve with ice cubes and mint sprigs.

IS-36. Iranian Almond and Pistachio Loaf

This rather rich nut loaf is often served to guests on holidays.

Yield: 1 loaf

Equipment needed: Sifter, food processor, mixing bowl, electric mixer with paddle, scraper, 9-inch loaf pan

Ingredients

1 teaspoon baking powder	1 cup almonds, ground
1 cup flour	1 cup pistachio nuts

4 eggs

1 cup sugar

¼ teaspoon salt

½ teaspoon cinnamon

1 teaspoon almond extract

1 ounce (¼ stick) butter, melted

¼ cup slivered almonds

Pan spray

Flour for dusting pan

Method

1. Sift baking powder and flour together and set aside.
2. Coarsely chop almonds and pistachios in food processor.
3. Blend eggs and sugar, stirring until sugar is completely dissolved.
4. Add remaining ingredients, except slivered almonds.
5. Pan-spray loaf pan and evenly dust inside with flour.
6. Pour batter into pan. Sprinkle top with slivered almonds.
7. Bake at 375 degrees for 40 minutes.

IS-37. Sweet Cardamom Rice (*Sevaiyya Kheer*)

Sevaiyya Kheer is a traditional dessert dish eaten in all the parts of the Muslim world.

Yield: 6 servings

Equipment needed: 2-quart saucepan, colander, stirring spoon

Ingredients

1 cup basmati rice

8 green cardamom pods, crushed

2 quarts milk

½ teaspoon salt

½ cup sugar

2 tablespoons rose water

2 tablespoons pistachio nuts, chopped

Method

1. Place rice in pot and cover with water. Bring to a boil, then drain.
2. Add cardamom pods, milk, salt, and 1 tablespoon of sugar to rice. Bring to a boil and simmer for 40 minutes, stirring occasionally.
3. Add rose water, remaining sugar, and pistachio nuts.
4. Serve at room temperature.

Iftar: Evening Meal

Once the sun sets, the daily fast is broken with a simple snack such as bread, cheese, or fruit. Evening prayers are said and are followed by iftar, the big evening meal. Dishes usually include a hearty stew or spiced vegetable dish. Once the meal is over, people will usually meet at the local mosque or visit at each other's houses.

IS-38. Oxtail and Okra Soup

This recipe is an African-American specialty.
Yield: 8 servings
Equipment needed: Roasting pan, 3-quart soup pot, skimmer, bowl, cutting board, French knife

Ingredients

3-pound oxtail, cut in pieces
1 tablespoon flour
1 bay leaf
½ teaspoon peppercorns
½ cup onions, diced
½ cup celery, diced
½ cup parsnips, diced

½ cup carrots, diced
⅛ teaspoon dried thyme
1 cup fresh okra, cut horizontally
    in ¼-inch slices
1 teaspoon salt
1 teaspoon Worcestershire sauce
2 quarts water

Method

1. Place oxtail in large roasting pan, sprinkle with flour, and roast in 375-degree oven until light brown, about 30 minutes.
2. Put oxtail pieces in large soup pot and cover with 2 quarts water. Add bay leaf and peppercorns.
3. Bring to a boil and simmer about 2½ hours, or until oxtails are tender.
4. Remove oxtails with skimmer and place in a bowl to cool.
5. Add all remaining ingredients to beef broth. Bring to a boil and simmer 30 minutes.
6. Remove all lean meat from oxtails and place in soup.
7. Serve with bread.

IS-39. Bosnian Apricot Soup

Bosnia is famous for dried apricots. Here they are combined with dried apples in a delicious soup.
Yield: 8 servings
Equipment needed: 2-quart soup pot, food processor, small bowl, mixing spoon, whisk

Ingredients

8 ounces dried apricots
4 ounces dried apples
6¼ cups water
½ cup sugar
2 tablespoons cornstarch

1 teaspoon lemon juice
1 cup sour cream
¼ cup hazelnuts, peeled,
    chopped, and lightly toasted

Method

1. Bring apricots, apples, sugar, and 6 cups water to a boil and simmer 30 minutes.

2. Make slurry with cornstarch and remaining ¼ cup of water.
3. Add to simmering fruit, bring to a boil, and cool.
4. Put fruit soup in food processor and process to chunky consistency.
5. Add lemon juice.
6. When soup is completely cold, stir in sour cream and refrigerate.
7. Serve sprinkled with hazelnuts.

IS-40. Moroccan Lentil Soup (*Harira*)

Moroccan households enjoy this soup at sundown throughout the month of Ramadan.

Yield: 8 servings

Equipment needed: 1-quart saucepan, 3-quart saucepan, cutting board, French knife

Ingredients

8 ounces lentils
1 tablespoon lemon juice
1 tablespoon salt
1 pound lamb stew meat, cut in small cubes
½ cup onions, sliced
2 cups canned crushed tomatoes, with juice
2 cups plus 4 tablespoons water
¼ cup olive oil

1 teaspoon turmeric
1 teaspoon pepper, ground
1 teaspoon cumin
1 teaspoon coriander seeds, crushed
1 pound pearl onions
1 bunch cilantro
1 bunch parsley
2 tablespoons cornstarch

Method

1. Cover lentils with water, bring to a boil, and simmer until tender and soft, but not mushy—about 40 minutes. Do not allow lentils to dry out; add water to cover as needed.
2. Add lemon juice and salt; set aside.
3. Combine meat with tomatoes, 2 cups water, olive oil, and spices. Bring to a boil and simmer 1 hour.
4. Soak pearl onions in hot water and peel. (Hot water makes removal of peels easier.)
5. Add peeled pearl onions to meat, blend, and simmer 20 minutes more.
6. Add lentils and stock. Bring to a boil and simmer 5 minutes.
7. Cut off stems from cilantro and parsley. Wash thoroughly to remove all sand. Drain well.
8. Chop greens and set aside.
9. Blend cornstarch with 4 tablespoons water and add to simmering soup. Stir well.
10. Add chopped greens and serve at once.

IS-41. Fava Bean Fritters (*Taamiya*)

This dish is traditional in Oman and popular throughout the Middle East. Native fava beans are made into fritters seasoned with garlic, onions, and coriander.
Yield: About 30 pieces
Equipment needed: 2-quart soup pot, strainer, food mill, mixing bowl, small pan, scraper, mixing spoon, small ice cream scoop, skimmer

Ingredients

2 cups dried fava beans	1 teaspoon salt
1 tablespoon oil	1 egg
1 teaspoon garlic, chopped	2 tablespoons farina
1 teaspoon coriander, ground	$\frac{1}{4}$ teaspoon cayenne pepper
1 teaspoon cumin, ground	Oil for frying

Method

1. Soak fava beans in cold water overnight.
2. Cover with additional water and simmer until soft, about an hour.
3. Drain beans and puree with food mill. (Do not use electric blender as tough skins will not fully disintegrate.)
4. Briefly cook garlic in oil without browning. Remove from heat and add coriander, cumin, and salt.
5. Add spices to bean paste.
6. Add remaining ingredients and let mixture rest 1 hour for farina to absorb moisture.
7. Using ice cream scoop, drop small fritters into hot oil and fry until brown on all sides.
8. Drain on paper towels.

IS-42. Turkish Spiced Liver Rice (*İç Pilâl*)

Turkey gets credit for introducing the term *pilaf* to the Western world. The concept of cooking rice together with other ingredients is alien to Chinese, Japanese, and East Asian cooking, where rice is always served plain, as an accompaniment, or stir-fried.
Yield: 6 to 8 servings
Equipment needed: Cutting board, knife, 2-quart heavy saucepan with lid, mixing spoon

Ingredients

6 ounces lamb liver (calf's liver can be substituted)	$\frac{1}{2}$ cup sultanas (small raisins)
	2 cups rice
2 tablespoons olive oil	4 cups canned chicken broth
$\frac{1}{2}$ cup pine nuts	1 teaspoon white pepper, ground
1 teaspoon fennel seeds	$\frac{1}{2}$ teaspoon cinnamon, ground

Method

1. Cut liver into ½-inch pieces.
2. Sauté pine nuts and fennel seeds in oil until pine nuts are golden brown.
3. Add liver and cook briefly. Add all other ingredients and bring to a boil. Cover and simmer 20 minutes.

IS-43. Semolina Cake (*Basbousa*)

Semolina is fine-ground wheat sold under the name "farina" in the United States. In Egypt it is the basis for a delicious dessert, served soaked in sweet syrup. It could also be topped with almonds or pistachio nuts.

Yield: 1 cake

Equipment needed: Electric mixer with whisk, spoon, spatula, 9 × 9-inch baking pan, 1-quart saucepan, ladle

Ingredients

4 ounces (1 stick) butter, room temperature	1½ cups water
1 cup sugar	1½ cups farina
1 teaspoon vanilla extract	Pan spray
2 eggs	½ cup honey
1 teaspoon baking powder	4 tablespoons lemon juice
	2 tablespoons rose water

Method

1. Cream butter with ¾ cup sugar. Add vanilla and eggs; cream until mixture is light yellow, smooth, and fluffy.
2. Stir in baking powder, ½ cup water, and farina. Blend well.
3. Pour batter into pan-sprayed cake pan and bake at 350 degrees for 40 minutes.
4. Bring remaining sugar, honey, and 1 cup of water to a boil.
5. Simmer 5 minutes; cool.
6. Add lemon juice and rose water to syrup.
7. Ladle over cake while still in pan. Let syrup soak in evenly. Refrigerate, cut cake in cubes, and serve directly from pan.

IS-44. Peanut Stew

This African-American recipe uses unsalted peanuts. If they are not available, salted peanuts should be rinsed in warm water to remove as much salt as possible.

Yield: 8 servings

Equipment needed: 2-quart heavy soup pot, stirring spoon, cutting board, French knife, 1-quart saucepan

(continued)

Ingredients

2 cups unsalted peanuts
1 tablespoon vegetable oil
1 tablespoon flour
1 cup leeks, washed and diced
1 cup celery, washed and diced
12 ounces canned chicken stock

1 cup canned black-eyed peas, drained
1 teaspoon chili powder
1 cup canned crushed tomatoes
1 tablespoon oil

Method

1. Toast peanuts in 350-degree oven until light brown. Set aside.
2. When cool enough to handle, rub peanuts between hands to loosen skins, then rinse several times to remove skins. Set peanuts aside.
3. Heat oil in heavy saucepan, add flour, and cook over medium heat until light brown.
4. Add leeks and celery. Stir briefly.
5. Add chicken stock, drained peas, chili powder, and tomatoes. Bring to a boil and simmer 10 minutes.
6. Add peanuts to stew and simmer 20 minutes longer.
7. Serve as main course with bread or as vegetable side dish.

IS-45. Chicken in Nut Sauce (*Cerkez Tavuğu*)

This is a classic cold chicken dish from Turkey.

Yield: 4 servings

Equipment needed: 3-quart soup pot, cookie sheet, kitchen towel, cutting board, knife, food processor, serving platter

Ingredients

1 chicken, 3 to $3^{1}/_{2}$ pounds
1 tablespoon salt
1 pound hazelnuts
8 slices white sandwich bread, crusts removed
1 cup light cream
2 tablespoons olive oil

1 teaspoon hot pepper
1 teaspoon garlic
2 cups chicken broth
$^{1}/_{2}$ cup black olives
$^{1}/_{2}$ cup canned pimento
Parsley for garnish

Method

1. Wash chicken, place in pot, and cover with salted water. Bring to a boil and simmer $1^{1}/_{2}$ hours. Cool in stock.
2. Bake hazelnuts on rimmed cookie sheet in 375-degree oven until brown, being careful not to burn.
3. Remove from oven and place on kitchen towel. Once nuts are cool enough to handle, rub against each other, in towel, to remove skins.
4. Put skinned hazelnuts in food processor.
5. Cube bread; add to nuts with cream, oil, and spices. Process to thick puree.

6. Gradually add chicken stock to form thick, smooth sauce. Refrigerate.
7. Remove all skin and bones from chicken, cut into serving-size pieces, and place on platter. Cover with chilled sauce. Decorate with olives and pimento strips; garnish with parsley.

Eid-al-Fitr (1 Shawwal)

Signaling the end of Ramadan, the three-day Breaking of the Fast is the most important and joyous Muslim festival, a sort of thanksgiving to Allah for giving believers an opportunity to observe the fast. When the new moon's arrival signals the end of Ramadan, there is a colossal celebration with unparalleled feasting and revelry. Eid-al-Fitr is a time when the whole community comes together to rejoice and, of course, eat! Also known as Sweet Id, this festival's foods include dishes such as sweet vermicelli pudding (see recipe on page 153) and sweet cardamom rice (see recipes on page 171). Meals traditionally begin by sharing bread served with a spicy dip.

IS-46. Hilbeh Dip

This Libyan dip is usually eaten with fried bread.
Yield: 1 cup
Equipment needed: Small bowl, cutting board, French knife

Ingredients

1 tablespoon fenugreek seeds
3 tablespoons garlic, chopped
1/4 cup olive oil

1 teaspoon salt
1 tablespoon lemon juice
1/2 cup cilantro, chopped

Method

1. Soak fenugreek seeds in 2 tablespoons water overnight.
2. Drain seeds and chop on cutting board as finely as possible.
3. Return to bowl, add remaining ingredients, and marinate in refrigerator at least 2 hours.

IS-47. Egyptian Mazza Dip

Appetizers known as *mazza*, or *mezze*, are popular throughout the Middle East and are usually accompanied by a tahini-based dip with a variety of seasonings.
Yield: 1 1/2 cups
Equipment needed: Mixing bowl, mixing spoon

(continued)

Ingredients

1½ tablespoons garlic, chopped
1 cup tahini (sesame) paste
3 tablespoons lemon juice
¼ teaspoon salt

1 teaspoon cumin, ground
½ cup water
½ cup parsley, chopped
¼ teaspoon cayenne pepper

Method

1. Combine all ingredients.
2. Serve with pita bread wedges.

IS-48. Egyptian Chickpea Fritters (*Falafel*)

These fritters are popular throughout the Middle East and have become common street food in many North American cities. Often prepared from a ready-to-use mix available in supermarkets, falafels are very tasty, especially when eaten with *mazza* dressing (see preceding recipe). Don't overcook them or they will become dry.

Yield: 10 side-dish servings
Equipment needed: Food processor, frying kettle or wide deep pot suitable for frying, small ice cream scoop, slotted spoon, paper towels for draining

Ingredients

1 cup dried lima or fava beans
1 cup dried chickpeas
2 tablespoons garlic, chopped
½ cup onions, chopped
¼ cup cilantro leaves, chopped
¼ cup parsley, chopped
½ tablespoon salt
1 teaspoon cumin, ground

1 teaspoon coriander, ground
2 tablespoons flour
¼ teaspoon cayenne pepper
1 teaspoon baking powder
Oil for frying
Shredded lettuce
Sliced tomatoes

Method

1. Soak legumes in cold water for 24 hours. Drain.
2. Blend all ingredients except oil, lettuce, and tomatoes in food processor to make smooth paste.
3. Heat oil in deep pot or fryer until a drop of water sizzles.
4. Using ice cream scoop, drop walnut-size balls into fat and fry over moderate heat until brown and cooked through.
5. Remove with slotted spoon and drain on paper towels. Serve with lettuce, sliced tomatoes, and mazza.

IS-49. Lamb and Lentil Soup (*Abgooshth*)

This substantial Pakistani soup may be served as main course when accompanied by flat bread.

Yield: 6 to 8 servings
Equipment needed: Cheesecloth, cutting board, French knife, 3-quart heavy soup pot, frying pan, tongs

Ingredients

1 cinnamon stick, about 3 inches	$\frac{1}{2}$ tablespoon plus 1 teaspoon salt
5 cardamom pods	1 large eggplant
5 cloves	3 tablespoons flour
1 teaspoon peppercorns, crushed	1 cup oil
2 pounds lean lamb stew meat	1 lime, sliced
1 pound lentils	$\frac{1}{4}$ cup mint, chopped
1 cup onions, chopped	2 quarts water
$1\frac{1}{2}$ cups canned crushed tomatoes	

Method

1. Place first four ingredients in small piece of cheesecloth and make bundle. (This will make retrieval easier later.)
2. Put spice bundle, next four ingredients, and $\frac{1}{2}$-tablespoon salt in pot.
3. Cover with 2 quarts water, bring to a boil, and simmer over low heat about an hour, until cooked and tender.
4. Peel eggplant; cut in $\frac{1}{2}$-inch slices. Sprinkle with remaining teaspoon of salt.
5. Dredge slices in flour.
6. Heat $\frac{1}{2}$ inch of oil in wide frying pan. Carefully fry eggplant slices on both sides. Set aside and keep warm.
7. Remove spice bundle from soup. Place one eggplant slice in each soup plate and ladle soup on top.
8. Float lime slices on soup. Sprinkle with mint leaves.

IS-50. Stir-Fried Scallops with Chicken, Mushrooms, and Cucumbers

This dish may have originated in Singapore, where seafood is popular and readily available and where many different cooking styles blend harmoniously.
Yield: 4 servings
Equipment needed: Small bowl, cutting board, knife, wok, spatula

Ingredients

4 large shiitake mushrooms, dried	$2\frac{1}{2}$ tablespoons light soy sauce
8 ounces chicken breasts, boneless and skinless	1 teaspoon salt
	$\frac{1}{2}$ teaspoon hot pepper
1 cucumber	$\frac{1}{2}$ cup chicken stock
8 ounces bay scallops	2 teaspoons cornstarch
4 tablespoons oil	

(continued)

Method

1. Soak mushrooms in warm water 30 minutes.
2. Cut mushrooms in quarters, discarding stems.
3. Dice chicken into ½-inch pieces.
4. Wash cucumber, but do not peel. Split and remove seeds. Cut into ½-inch pieces.
5. Sauté scallops, chicken, and cucumber in oil over high heat. Add mushrooms, soy sauce, and spices.
6. Cook over low heat for 2 minutes. Make slurry with chicken stock and cornstarch and pour into simmering stew.

IS-51. Iranian Lemon Chicken with Roasted Garlic
(*Tahsreeb Dijaj*)

Lemons, cultivated in the Middle East since 100 CE, are an important part of that region's cuisine.
Yield: 4 servings
Equipment needed: Roasting pan, cutting board, knife

Ingredients

1 roasting chicken, about 3 pounds	Freshly ground black pepper to taste
2 lemons	4 whole heads of garlic
Salt to taste	2 tablespoons ghee or oil

Method

1. Rub chicken with lemon juice inside and out. Set aside in refrigerator for 1 hour.
2. Season with salt and pepper according to taste.
3. Rub chicken and whole garlic heads with ghee or oil.
4. Put in roasting pan and bake at 350 degrees for about an hour.
5. Cut chicken in serving-size pieces and serve with roasted garlic heads. (Inside of garlic will be soft and mushy and the strong garlic taste greatly reduced.)

IS-52. Lamb in Almond Sauce (*Roghan Josh*)

Of Bedouin origin, this recipe uses typical Arabic ingredients.
Yield: 4 to 6 servings
Equipment needed: 2-quart heavy-bottomed saucepan, wooden spoon, slotted spoon, small frying pan, electric blender

Ingredients

¼ cup ghee or oil	¼ teaspoon mace, ground
10 cloves	3 tablespoons almonds, chopped
1 dried hot pepper	¾ cup onions, chopped
1 teaspoon peppercorns	2 tablespoons garlic, chopped
6 cardamom pods	1 tablespoon ginger, chopped
2 pounds lean lamb stew meat	2 cups water
2 tablespoons coriander, ground	1 teaspoon salt
½ teaspoon turmeric	8 ounces dried dates
¼ teaspoon nutmeg, ground	¼ cup yogurt

Method

1. Heat oil and cook cloves, hot pepper, peppercorns, and cardamom briefly (without burning spices).
2. Add lamb and brown over moderate heat. Remove meat with slotted spoon and set aside.
3. Add remaining dry spices to oil. Cook over moderate heat until light brown, being careful not to burn.
4. Add almonds, chopped onions, garlic, and ginger. Cook until onions are brown.
5. Add meat, water, and salt. Bring to a boil and simmer until meat is tender. If stew gets too dry, add more water.
6. Add dates.
7. Remove from heat and stir in yogurt. Serve with bread.

IS-53. Rainbow Rice Dessert

This colorful dessert, a favorite of African-American Muslims, consists of three flavored layers of rice: white (toasted coconut sprinkles), yellow (orange peel), and green (pistachios).

Yield: 10 servings

Equipment needed: 2-quart saucepan, colander, cookie sheet, three 1-quart mixing bowls, mixing spoon, small pot, three containers, pastry brush, 1-quart glass baking dish

Ingredients

2 cups rice	2 tablespoons candied orange peel, chopped
2 quarts plus ¾ cup water	
2 cardamom	6 tablespoons sugar
½ teaspoon nutmeg, ground	Assorted food colors—red, yellow, and green
1 teaspoon salt	
8 ounces sweet shredded coconut	2 tablespoons oil
1 cup pistachio nuts	

(continued)

Method

1. Boil rice for 20 minutes, drain, rinse, and set aside.
2. Blend rice with cardamom, nutmeg, and salt. Divide spiced rice into three mixing bowls.
3. Spread coconut on cookie sheet and toast in oven until light brown.
4. Add toasted coconut to one bowl of rice, pistachio nuts to second bowl, and orange peel to third.
5. Bring sugar and water to boil; divide equally into three containers.
6. Mix one container of sugar-water into coconut-flavored rice.
7. Color second container of sugar-water with green food coloring and mix into pistachio rice.
8. Color remaining container of sugar-water with yellow food coloring and mix into orange-flavored rice.
9. Brush sides and bottom of baking dish with oil.
10. Layer rice in dish, making sure there are three distinct layers.
11. Cover with aluminum foil and bake in 350-degree oven for 25 minutes.

IS-54. Quince Sorbet

This traditional Arabic *sharab* (sorbet) is made with sugar and quince, a native Asian fruit. Before the invention of mechanical refrigeration, this dish was made by blending fruit puree with shaved ice, the latter brought down from the high Atlas mountaintops and preserved in cold basements. In the United States, quinces ripen in the fall.

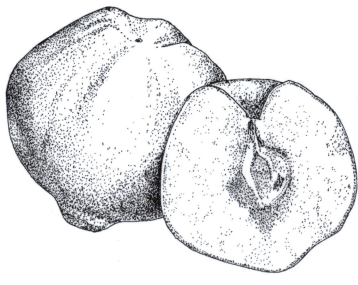

QUINCE

Yield: 4 to 6 servings
Equipment needed: Cutting board, French knife, paring knife, large saucepan, food processor, strainer, small bowls or ice cream machine

Ingredients

2 pounds ripe quince
3 cups water

2 cups sugar
$\frac{1}{4}$ cup lemon juice

Method

1. Carefully quarter quince, peel, remove center core, and cube.
2. Combine quince, water, and sugar in saucepan.
3. Bring to a boil. Simmer about 30 minutes or until fruit is mushy. Cool.
4. Blend with food processor to make smooth puree.
5. Strain mixture to remove all pieces, or process through food mill.
6. Add lemon juice. Place in small bowls in freezer and stir occasionally until mixture is frozen like slush, or use ice cream machine if available.

IS-55. Peach Condiment

In Turkey, the festival of Eid-al-Fitr is called Seker Bayrami. Before prayers begin, customary offerings are made of wheat, dates, and fruit. Special delicacies prepared for this joyous occasion are shared with family, friends, and neighbors.
Yield: 8 to 10 servings as condiment
Equipment needed: 3-quart saucepan, large kettle, wire basket to fit kettle, large bowl, paring knife, cutting board, French knife

Ingredients

$\frac{1}{2}$ cup vinegar
2 tablespoons ginger, chopped
3 teaspoons coriander, ground
1 tablespoon garlic, chopped
2 teaspoons tamarind paste
1 teaspoon fenugreek, ground

1 cup honey
1 teaspoon cayenne pepper
1 teaspoon salt
1 teaspoon cinnamon
2 pounds fresh ripe peaches

Method

1. Combine all ingredients except peaches. Bring to a boil in saucepan.
2. To peel peaches, bring pot of water to boil. Using basket or strainer, dip several peaches in boiling water for about 20 seconds.
3. Remove and immediately submerge peaches in ice water.
4. Peel off skin. Remove pits, cut peaches in chunks, and add to spice and vinegar mixture.
5. Bring to a boil; simmer 5 minutes. Chill; transfer to stainless steel or glass container.
6. Cover and keep refrigerated at least one week before use.

IS-56. Shiebiat Pastry

This Syrian pastry uses filo (or phyllo) dough, which is available in 16-ounce packages in the frozen food section of most supermarkets. Each package consists of two rolls of dough. As this recipe uses only one roll, the other can be kept frozen for future use.

Yield: 24 pieces

Equipment needed: 1-quart saucepan, small bowl, stirring spoon, small wire whisk, small pot, pastry brush, two glass 8 × 12-inch baking dishes, spoon, baking sheet, ½-quart saucepan

Ingredients

½ package (8 ounces) filo (phyllo) dough
1 pint heavy cream
4 tablespoons cornstarch
2 cups sugar

1 teaspoon cinnamon, ground
2 tablespoons rose water
4 ounces (1 stick) butter, melted
1 cup water
1 tablespoon lemon juice

Method

1. Defrost dough in refrigerator (about 2 hours).
2. Bring heavy cream to boil. Make slurry with cornstarch and a little water; add to boiling cream. It will thicken immediately. Remove from heat.
3. When cooled, stir in 1 cup sugar, cinnamon, and rose water. Chill to consistency of very thick cream.
4. Melt butter and set aside.
5. Brush baking dishes with butter. Place two sheets of dough in first dish. Brush with melted butter. Add two more sheets.
6. Spread about three-quarters of cold filling on top.
7. Put two pastry sheets on top of filling. Brush with melted butter.
8. Repeat process in second baking dish.
9. Bake at 350 degrees about 30 minutes, until brown on top.
10. Chill. When cold, cut into squares. Leave in baking dishes.
11. Bring remaining (1 cup) sugar to boil in 1 cup water. Remove from heat and add lemon juice.
12. When syrup has cooled, ladle it over the pastry.

IS-57. Malaysian Rice Flour Dessert

This dish is influenced by Indian cooking.

Yield: 6 to 8 servings

Equipment needed: 2-quart saucepan, wooden spoon, 2-quart soup pot, wire whisk, shallow serving pan

Ingredients

3 tablespoons mild sesame oil
3 tablespoons vegetable oil

1 cup rice flour
1 quart milk

2 tablespoons rose water

2 tablespoons almond extract

1/2 cup sugar

1/2 teaspoon cardamom, ground

1/2 teaspoon cinnamon, ground

Method

1. Heat oils together and add rice flour.
2. Cook over low heat, stirring constantly, until rice flour is light brown.
3. Heat milk to about 180 degrees.
4. Add milk to rice flour mixture, stir with wire whisk, and bring to a boil. It will become a thick cream.
5. Add remaining ingredients. Pour mixture into shallow pan and refrigerate.
6. Serve cold, cut in squares.

What Would Muhammad Have Eaten?

Nomadic shepherds of the pre-Islamic period lived on dairy products, a small amount of meat, and dates. In the oasis and the southern part of the Arabian Peninsula, where the climate was less arid, the food was more varied. Grains, vegetables, and fruits were eaten. In poorer, harsher environments, people were obliged to eat what they found, including grasshoppers and roasted lizard.

IS-58. Tharid

This simple dish, which was praised by the Prophet, consisted of slices of bread soaked in a spicy meat stock. More elaborate versions included pounded meat and vegetables. Flour and rice were used to thicken the mixture, and eggs served as binding agents.

Yield: 6 servings

Equipment needed: 3-quart soup pot, cutting board, knife, strainer

Ingredients

1 pound lamb neck bones

1 teaspoon salt

4 cardamom

1 teaspoon fennel seeds

1 teaspoon peppercorns, crushed

1 teaspoon coriander seeds, crushed

1 pound chicken bones (necks and backs)

1 onion, about 4 ounces

1 whole leek, about 3 ounces

1/2 cup carrots, coarsely diced

12 slices bread, white and crusty

1 teaspoon cinnamon, ground

Method

1. Wash lamb bones, put in soup pot, and cover with 3 quarts water. Bring to slow boil.
2. Add salt, cardamom, fennel seeds, peppercorns, and coriander seeds. Simmer 1 hour.
3. Wash chicken bones in hot water to remove all blood; add to lamb stock.

(continued)

4. Cut unpeeled onions in quarters and add to soup. Split leek horizontally. Separate leaf layers and wash thoroughly. Add leek and carrots to soup.
5. Simmer 1 hour and strain, discarding bones and vegetables. Adjust seasoning if necessary.
6. Toast bread and put two slices in each soup bowl. Ladle soup over bread and sprinkle with cinnamon.

IS-59. Hais

Hais is a medieval Middle Eastern sweet made of dates, crumbled cakes, ground nuts, and sugar. It is referred to in the Hadith (sayings and actions of Muhammad). This recipe is an adaptation from a thirteenth-century Islamic cookbook.

Yield: 35 to 40 pieces
Equipment: Food processor

Ingredients

12 ounces ginger snaps	$1/2$ cup butterfat, melted
8 ounces dates, pitted	1 tablespoon mild sesame oil
8 ounces dried figs	$1/2$ cup brown sugar
$1/3$ cup almonds, ground	1 teaspoon cinnamon, ground
$1/3$ cup pistachio nuts, ground	Powdered sugar for dusting

Method

1. Combine ingredients, except powdered sugar, in food processor.
2. Roll into 1-inch balls with wet hands.
3. Refrigerate until solid. Dust with powdered sugar.
4. Serve as snack.

IS-60. Fruit Refreshment

Muhammad loved to eat fresh dates with melon. A saying attributed to him is, "The heat of the one is broken by the coolness of the other, and the coolness of the one by the heat of the other." Fresh dates have a very short season in the United States and are not universally available. Those used in this recipe are dried.

Yield: 4 servings
Equipment needed: Cutting board, knife, 1-quart saucepan, strainer, melon baller, bowl

Ingredients

1 small bunch fresh mint	$1/2$ cup honey
1 cup water	$1/2$ teaspoon cardamom, ground

1 teaspoon pepper, ground   8 ounces dates, pitted

2 cantaloupes

Method

1. Wash mint thoroughly. Chop coarsely, saving four sprigs for garnish.
2. Cover with water, bring to a boil, and steep 5 minutes.
3. Strain carefully into bowl and add honey, cardamom, and pepper.
4. Chill liquid until ice-cold. (Put in freezer, if possible.)
5. Cut melons in half; remove seeds.
6. Scoop into balls with melon baller.
7. Place in ice-cold liquid. Blend with dates.
8. Garnish with mint sprigs.

5

JUDAISM

Judaism is the oldest of the monotheistic world religions. It has no single founder, and its historical origins are uncertain. Biblical accounts suggest that it arose in the Middle East sometime between 1700 and 1900 BCE under the leadership of Abraham, who was commanded by God to leave his homeland and forsake worship of the old gods in obedience to the one true God. In return for this obedience, Abraham was promised divine protection for his people and his descendants, who came to see themselves as the chosen people of God. But it wasn't until the twelfth century BCE that Judaism emerged as an established religion. Having led the Israelites out of slavery in Egypt, the prophet Moses received divine guidance on righteous living in the form of the Ten Commandments, ethical statements that have remained for Jews and Christians as fundamental religious principles governing human morality and behavior. Observant Jews live according to the laws of God that are written in their holy books, which include detailed food-related rules.

In 70 CE, the Roman conquest of the Israelite capital of Jerusalem marked the end of the ancient Jewish state. Though the Jews were to remain without a homeland until the modern state of Israel was established in 1948, traditions were kept alive by their rabbis. Over the next few hundred years, as Jews settled in regions throughout the Roman Empire and beyond, they maintained their faith communities. One group, known as the Sephardim, settled in present-day Spain. As a result of renewed religious persecution in 1492, these Jews were expelled from Spain and fled to other areas of Europe or to Turkey and North Africa. Central and Eastern European Jews are known as the Ashkenazi branch.

Modern Jewish history has continued to be marked by oppression and displacement. Israel was founded after World War II as an independent Jewish state, and Jewish people from more than 70 countries returned to the ancient homeland. The demographics of Israel are constantly changing because the country grants immigration rights and citizenship to all Jews regardless of nationality and background.

The first North American Jewish settlement was founded by exiles from Spain who came to the Dutch colony of New Amsterdam (New York) in 1654. In the mid-nineteenth century, large numbers of Jewish immigrants arrived from Germanic Europe, followed later that century by hundreds of thousands of Eastern European Jews. The United States has the largest Jewish population in the world, numbering around six million. New York City itself has the highest Jewish population outside Israel. There are an estimated 370,000 Jews in Canada.

Contemporary Jews belong to one of several groups. Hasidic Jews are one of the ultraorthodox congregations that observe detailed Biblical dietary rules and have flourishing communities in Israel and New York City. They are easily recognizable by their conservative black clothing, long beards, wide brimmed hats, and prayer shawls. Conservative Jews (the largest branch in the United States), Reform Jews, and Reconstructionist Jews differ in the way in which they interpret and practice Jewish law. There are also many Jews who do not observe religious practices, but who still maintain a Jewish identity and follow cultural traditions.

Food, Diet, and Cooking

Judaism probably has the most extensive dietary rules of any religion. These rules are described in detail in the Bible's Old Testament books of Leviticus and Deuteronomy. The dietary rules are called *kashrut*, or kosher; this Hebrew word is best translated as "right," "fit," or "clean." Kosher rules are rather complicated and describe what animals can be eaten, how they are to be slaughtered, how long the meat can be stored, the parts of an animal that can be used, and how these parts must be prepared. They also stipulate what kind of fish and fowl can be eaten and restrictions on what foods can be prepared and eaten together. To understand Jewish eating habits and recipes, knowledge of kosher dietary rules is essential.

Basic Kosher Rules

- Only animals that have cloven hooves and chew their cud are permitted for consumption: Sheep, goats, and cattle are allowed, but pigs are not.
- The animal must be slaughtered with a swift cut by a very sharp knife so that the blood is completely drained. The slaughter must be done by a trained and certified butcher known as a *shoshet*.
- The meat must be eaten fresh.
- Only the forequarters can be used.
- The meat must be cooked until it is well-done; no blood can be eaten.
- Chicken, turkey, and duck are permitted.
- Meat and dairy products can never be served at the same meal, be cooked in the same pots, or touch any utensils used by the other.
- Food that is neither meat nor dairy is *parve* (neutral) and can be served any time with meat, fish, or dairy products. Parve items are vegetables, fruits, salads, cereals, eggs, sugar, and approved spices.
- Only fish with scales are allowed; any kind of shellfish is prohibited. Permitted fish is considered parve and can be served with meat or with dairy dishes.
- Cheese can be kosher if made without rennet, an animal coagulant.

In Jewish households the extent to which dietary rules are followed depends on religious strictness and family tradition. Many Jewish families observe abbreviated versions of kosher restrictions. To help families choose kosher foods at the supermarket, many packaged foods have a special symbol certifying that the food is kosher, as approved by a board of rabbis, such as the Orthodox Union (OU) located in Manhattan. Manufactured foods may contain many additives, colors, preservatives, and enzymes, and each has to be carefully checked before being approved.

Celebration Recipes

Jewish cooking reflects a mixture of cultural influences from countries around the world where Jews have settled. Jewish food is associated as much with ethnic identity as it is with specific religious meanings, though certain foods are essential parts of some religious celebrations. The Jewish year follows a twelve-month lunar calendar. Periodically a "leap month" is added to keep in harmony with the solar year that is the basis of the common 365-day calendar. Consequently, the dates of Jewish holidays as measured by the Gregorian solar calendar vary from year to year. The holy days are listed below by the solar calendar month in which they usually occur. The Hebrew date is also given.

Rosh Hashanah (September or October/1 Tishrei)

The Jewish New Year is a holiday of remembrance and prayer: The blowing of a ram's horn—the *shofar*—at synagogue services reminds congregation members of their obligations to God. Rosh Hashanah is also a festive holiday, when large family dinners are customary. Sweet dishes are symbolic of a good, sweet new year, and apples, honey, carrots, pomegranates, and nuts appear on many tables or as ingredients in recipes. One North African custom spreading to the United States is the Blessings Tray. Seven edible items, usually fruits or vegetables in different shapes, are put on a tray to serve as symbols for the next year. Family members and guests make up puns about the offerings.

J-1. Chicken and Date Patties

Autumn is the season for fresh dates in Israel, and the combination of chicken with sweet dates is popular. Since fresh dates are not readily available in the Unites States, this recipe uses dried dates instead.

Yield: 8 servings

Equipment needed: Cutting board, French knife, colander, food processor, large mixing bowl, 4-ounce ice cream scoop, two large cast-iron pans, spatula

Ingredients

2 pounds boneless, skinless
  chicken breasts

1 egg
1 teaspoon garlic, chopped

(continued)

½ teaspoon allspice
½ teaspoon coriander, ground
½ teaspoon fenugreek, ground
¼ teaspoon cayenne pepper
1½ teaspoons salt

1 cup bread crumbs
½ cup cold water
4 ounces dried dates, pitted
½ cup olive oil

Method

1. Trim chicken breast of any fat and gristle. Cut in 1-inch chunks.
2. Wash chicken breasts in cold water and drain in colander.
3. Blend chicken pieces, egg, garlic, and spices in food processor to medium-fine consistency.
4. Add ¼ cup of bread crumbs and cold water. Process once more.
5. Cut dates into ¼-inch pieces.
6. Blend chicken mix with dates in large bowl.
7. Using ice cream scoop, shape into eight patties.
8. Dredge patties in remaining bread crumbs.
9. Heat oil. Carefully put patties in pans and cook over medium heat until underside is light brown. Turn patties.
10. Place pans in 375-degree oven and bake 25 minutes.
11. Serve with stewed fruits.

J-2. Braised Brisket with Pomegranate

According to legend, pomegranates contain 613 seeds, the number of good deeds mentioned in the Torah. Dishes containing pomegranate seeds and juices are often served on this holiday. Brisket is a stringy yet moist piece of meat that

POMEGRANATES

requires long braising or simmering. Experience is needed to slice the meat properly, as the grain runs in two perpendicular directions. This dish was traditionally prepared on Fridays and simmered overnight; it is a favorite of New York's Ashkenazim. When pomegranates are not available, dried apricots are usually substituted.

Yield: 8 to 10 servings

Equipment needed: Large Dutch oven, kitchen fork, ladle, 1-quart saucepan, cutting board, peeler, knife, slicing knife, serving platter

Ingredients

2 tablespoons oil
4 pounds lean beef brisket
1 cup carrots, diced small
1 cup onions, diced small
½ cup celery, chopped
½ tablespoon garlic, chopped
½ teaspoon ginger, ground
1 teaspoon pepper, ground

1 teaspoon salt
½ teaspoon coriander, ground
1 cup canned stewed tomatoes
2 cups canned beef stock
3 pomegranates (about 1½ pounds)
1 tablespoon cornstarch
2 tablespoons cold water

Method

1. Put oil in Dutch oven; add brisket and cook, uncovered, in 400-degree oven until top is browned.
2. Carefully turn over.
3. Add vegetables and spices.
4. Lower heat to 375 degrees. Bake until vegetables are slightly browned.
5. Add tomatoes and 1 cup beef stock. Cover Dutch oven and bake at 375 degrees for 1½ hours.
6. Remove meat from Dutch oven and keep warm.
7. Ladle pan gravy into saucepan. Let sit for 10 minutes; using ladle, remove as much fat as possible.
8. Halve pomegranates and scoop out juices and seeds. Add to pan gravy.
9. Add remaining beef stock and simmer 10 minutes.
10. Make slurry with cornstarch and 2 tablespoons cold water. Add to simmering pan gravy.
11. Slice meat and serve with sauce.

J-3. Carrots and Prunes Tzimes

The Yiddish term *tzimes* applies to anything mixed, such as stewed vegetables or fruits served as hot accompaniments to meat dishes. The best-known and most traditional Rosh Hashanah combination consists of carrots and prunes. *Merren*, the Yiddish word for carrots, also means "more" and "increased." The carrot slices in this recipe represent coins.

Yield: 8 servings

Equipment needed: Potato peeler, French knife, cutting board, heavy saucepan, paring knife

(continued)

Ingredients

2 pounds carrots	1 teaspoon salt
¼ cup margarine (parve)	½ teaspoon nutmeg
½ cup onions, chopped	⅛ teaspoon cumin
2 tablespoons honey	8 ounces dried prunes
1 teaspoon pepper	

Method

1. Peel carrots and cut into ¼-inch rounds or slices.
2. Melt margarine in saucepan and add onions. Sauté until transparent.
3. Add carrots and spices. Cover with water and simmer about 30 minutes.
4. Remove pits from prunes, cut into halves, and combine with carrots.
5. If necessary, add more water to cover prunes.
6. Simmer for 20 minutes, until most of the water has evaporated.

J-4. Kasha Varnitchekes

Kasha is the Jewish term for buckwheat grits, a popular starch in Eastern Europe. Popular in New York, this particular dish consists of kasha blended with bow-tie pasta and is often served with braised beef.

Yield: 6 to 8 side-dish servings

Equipment needed: 2-quart heavy pot with lid, wooden spoon, small bowl

Ingredients

1 cup kasha (buckwheat grits)	1 teaspoon salt
1 egg	3 cups water
4 tablespoons chicken fat or oil	2 cups bow-tie pasta, cooked

Method

1. Dry-roast kasha in heavy 2-quart pot, stirring over moderate heat until nutty smell develops. Remove from heat and cool.
2. Beat egg and add to cold kasha.
3. Use hands to blend evenly, coating all kernels.
4. Put mixture back on stove; add fat, salt, and water. Bring to a boil, cover, and simmer 45 minutes.
5. Blend with cooked pasta.

Yom Kippur (October/10 Tishrei)

Rosh Hashanah is followed ten days later by Yom Kippur, which is the holiest day of the Jewish year. Known as the Day of Atonement, it is a time for individuals and congregations to ask forgiveness from their neighbors and from God.

Yom Kippur is a twenty-four-hour period of complete fasting, lasting from sundown to sundown.

J-5. Farfel

On the evening before Yom Kippur it is customary to serve nonspicy foods after the Kiddush, the blessing said over the wine. A popular Ashkenazic dish is chicken soup with homemade pasta called *farfel*. Traditionally grated with the coarse blade of a grater, this dough may also be flattened and coarsely chopped with a heavy knife.

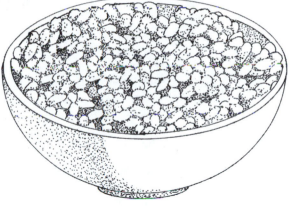

FARFEL

Yield: 4 to 6 servings

Equipment needed: Food processor with dough blade, cutting board, French knife or grater, soup pot, stirrer

Ingredients

1½ cups flour
1 egg

1 tablespoon water
Soup

Method

1. Combine flour, egg, and water at slow speed in food processor.
2. Do not overprocess. The dough will be very stiff. (If necessary, dough may also be kneaded on floured work surface.)
3. Shape dough into ball, cover, and let rest 1 hour.
4. Cut dough in slices, then chop into smaller pieces. (Dough can be dried and stored.)
5. Sprinkle farfel into boiling chicken or beef soup.
6. Simmer 5 minutes. Serve soup and farfel together.

Sukkot (November/15–23 Tishrei)

Also known as Succoth, or the Feast of the Tabernacles, this nine-day harvest-thanksgiving celebration begins five days after Yom Kippur. Traditionally, it is celebrated in temporary thatched sheds that recall the portable huts built by the ancient Israelites during their sojourn in the desert after they fled persecution in Egypt. The huts are called *sukkahs* and are made with willows and branches decorated with fruits, corn, squashes, apples, and grapes. Children sometimes build model sukkahs using crackers, pretzel sticks, and green icing. In Israel, sukkahs can be seen on apartment balconies, but New York City apartment-dwellers must make do with table decorations of autumn fruits—which always include grapes and fresh dates, if available.

J-6. Frosted Grapes

Although grapes are often part of the table decorations, served frosted they make a tasty appetizer.
Yield: 4 to 6 servings
Equipment needed: Paring knife or scissors, colander, small bowl, large bowl, cookie sheet

Ingredients

3 pounds seedless grapes, green or red
2 egg whites

2 tablespoons cold water
1 pound sugar

Method

1. Divide grapes into small clusters, rinse, and then air-dry.
2. Combine egg whites with water.
3. Dip each cluster first in egg-white blend and then in sugar.
4. Coat evenly with sugar, shaking off excess.
5. Let grape clusters air-dry. Do not refrigerate.
6. Use within 2 hours on humid days.

J-7. Stuffed Cabbage (*Holishkes*)

This dish, of Ukrainian origin, is traditionally served on Sukkot, when sweet and sour dishes are especially popular.
Yield: 5 to 6 servings
Equipment needed: Large pot, slotted spoon, large bowl, small mixing bowl, mixing spoon, work surface, Dutch oven

Ingredients

10 large cabbage leaves
1 pound ground beef
2 ounces rice
1/2 cup water
1 egg
1/2 cup onions, chopped
1/2 cup carrots, grated

1 teaspoon salt
1 teaspoon garlic, chopped
1/4 cup vinegar
1/2 cup brown sugar
1 cup canned tomato sauce
2 ounces raisins

Method

1. Fill pot with water and bring to a boil.
2. Add cabbage leaves; boil for 5 minutes.
3. Remove cabbage leaves with slotted spoon, plunge into cold water, and drain.
4. Combine meat with rice, water, egg, onions, carrots, salt, and garlic.

5. Set cabbage leaves on work surface and fill with meat mixture. Roll up and tuck in ends to make bundles.
6. Place rolls closely together in Dutch oven, seam side down.
7. Add remaining ingredients and water to cover.
8. Bring to simmer on stove, then transfer pot to 375-degree oven and bake 45 minutes.

J-8. Unstuffed Cabbage

Sometimes stuffing cabbage rolls is too much trouble! This dish uses the leftover cabbage from the previous recipe.
Yield: 8 servings
Equipment needed: 2-quart soup pot, colander, 2-inch-high baking pan, mixing bowl

Ingredients

½ cup rice
3 cups shredded cabbage
2 pounds ground beef
¼ cup onions, chopped
1 teaspoon garlic, chopped

Salt and pepper
Pan spray
1 cup whole-berry cranberry sauce
2 cups canned tomato sauce

Method

1. Bring 2 quarts water to a boil and stir in rice; simmer about 20 minutes.
2. Carefully drain off water, rinse rice in cold water, and drain well again.
3. Spray rectangular baking dish with pan spray.
4. Add cabbage, making flat bed.
5. Combine meat with cooked rice, onions, and garlic. Season with salt and pepper.
6. Shape 32 meatballs and place on cabbage.
7. Put cranberry sauce, and then tomato sauce, around meatballs.
8. Cover with aluminum foil and bake in 350-degree oven for 1½ hours.
9. Carefully remove from oven and let sit 15 minutes before removing foil.

J-9. Fillet of Perch with Almonds and Avocados

Perch is a kosher fish that is readily available, but other fish fillets can be substituted.
Yield: 8 servings
Equipment needed: Small sauté pan, cutting board, French knife, wide soup plate, small cookie sheet, large frying pan, serving platter, 8-inch frying pan

(continued)

Ingredients

¹⁄₂ cup sliced almonds	¹⁄₂ cup flour
3 pounds perch fillets, skin-on	1 lemon
¹⁄₄ cup light cream	4 ounces (1 stick) butter
Oil for frying	2 medium-size, ripe avocados

Method

1. Put almonds in dry sauté pan and cook over medium heat, turning continuously, until light brown. Set aside.
2. Wash fish fillets, drain, and dry.
3. Divide fish fillets into eight equal servings of 6 ounces each.
4. Pour light cream into shallow bowl. Put flour on cookie sheet next to it.
5. Heat ¹⁄₄ inch of oil in frying pan until a drop of water sizzles.
6. Dip fish fillets first in cream and then in flour, shaking off excess.
7. Put fish fillets skin-side down in pan and fry over medium heat. Turn over when light brown and cook other side.
8. Place cooked fish fillets on platter; keep warm. Cut lemon in half and squeeze over fish.
9. Peel and dice avocado.
10. Cook butter in 8-inch frying pan over medium heat until it starts to brown.
11. Quickly toss in almonds, then immediately pour over fish fillets.
12. Sprinkle with diced avocado.

J-10. Date Nut Loaf

This delicious recipe is of Israeli origin and uses ingredients indigenous to the area.

Yield: 6 to 8 servings

Equipment needed: Cutting board, French knife, mixing bowl, sifter, electric mixer with bowl, whisk, loaf pan

Ingredients

12 ounces dried dates, pitted	¹⁄₄ cup water
¹⁄₂ cup walnuts, chopped	1 teaspoon ginger, ground
¹⁄₂ cup raisins	¹⁄₂ teaspoon allspice
1 cup flour	¹⁄₄ teaspoon salt
1 teaspoon baking powder	¹⁄₂ cup sugar
4 eggs	Pan spray

Method

1. Cut dates into small pieces; combine with walnuts and raisins.
2. Sift flour and baking powder.
3. Separate eggs; blend yolks together with date mixture and remaining ingredients.

4. Beat egg whites and salt until stiff. Beat in sugar.
5. Fold egg whites, flour, and date mixture together.
6. Pan-spray loaf pan. Add batter.
7. Bake at 350 degrees for about 40 minutes.

J-11. Mandelbrot

Jews of Eastern European origin, the Ashkenazim, developed their own language—Yiddish—based on medieval German. The word *mandelbrot* comes from the German words for almonds (*mandel*) and bread (*brot*).
Yield: 40 slices
Equipment needed: Flour sifter, bowl, cutting board, French knife, grater, juice extractor, electric mixer with paddle, scraper, work surface, cookie sheet

Ingredients

3 cups flour
1 tablespoon baking powder
1 orange
3 eggs
1½ cups sugar
8 ounces margarine (parve), room
   temperature

½ teaspoon salt
1½ cups almonds, chopped
Flour for dusting
Pan spray

Method

1. Sift flour and baking powder together. Set aside.
2. Grate orange peel and add to flour.
3. Cut orange in half and squeeze ¼ cup juice.
4. Blend juice, at slow speed, with eggs, sugar, salt, and margarine until mixture is smooth.
5. Blend in flour and almonds.
6. Place soft dough on floured work surface.
7. Pan-spray cookie sheet.
8. Shape dough into 2-inch bars and place on cookie sheet.
9. Bake at 350 degrees until brown, about 20 minutes.
10. Cut bars into slices while still warm.

J-12. Rugelach

These cookies come from Eastern Europe and are popular in New York City. Since the dough is made with cream cheese, the cookies cannot be served with or after a meat dish.
Yield: 30 pieces
Equipment needed: Electric mixer with paddle, work surface, small bowl, rolling pin, pastry brush, French knife, cookie sheet

(*continued*)

Ingredients

8 ounces (2 sticks) butter
8 ounces cream cheese
1 pound flour
1 teaspoon baking powder
1 teaspoon salt
½ cup honey

1 cup walnuts or almonds,
  chopped
1 teaspoon cinnamon
Flour for dusting
Pan spray

Method

1. Cream butter together with cream cheese.
2. Add flour, baking powder, and salt. Blend at slow speed with mixer to form dough. Refrigerate.
3. Roll dough on floured work surface to thickness of about ½ inch. Shape into rectangle and brush with honey.
4. Blend nuts with cinnamon; sprinkle mixture evenly on top of dough.
5. Roll dough into sausage shape.
6. Cut roll into 1-inch pieces and place on cookie sheet. (Since dough is rather soft, it might be easier to chill it before slicing.)
7. Bake at 375 degrees until brown, about 15 minutes.

Hanukkah (November or December/ 25 Kislev–2 Tevet)

The eight-day winter festival of Hanukkah, or the Feast of Lights, commemorates the historic victory of the Jewish Macabees over a Greek army in the second century BCE. An oil lamp found in the rubble after the battle is said to have miraculously burned for eight days although it only had sufficient oil for one day. This gave rise to the custom of lighting a series of candles, called a *menorah*, over the course of the holiday. Many traditional Hanukkah foods are fried—symbolizing the importance of oil to the holiday.

J-13. Sufganiyot

In celebration of the miracle of the burning oil lamp, deep-fried yeast doughnuts are prepared in many households for breakfast.
Yield: 30
Equipment needed: Electric mixer with paddle, dough scraper, work surface, rolling pin, 2½-inch cookie cutter, kitchen towel, 12-inch deep-frying pan

Ingredients

1 package dry yeast
4 tablespoons sugar
1 cup milk
½ teaspoon salt

3 egg yolks
2 ounces butter, melted
3 cups bread flour
Flour for dusting

Fat for frying   Ground cinnamon
Powdered sugar

Method

1. Combine yeast with 1 tablespoon sugar and $\frac{1}{2}$ cup warm milk. Set aside in warm place to ferment, about 10 minutes.
2. Blend remaining milk, sugar, salt, egg yolks, and butter with electric mixer at low speed.
3. Add yeast blend. Mix again at low speed, adding flour, until dough begins to form. Increase speed to medium to obtain smooth, silky dough.
4. Knead into smooth ball on floured work surface. Dust dough with flour and cover with clean kitchen towel.
5. Let ferment for about an hour. Punch dough down and let ferment a half-hour longer.
6. Roll dough to thickness of about $\frac{1}{4}$ inch. Cut into circles with cookie cutter and place, upside down, on floured cookie sheet. Cover with kitchen towel again; let rise in warm location.
7. In frying pan, heat 2 inches of fat to about 325 degrees. Carefully place doughnuts upside down into hot fat. Fry until light brown, turn over, and fry other side. Doughnuts will float.
8. Drain on absorbent paper. Serve warm, dusted with powdered sugar and cinnamon.

J-14. Chicken Legs with Kumquats

In season during the winter, kumquats are small, tart citrus fruits of the orange family that are edible only when cooked. This recipe uses chicken legs because they have more flavor than chicken breasts.

Yield: 6 servings

Equipment needed: Cutting board, French knife, wide baking pan, aluminum foil, 1-quart saucepan, fork, deep serving dish, mixing spoon, small bowl

Ingredients

6 chicken legs, about 6 to 8 oun- $\frac{1}{4}$ cup apricot jam
   ces each $\frac{1}{2}$ teaspoon cayenne pepper
1 tablespoon olive oil $\frac{1}{2}$ teaspoon allspice
1 teaspoon salt $\frac{1}{4}$ cup sugar
1 cup orange juice   1 tablespoon cornstarch
$\frac{1}{2}$ cup water   1 pound fresh kumquats, without
$\frac{1}{4}$ cup lemon juice   leaves and stems

Method

1. Wash chicken legs and pat dry.
2. Separate drumsticks from thighs with sharp knife.

(continued)

3. Trim off excess fat. Put chicken in baking pan and sprinkle with oil and salt.
4. Brown in 400-degree oven.
5. Carefully add all ingredients except cornstarch and kumquats.
6. Cover with aluminum foil and bake at 300 degrees for 10 minutes.
7. Wash kumquats and halve lengthwise. Put in saucepan, cover with water, and boil for 5 minutes.
8. Drain and add to chicken. Bake 10 minutes longer.
9. Carefully remove aluminum foil.
10. Use fork to transfer chicken pieces to serving dish; keep warm.
11. Blend cornstarch with 3 tablespoons cold water.
12. Place baking pan on stove, bring to simmer over low heat, and add cornstarch slurry.
13. Serve sauce over chicken. (If sauce is too fatty, use small ladle to skim.)

J-15. Potato Latkes

In the kosher system, latkes are parve (neutral) and can be served with applesauce and sour cream or as a side dish with meat. Latkes are a popular dish at receptions. It is important to use russet (baking) potatoes.
Yield: 4 to 6 servings
Equipment needed: Potato peeler, food processor, strainer, stirring spoon, deep-frying pan, slotted spoon

Ingredients

3 pounds russet potatoes	4 eggs
1/4 bunch parsley	1/2 cup matzo meal
1/2 cup chopped onions	Oil for frying

Method

1. Peel and wash potatoes; cut into large chunks.
2. Wash parsley and discard stems. Make sure all sand is removed.
3. Blend potatoes, onions, and parsley in food processor until mixture is evenly coarse. Do not overprocess.
4. Place in strainer and drain out as much juice as possible. The mixture will turn brownish. (Some lemon juice will prevent this, but will affect the taste.)
5. Blend in eggs and matzo meal. If mixture is too wet, add more matzo meal. (Batter should hold together well.)
6. Heat about 3/4 inch of oil in frying pan. Using a spoon, carefully drop small pancakes into oil.
7. Fry on both sides, remove with slotted spoon, and place on paper towels to remove excess oil.

J-16. Stuffed Kishke or Derma

This old-fashioned winter dish originated in Eastern Europe and was served as an accompaniment to braised meat dishes. The *derma* (stomach casings) and beef suet used in the original recipe have been replaced with plastic wrap and healthier vegetable shortening.

Yield: One 12-inch roll

Equipment needed: Large mixing bowl, mixing spoon, parchment paper, wide pot or baking pan about 4 inches high

Ingredients

1 cup flour	1 tablespoon paprika
½ cup matzo meal	1 teaspoon salt
¾ cup shortening	1 teaspoon pepper
½ cup onions, chopped	½ cup water

Method

1. Combine all ingredients to form rather stiff dough.
2. Place sheet of plastic wrap about 16 inches long on work surface.
3. With wet hands, shape dough into 12-inch roll; wrap in plastic wrap, twisting ends.
4. Do not roll too tightly as the derma will expand.
5. Place in shallow pan, cover with water, and simmer for 1 hour.

Tu Bishvat (January or February/15 Shvat)

Also known as Chamiso Oser B'sh'vat, or New Year of the Trees, this spring festival resembles Arbor Day and is celebrated when the trees are blooming in Israel. Favorite foods include fried flower blossoms and carob beans. These long, sweet, and succulent brown pods, from an evergreen tree native to the Middle East, are chewed as a sweet treat.

J-17. Zucchini Flower Fritters

While this recipe uses chopped blossoms, whole blossoms can also be dipped in batter and fried. These fritters can be served as an appetizer or as accompaniment to a main course such as a lean roast.

Yield: 12 to 14 fritters

Equipment needed: Cutting board, French knife, mixing bowl, wire whisk, frying pan, spoon

Ingredients

12 zucchini flowers	1 teaspoon salt
3 eggs	Oil for shallow frying
¾ cup flour	

(continued)

Method

1. Wash zucchini flowers and drain.
2. Remove green stem and chop flowers medium-fine.
3. Make batter with eggs, flour, and salt.
4. Add chopped flowers.
5. Heat oil.
6. Carefully drop small fritters in oil with tablespoon. Turn over when brown on one side.

J-18. Carciofi alla Giudea

This recipe originated with the Jewish population in Venice, Italy. Very young, small artichokes should be used because the leaves must be tender enough to be eaten. These could be made the same day as the zucchini fritters and the same fat used for frying.

Yield: 20 pieces (4 servings)

Equipment needed: Large bowl, paring knife, French knife, cutting board, paper towels and tray, slotted spoon, deep fat fryer or 3-quart heavy saucepan

Ingredients

1 lemon	20 very small, fresh artichokes
1 tablespoon salt	Fat for frying

Method

1. Fill large bowl with cold water, squeeze lemon into water, and add salt.
2. Shorten artichoke stems to about an inch and a half. Cut off tips. Peel stems. Place trimmed artichokes in lemon water for about an hour.
3. Drain upside down on paper towels. Pat dry.
4. Heat fat to 375 degrees.
5. Stem up, carefully lower dry artichokes, one at a time, into fat. Do not crowd.
6. Turn with slotted spoon until leaves are opened and artichokes are light brown.
7. Remove to drain. Sprinkle with salt, and serve hot as appetizer.

Purim (March/14 Adar)

This joyous and fun-filled spring holiday is based on a story from the Biblical book of Esther. The Persian king Ahasuerus was goaded by his advisor Haman to kill all Jews. Esther, the king's wife—whose Jewish ancestry was a secret guarded even from the king—managed to change her husband's mind, and Haman was executed instead. At Purim, three commandments must be observed: giving gifts to the poor, exchanging food gifts between friends, and holding a joyous feast. The latter, called Seudat Purim, is served in the after-noon, and adults are encouraged to drink wine with the meal. Children dress as historic figures from this Biblical story and make fun of the evil Haman.

J-19. Hamantaschen

These three-cornered cookies are named after the type of hat worn by Haman. Fillings may vary; in New York, hamantaschen are traditionally filled with poppy seeds and honey. Other filling options are chopped dried prunes and apricots. Since this recipe uses butter, it cannot be served with a meal that includes meat.

Yield: About 40 cookies

Equipment needed: 1-quart saucepan, electric mixer with paddle, work surface, rolling pin, 2½-inch round cookie cutter, cookie sheet

Ingredients

1 cup milk
½ cup honey
1 cup poppy seeds, ground
1 cup cake crumbs
½ teaspoon salt
2 eggs
1 cup sugar
4 ounces (1 stick) butter

3 tablespoons lemon juice
1 tablespoon grated lemon peel
1 teaspoon vanilla extract
1 tablespoon baking powder
4 cups flour
Flour for dusting
Pan spray

Method

1. To make filling, combine milk and honey; bring to a boil.
2. Add poppy seeds and simmer 5 minutes.
3. Remove from heat; add cake crumbs and salt.
4. Refrigerate filling before using.
5. Combine all dough ingredients, except flour, in mixing bowl and blend well.
6. Add flour in stages at slow speed until stiff dough forms.
7. Remove dough from mixer bowl and refrigerate for at least 3 hours.
8. On floured work surface, divide dough into smaller sections and roll about ½-inch thick.
9. Cut out 2-inch circles with cookie cutter.
10. Put ½ teaspoon filling in center of each circle.
11. Fold edges inward to make triangles resembling Haman's hat. Some filling should show in the center where edges meet.
12. Place on cookie sheet and bake at 350 degrees until light brown.

Passover (April/15–22 Nisan)

Passover, or Pesach, celebrates the Israelites' escape from slavery in Egypt. To avoid the divine punishment dealt to the Egyptians resulting in the death of each firstborn son, the Israelites were told to slaughter a lamb and mark their doors with its blood so that death would "pass over." The lamb was to be roasted and eaten with bitter herbs. During their hurried escape from Egypt, families did not have time to let their bread dough rise and were forced to take unleavened dough, which baked in the sun as they fled. Today, in remembrance of these events, no leavening agents except eggs are used in Passover foods. On the eve of Passover, homes are carefully cleaned of all *chometz* (yeast). Orthodox families conduct a symbolic search for the last crumbs of leavened bread.

The Seder

Although Passover traditions vary depending on local customs, all celebrations center on the Seder meal—an occasion rich with religious symbolism. The holy book known as the Haggadah is read at the table by the oldest male member of the family, and children ask ritual questions designed to help understand the meaning of these historical events. The elements of the Seder include:

- *Baytza*. A hard-boiled egg, with its oval shape, symbolizes the life cycle.
- *Charoset* (*haroset*). A condiment of minced fruit (such as apples), nuts, and wine, it symbolizes the mortar the Hebrew slaves used to set bricks during their forced labor in Egypt.
- *Karpas*. A green vegetable celebrates the arrival of spring; dipped in salt water, it represents the tears shed in slavery. In America, parsley or celery is commonly used.
- *Maror* or *chrain*. Literally "bitter herbs," they represent the bitterness of slavery. Horseradish is the most commonly used item.
- *Matzo*. This unleavened bread is the central symbol of the meal. Three matzos are placed on the plate under a cover, to symbolize the hasty departure of the Jews from Egypt. Today, it is a custom at the Seder to add a fourth matzo in honor of the still-oppressed Jews.
- *Zeroa*. A roasted shank bone symbolizes the paschal lamb sacrifice. A roasted chicken bone is also sometimes used.
- Four cups of wine symbolize the four Biblical expressions of redemption. They also honor the four matriarchs: Sarah, Rebecca, Rachel, and Leah.
- A fifth cup of wine is poured for Elijah, a Jewish prophet, who is a hoped-for guest.

Matzos

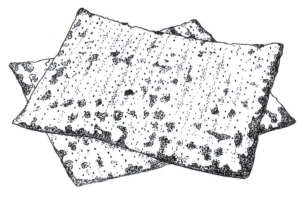

MATZOS

Symbols of liberation from slavery, these unleavened wheat crackers are eaten year-round and used in many recipes. Most matzos consist of wheat-flour and water, but egg matzos are also available. Matzos are never made at home. By tradition, they must leave the oven exactly eighteen minutes from the moment water is blended with the dough, to avoid all possible contamination from wild yeast. These baked crackers are also ground and used as a cooking ingredient called matzo meal.

J-20. Breakfast Matzo Fritters

This is a traditional family breakfast dish.

Yield: 10 fritters

Equipment needed: Two kitchen towels, 1-quart saucepan, 10-inch frying pan, spatula, wide china dish

Ingredients

2 cups sugar	½ teaspoon cardamom, ground
1½ cups water	¼ cup lemon juice
1 tablespoon grated lemon peel	10 matzos
½ teaspoon fenugreek, ground	Oil for frying

Method

1. Combine sugar with water, lemon peel, and spices.
2. Bring to a boil and simmer 20 minutes. Add lemon juice and keep sugar syrup hot.
3. Soak kitchen towels in cold water and wring fairly dry.
4. Put one towel on work surface.
5. Place matzos on top and sprinkle lightly with water. (Matzos should be moist, but not soaked.)
6. Cover with second towel and press down lightly.
7. Heat ¼ inch of oil in frying pan.
8. Remove towel from matzos and use spatula to carefully lower one matzo at a time into hot oil.
9. Fry on both sides. Place matzo in a wide dish.
10. Pour hot syrup over matzo and let soak 2 minutes, before removing to a serving platter.
11. Repeat process with each matzo individually.

J-21. Ashkenazic Charoset

Eastern European Jews used walnuts, raisins, dates, and locally grown apples to make this recipe. Since dates and raisins were a luxury, some older recipes use grated carrots and apples blended with nuts and honey instead.

Yield: 3 cups

Equipment needed: Peeler, paring knife, cutting board, French knife, food processor, small bowl, mixing spoon

Ingredients

1 teaspoon ginger, chopped	1 tablespoon honey
2 medium apples	8 ounces dates, pitted
¼ cup lemon juice	1½ cups raisins
1 teaspoon cinnamon, ground	½ cup walnuts, chopped

(continued)

Method

1. Peel ginger and chop as finely as possible.
2. Peel and core apples. Cut in chunks and place in food processor with ginger.
3. Add all remaining ingredients except walnuts.
4. Process to coarse consistency.
5. Put mixture in bowl and blend in walnuts.
6. Refrigerate overnight.

J-22. Sephardic Charoset

Since the Sephardim lived in Spain and North Africa, they were able to use semitropical fruits and ingredients in their recipes.

Yield: 4 to 6 cups
Equipment needed: Cutting board, French knife, mixing bowl

Ingredients

2 pomegranates	2 tablespoons grated orange peel
6 ounces dates, pitted	1 teaspoon allspice, ground
$\frac{1}{2}$ cup almonds, chopped	1 teaspoon ginger, ground
2 tablespoons honey	1 tablespoon lemon juice

Method

1. Halve pomegranates; remove seeds and juice. Discard shell.
2. Chop dates.
3. Combine all ingredients and let marinate in refrigerator for at least 2 hours.

J-23. Beet Horseradish

Beet-colored horseradish is a popular and almost indispensable relish. Most people buy it at the supermarket, but the homemade version tastes better!

Yield: 3 cups
Equipment needed: Peeler, paring knife, food processor with fine grating attachment, stainless steel bowl

Ingredients

1 pound fresh horseradish	$\frac{1}{4}$ cup sugar
$\frac{1}{2}$ pound fresh, small beets	$\frac{1}{2}$ tablespoon salt
$\frac{1}{2}$ cup vinegar	$\frac{1}{4}$ cup water

Method

1. Peel horseradish and beets.
2. Grate horseradish using fine blade of food processor. (*Note:* Horseradish is stringy and difficult to grate.)
3. Grate beets.
4. Combine with remaining ingredients and refrigerate overnight so flavors will blend evenly.

J-24. Chickpea Dip (*Nahit*)

This popular appetizer is known throughout the Middle East, often under the name hummus.
Yield: 2 cups
Equipment needed: Food processor

Ingredients

1½ cups canned chickpeas, drained
½ cup tahini (sesame paste)
½ cup lemon juice
1 tablespoon garlic, chopped
2 tablespoons olive oil
1 teaspoon salt

Method

1. Blend all ingredients in food processor.
2. Serve with pita bread or crackers.

J-25. Stuffed Chicken

Only chickens slaughtered according to Kashrut laws are used in Jewish households. The dressing will taste just as good if baked separately and basted with chicken juices.
Yield: 6 servings
Equipment needed: Cutting board, colander, French knife, food processor, heavy saucepan, wooden spoon, mixing bowl, butcher's twine, roasting pan, brush, small sauce pan, strainer

Ingredients

8 ounces chicken livers
8 ounces mushrooms
4 matzos
½ cup oil
½ cup onions, chopped
1 teaspoon garlic, crushed
1 tablespoon parsley, chopped
2 eggs
1 tablespoon paprika
2 tablespoons bread crumbs
1 roasting chicken, about 4 or 5 pounds

(continued)

2 tablespoons chicken fat or oil	1 cup apple juice
1 teaspoon salt	1 teaspoon cornstarch

Method

1. Wash chicken livers in warm water and drain in colander.
2. Trim fat and cut livers into 1/4-inch pieces. Set aside.
3. Wash mushrooms, carefully removing any sand.
4. Break matzos into smaller pieces; soak in warm water.
5. Cook onions and garlic in oil until light brown. Add chicken livers and cook lightly. Set aside.
6. Chop mushrooms in food processor to coarse consistency.
7. Squeeze water from matzos and add to mushrooms with parsley, eggs, paprika, salt, and bread crumbs.
8. Blend briefly, but do not overmix.
9. Place stuffing in bowl and blend in chicken livers. Chill.
10. Make sure chicken is dry inside and out. Remove excess fat.
11. Stuff chicken cavity and under breast skin.
12. Truss with butcher's twine.
13. Place chicken in roasting pan, breast up, and brush with oil.
14. Roast in 350-degree oven for 40 minutes.
15. Cover with aluminum foil and roast at 375 degrees for another hour.
16. Check inside of bird with meat thermometer; temperature should register 170 degrees.
17. Carefully remove roasting pan from oven. Turn chicken upside down in pan to let the juices collect in breast.
18. Turn bird breast-up after 10 minutes and place on warm platter or cutting board.
19. Pour all pan juices into small saucepan. Wait a few minutes, then skim off fat that rises to top.
20. Add apple juice. Bring liquid to boil. Blend cornstarch with 1 tablespoon cold water. Add to boiling gravy.
21. Strain gravy. Carve chicken into portions and serve with gravy.

J-26. Pineapple Carrot Soufflé

Jewish cooking often combines sweet side dishes with meat.
Yield: 6 servings
Equipment needed: Potato peeler, French knife, saucepan, food processor, bowl, whisk, spatula, 3-quart baking dish

Ingredients

2 pounds carrots	4 tablespoons matzo meal
2 ounces (1/2 stick) margarine (parve)	1/2 teaspoon cinnamon, ground
	1 cup canned crushed pineapple
1/2 cup sugar	4 tablespoons cornstarch
1 teaspoon salt	6 eggs
1/2 teaspoon nutmeg, ground	Pan spray

Method

1. Peel carrots and cut into small pieces.
2. Put carrots in pot, barely cover with water, and simmer until tender. Do not overcook.
3. Carefully drain carrots, cool, and puree in food processor.
4. Add all remaining ingredients except eggs.
5. Pulse-process to blend.
6. Carefully separate egg yolks from whites. Blend yolks into carrot mix.
7. Beat egg whites in large stainless steel bowl until stiff.
8. Fold carrot blend into egg whites.
9. Pan-spray baking dish. Spread mixture evenly in dish. (Note that mixture will rise and baking dish should have about an inch of room left above filling.)
10. Bake at 350 degrees for about an hour.

J-27. Azerbaijani Roasted Eggs

Jewish traders lived along the Silk Road that led from China to Europe, passing through Azerbaijan. This roasted-egg recipe shows the influence of Chinese cooking as it resembles preserved hundred-day eggs. These eggs are served unpeeled at tableside and have a marble-like color.

Yield: 10 eggs

Equipment needed: 1-quart saucepan with lid, cutting board, French knife, wooden spoon

Ingredients

10 eggs	1 teaspoon fenugreek
1 tablespoon salt	1 teaspoon cumin, ground
1 large onion	1 teaspoon peppercorns
¼ cup oil	½ teaspoon cardamom, ground
1 bay leaf	Juice of one lemon

Method

1. Cover eggs with water; add salt. Bring to a boil and simmer 10 minutes.
2. Drain eggs and plunge into cold water.
3. Crack eggs, but do not peel.
4. Peel and dice onion, saving the peel.
5. Sauté diced onion and peel in oil until slightly transparent.
6. Add spices, onion peel, and 3 cups water.
7. Add eggs, bring to a boil, cover pot, and simmer 2 hours. Stir occasionally and add water if necessary.
8. Let cool; serve in quarters sprinkled with lemon juice.

J-28. Eastern European Seed Cake

The flavors of several aromatic spices come together in this tasty dessert. Lemon extract can be substituted for the vanilla if desired.
Yield: 6 servings
Equipment needed: Electric mixer with paddle, scraper, flour sifter, 9-inch cake pan

Ingredients

8 ounces (2 sticks) butter, room temperature
1 cup sugar
5 eggs
1 teaspoon vanilla extract
1/2 teaspoon salt
2 cups flour
1 teaspoon baking powder

1/2 teaspoon allspice
1/2 tablespoon caraway seeds
2 tablespoons sesame seeds
1/2 tablespoon anise seeds
1/4 cup milk
Pan spray
Powdered sugar

Method

1. Cream butter, sugar, salt, eggs, and vanilla extract.
2. Sift flour together with baking powder and allspice.
3. Add milk, seeds, and flour to butter mixture at low speed.
4. Pan-spray cake pan and add batter.
5. Bake at 375 degrees for 40 minutes.
6. Sprinkle with powdered sugar when cool.

J-29. Brazilian Cashew and Guava Cake

This cake recipe uses typical Brazilian ingredients. Guava is a tropical fruit that can be eaten raw but is often made into a solid paste sold in flat cans or boxes.
Yield: 40 pieces
Equipment needed: Food processor, baking dish, cutting board, knife

Ingredients

4 cups cashews, roasted
1 1/2 cups matzo meal
2 cups sugar
1 tablespoon grated lime peel
1/2 cup lime juice

1/2 cup vegetable oil
4 eggs
1 pound canned guava paste
Pan spray
Powdered sugar

Method

1. Chop cashews in food processor until medium-fine.
2. Add all other ingredients, except guava paste, and pulse to blend.
3. Pan-spray 8-by-12-inch baking dish. Add about half the batter.

4. Cut guava paste into thin slivers and put on top of batter layer. Fill with remaining batter.
5. Bake at 400 degrees until light brown, about 45 minutes.
6. Dust with powdered sugar. Cut into 40 pieces when cold.

Shavuot (May or June/6 Sivan)

This early summer holiday, sometimes called the Feast of Weeks, occurs seven weeks after Passover in the Jewish calendar. Originally an agricultural festival celebrating the wheat harvest and first fruits of the season, it now commemorates the giving of the Ten Commandments to Moses on Mount Sinai. Traditionally honey and dairy foods are served.

J-30. Blintzes

These cheese pancakes, usually served with stewed fruits, are a popular Ashkenazi dish.

Yield: 20 pancakes
Equipment needed: Sifter, mixing bowl, wire whisk, strainer, bowl, ladle, 5-inch crepe pan, teaspoon, spatula, cookie sheets, tablespoons, frying pan

Ingredients

³/₄ cup flour	4 ounces cream cheese
1 cup milk	4 ounces baker's cheese
4 eggs	3 egg yolks
¹/₂ teaspoon salt	2 teaspoons grated lemon rind
8 ounces (2 sticks) butter	¹/₂ cup sugar
4 ounces ricotta cheese	1 teaspoon vanilla extract

Method

1. Sift flour into bowl; add milk, eggs, and salt, blending together with wire whisk.
2. Strain batter to remove all lumps.
3. Refrigerate for 1 hour.
4. Melt butter in water bath to separate whey from butterfat. (Only clarified butter that rises to top is used here.)
5. Heat crepe pan until water droplet sizzles.
6. Swirl 1 teaspoon clarified butter in pan to coat evenly.
7. Add 2 tablespoons batter and swirl it around to coat bottom of pan.
8. Cook over medium heat until batter is firm.
9. Slide crepe onto cookie sheet to cool; continue baking crepes.
10. Blend remaining ingredients together to make filling.

(continued)

11. Place about 2 tablespoons of filling in each crepe; roll and tuck in sides to make rectangular package.
12. Chill until ready to serve.
13. Just before serving, pan-fry blintzes in butter until golden brown on both sides.

J-31. Crisp Cornmeal Waffles

Sephardic Jews eat corn, while Ashkenazim usually shun it.
Yield: 8 to 10
Equipment needed: Sifter, large bowl, wire whisk, pan spray, waffle iron

Ingredients

1 cup flour, sifted
2 teaspoons baking powder
1 teaspoon baking soda
1 teaspoon sugar
$1/2$ teaspoon salt

1 cup yellow cornmeal
2 eggs
2 cups buttermilk
$1/4$ cup oil

Method

1. Sift all dry ingredients, except cornmeal, into a bowl.
2. Mix in cornmeal, then add eggs, buttermilk, and oil to make a batter.
3. Bake waffles; serve with honey or syrup.

Sabbath Celebrations

In addition to high holidays, Jews observe a weekly day of rest known as the Sabbath, which lasts from sundown on Friday to sundown on Saturday. Traditionally, it is a time of prayer and repose, when no manual labor should be carried out. The interpretation of what is manual labor varies greatly; many Jewish-owned stores close on Saturdays, and some very pious Jews do not activate any mechanical device. However, for some less-observant Jews, it is just another day. Since the Sabbath is also a day of hospitality, it is customary to invite a guest for dinner and to wish them *"ess gesindeheit"* which means "eat in good health" in Yiddish.

J-32. Challah

Sabbath eve often begins with a special ritual meal that includes challah, an egg-rich braided bread that symbolizes the manna given to the ancient Israelites by God during their years wandering in the desert. *Challah* means "the priest's share." Traditionally, a little bit of dough is pinched off, baked separately, and then burnt so it cannot be consumed. The bread's golden color comes from egg yolks and, sometimes, a pinch of costly saffron.

Yield: 1 loaf
Equipment needed: Small bowl, electric mixer with dough hook, sifter, work surface, baking sheet, pastry brush

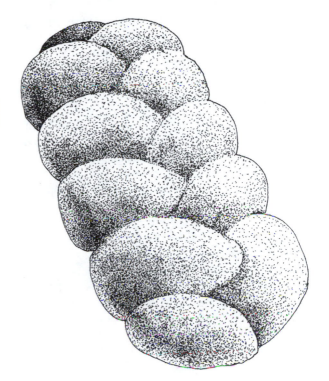

CHALLAH

Ingredients

1½ cups milk	1 teaspoon
1 envelope	grated lemon
yeast	peel
¼ cup sugar	2 tablespoons
4 egg yolks	heavy cream
½ teaspoon salt	Flour for
2 ounces butter, melted	dusting
3 cups flour, sifted	

Method

1. Warm milk to about body temperature. Add yeast. Let stand in warm place for about 10 minutes.
2. Mix milk-and-yeast blend together with sugar, three egg yolks, and salt at medium speed.
3. Combine all remaining ingredients, except heavy cream and last egg yolk.
4. Using dough hook, blend at medium speed to make smooth dough.
5. Scrape down dough from sides of mixing bowl and cover with clean kitchen towel.
6. Let dough rise in warm place for 1 hour.
7. Briefly knead dough on flour-dusted work surface and divide into five strands of equal length.
8. Braid three strands together, place on baking sheet, and then braid two strands and place on top.
9. Let challah rise for 45 minutes in a warm place.
10. Blend cream with remaining egg yolk and evenly brush on challah.
11. Bake at 375 degrees for about 55 minutes.

J-33. Cholent

Because of the prohibition against manual labor, observant Jews do not cook on the Sabbath. Instead, one-pot covered casserole dishes called *cholent* are prepared on Friday and baked overnight in a slow oven. In the past, Jewish women took the dish to the local baker, where it oven-cooked slowly overnight, a custom that saved scarce fuel.

(continued)

Yield: 8 to 10 main-course servings
Equipment needed: Bowl, cutting board, French knife, Dutch oven, potato peeler, meat slicing knife

Ingredients

8 ounces dried baby lima beans	1 teaspoon coriander seeds,
8 ounces dried red kidney beans	ground
4 tablespoons olive oil	2 tablespoons paprika
1 pound onions, peeled	4 pounds fresh beef brisket,
2 tablespoons garlic, chopped	trimmed
1 teaspoon cayenne pepper	1 pound Maine potatoes
1 teaspoon cumin	8 ounces dried lentils
1 tablespoon salt	

Method

1. Combine beans, cover with cold water, and soak overnight.
2. Heat oil in Dutch oven.
3. Cut onions into large chunks; cook in oil until evenly browned.
4. Drain beans and add to onions. Reduce heat.
5. Add spices and meat.
6. Cover with water and simmer slowly for 1 hour.
7. Peel potatoes and cut into 1-inch cubes.
8. Arrange potatoes and lentils evenly around meat.
9. Add water to cover and bring to simmer again.
10. Cover, place in 350-degree oven, and bake for 2 hours. Since dried legumes will absorb a lot of liquid, check periodically. Add more water as needed.
11. Remove from oven, check meat for tenderness. Let cool.
12. Slice meat and serve with legumes.

J-34. Hungarian Sólet (Bean and Goose Cholent)

No two cholent recipes are alike; some contain a variety of legumes, some contain potatoes, and some even barley. This Hungarian version uses smoked beef and goose. Geese are kosher if slaughtered by Kashrut laws. If soaked beans are used, this recipe can be prepared in about three hours.

Yield: 8 servings
Equipment needed: Dutch oven, wooden spoon, meat fork, tray, cutting board, French knife

Ingredients

1 pound dry beans, such as navy	1 tablespoon garlic, chopped
beans	1 tablespoon medium-sharp
2 tablespoons oil	paprika
½ cup onions, chopped	

1 pound smoked or corned beef
  brisket
1 pound smoked goose or duckling legs (about two)

¹/₂ cup bread crumbs
2 eggs, hard-boiled
Salt and pepper to taste

Method

1. Soak beans overnight.
2. Sauté onions and garlic in oil in Dutch oven. Drain beans and add to onions with paprika and beef. Cover with three times as much water as there are beans. Bring to simmer, close lid, and simmer for 1¹/₂ hours.
3. Check water level occasionally to be sure meat and beans have sufficient liquid to cook.
4. Add smoked goose or duckling legs and continue simmering.
5. Remove lid after an hour. There should be relatively little liquid, and beans and meats should be fully cooked.
6. Carefully remove meats with fork and place on tray to cool.
7. Sprinkle beans with bread crumbs; bake in 350-degree oven for 20 minutes.
8. Cut meat in portion-sized chunks and fold into beans.
9. Bake 10 minutes longer before serving.

J-35. *Powidltascherln*

Lekvar, known in the U.S. as prune butter, is called *powidl* by Czechs and Austrians. Czech Jews who brought their food traditions to New York occasionally included it in their Sabbath dishes. Lekvar is used in pastry fillings and hot Bohemian desserts. This dish is made with lekvar-filled potato dough and is similar in appearance to ravioli.

Yield: 20
Equipment needed: Saucepan, paring knife, potato ricer, work surface, teaspoon, dough scraper, wide saucepan, large sauté pan, slotted spoon

Ingredients

2 pounds russet (baking) potatoes
1 egg yolk
1 tablespoon oil
1 teaspoon salt
1¹/₂ cups flour
4 ounces prune butter (available
  canned)

6 ounces (1¹/₂ sticks) butter
3 ounces bread crumbs
3 ounces sugar
Extra flour for dusting

Method

1. Wash potatoes, cover with water, and simmer ¹/₂ hour or until cooked all the way through.
2. Peel potatoes when cool enough to handle; skin should slip off easily.

(continued)

3. Press warm potatoes through ricer directly onto flour-dusted work surface.
4. Make a well in center and add egg yolk, oil, and salt to cooled potatoes.
5. Blend in 1½ cups flour, starting at center and gradually working flour into potato dough.
6. Using dough scraper, move flour and potatoes toward center. Continue kneading until all flour is absorbed and dough rather stiff. (If too soft, add a little more flour.)
7. Shape dough into thick roll; divide into 20 pieces.
8. Flatten each piece and fill with a little prune butter. Fold over and close rim to tightly seal dough pockets.
9. Fill large saucepan three-quarters full with water; bring to a boil. Carefully drop dough pockets into boiling water; loosen any that stick to the bottom with a spatula.
10. Simmer until all pockets float to top (about 10 minutes).
11. Remove pockets with slotted spoon and place on serving dish.
12. Heat butter in sauté pan until golden brown. Brown bread crumbs over low heat.
13. Pour browned bread crumbs over dough pockets, then sprinkle with sugar.

Religious Rites

Religious ceremonies are often associated with important rites of passage such as birth, marriage, and death.

J-36. Nahit with Rice

Ben Zohor is celebrated on the Friday evening following the birth of a son. This Romanian chickpeas-and-rice dish is a tasty addition to the kosher table for a family celebration.

Yield: 10 appetizer servings
Equipment needed: Heavy saucepan, wooden spoon, baking dish

Ingredients

1 pound chickpeas	1 teaspoon salt
½ cup rice	½ cup brown sugar
½ cup honey	Pan spray

Method

1. Cover chickpeas with cold water and soak overnight.
2. Rinse, cover with water again, and bring to a boil.
3. Simmer 1½ hours. Add water as needed to keep peas covered.
4. Add rice; simmer 20 minutes until rice is soft. Add extra water as needed to reach thickness of rich porridge.

5. Add honey and salt.
6. Pan-spray baking dish, pour in porridge, and sprinkle with brown sugar.
7. Put under broiler until top browns.

J-37. Honey Cake

This cake is served at family gatherings for the ritual of Brith Millah, the circumcision of a male child one week after birth.

Yield: 20 slices

Equipment needed: Sifter, electric mixer with whisk, stainless steel bowl, wire whisk, mixing spoon, baking pan

Ingredients

2 cups flour
$\frac{1}{2}$ teaspoon cinnamon
$\frac{1}{2}$ teaspoon allspice
$\frac{1}{2}$ teaspoon salt
$\frac{1}{4}$ teaspoon baking soda
1 teaspoon baking powder
3 eggs
1 tablespoon instant coffee
2 tablespoons hot water
$\frac{1}{4}$ teaspoon vanilla extract

$\frac{1}{4}$ cup oil
1 cup honey
$\frac{1}{4}$ cup sugar
1 teaspoon grated lemon rind
2 ounces raisins
2 ounces candied orange peel, in pieces
$\frac{1}{2}$ cup slivered almonds
Pan spray
Flour for dusting

Method

1. Sift flour with dry spices, salt, baking soda, and baking powder.
2. Separate egg yolks from egg whites. Put egg whites in bowl and set aside.
3. Dissolve instant coffee in hot water; add egg yolks, vanilla extract, oil, and honey.
4. Blend at medium speed until batter is creamy.
5. Add lemon rind, raisins, and orange peel.
6. Whip egg whites until foamy; add sugar and whip until stiff.
7. Alternately fold flour and egg whites into batter.
8. Pan-spray baking pan, add batter, and sprinkle with almonds.
9. Bake at 375 degrees for about 45 minutes.

Coming of Age

The Jewish coming-of-age ceremony is called Bar Mitzvah for boys and Bat Mitzvah for girls. Wealthy liberal Reform Jewish families are expected to provide lavish celebrations, comparable to weddings, which commonly take place in hotel ballrooms, restaurants, or clubs and often include dancing, buffets, and open bars. In contrast, Orthodox Jewish ceremonies take place in the temple.

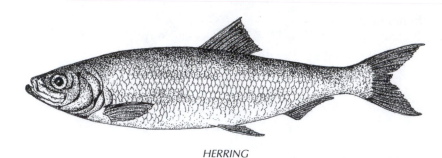

HERRING

Though joyous, these festivities are much more subdued than the parties held by Reform Jews. Both types, though, serve the same ritual purpose. All males attending, including non-Jewish guests, are expected to wear a yarmulke, the Jewish skullcap.

J-38. Chopped Herring

While there are no traditional Bar Mitzvah recipes, conservative Ashkenazi Jews might expect a caterer to serve this appetizer at the buffet.
Yield: Approximately 1 pound
Equipment needed: Cutting board, peeler, knife, small bowl, electric blender

Ingredients

10-ounce jar marinated Bismarck
  herring
2 slices white bread, crusts
  removed

2 medium apples
1 tablespoon oil
1 teaspoon pepper
4 eggs, hard boiled

Method

1. Drain herring; save marinade and onions.
2. Soak bread in herring marinade.
3. Peel and core apples; cut into small chunks.
4. Puree herring with onions, soaked bread, apples, oil, and pepper.
5. Coarsely chop eggs; blend with herring puree.
6. Serve with toast or crackers.

J-39. Gefilte Fish

This Yiddish term, meaning "stuffed fish," refers to the way the dish was originally prepared. Traditionally, the fish was boned, stuffed with ground fish, and poached with vegetables and spices. The bones and head added to the broth make it gelatinous when cold. Today the stuffing, which can be made ahead of time, is shaped into oval dumplings and poached in an aromatic broth. Most families purchase the product in jars. Gefilte fish is customarily served with beet horseradish (see recipe on page 208).
Yield: 12 servings

Equipment needed: Large pot, strainer, wide saucepan with lid, cutting board, French knife, food processor with sharp blade

Ingredients

1 pound bones and heads from kosher fish	3 pounds fish fillets, preferably carp, pike, flounder, or striped bass
1 teaspoon peppercorns	
½ tablespoon salt	½ cup onions, chopped
1 cup onions, sliced	½ cup carrots, grated
1 cup carrots, sliced	3 eggs
1 tablespoon sugar	1 teaspoon salt
¼ cup vinegar	1 teaspoon white pepper, ground
1 teaspoon coriander seeds	½ cup matzo meal

Method

1. Wash fish bones. Place in large pot and cover with water.
2. Add peppercorns and salt. Bring to a boil; simmer 25 minutes.
3. Strain into wide saucepan. Discard fish bones.
4. Add sliced onions, carrots, sugar, vinegar, and coriander to fish stock.
5. Bring to a boil; simmer 10 minutes. Set stock aside.
6. Cut fish into large chunks; freeze briefly.
7. Blend to smooth paste in food processor. (Do not overprocess.)
8. Chill in refrigerator in processor bowl.
9. When thoroughly cold, add chopped onions, grated carrots, eggs, salt, pepper, and matzo meal.
10. Process briefly to blend. Refrigerate.
11. Bring fish stock to simmer.
12. Shape fish mixture into egg-size dumplings; drop carefully into stock.
13. Simmer 40 minutes.
14. Let dumplings cool in stock; refrigerate until ready to use.
15. Serve on lettuce leaves with jelled stock, carrot rounds, and onion slices.

J-40. Chopped Liver

Popular because it can be made a day ahead and refrigerated, this cold appetizer originated in Eastern Europe. It has since become a standard item in delis and a popular fixture at traditional holiday buffets. Caterers love to present the chopped liver shaped like a fat chicken, surrounded by boiled eggs. Although tradition dictates the dish be made with beef liver, there is no reason why chicken liver cannot be substituted. For an authentic flavor, this recipe requires rendered chicken fat called *schmaltz* in Yiddish.

Schmaltz

Yield: 14 ounces
Equipment needed: Cutting board, knife, 1-quart heavy saucepan

(*continued*)

Ingredients

1½ pounds chicken fat, available in supermarkets
1 cup cold water

1 small onion, peeled and halved

Method

1. Wash chicken fat, removing any bloody skin and veins.
2. Cut into 1-inch squares.
3. Place in heavy saucepan with water and onion.
4. Slowly bring to simmer, cooking over very low heat for at least an hour, until fat is clear and onion slightly browned.
5. Cool briefly and strain through fine sieve. Discard onion. Save cracklings (called *greben*), as they are excellent with mashed potatoes or blended into chopped liver.
6. Store refrigerated.

Chopped Liver

Yield: 8 to 10 appetizer servings
Equipment needed: Pot, cutting board, French knife, roasting pan, food processor

Ingredients

6 eggs
3 pounds beef liver
8 ounces schmaltz (rendered chicken fat)

1 cup onions, chopped
2 teaspoons salt
2 teaspoons pepper, ground

Method

1. Cover eggs with water. Bring to a boil and simmer 10 minutes.
2. Drain off water and chill eggs under cold running water.
3. Peel while still submerged.
4. Wash liver, removing any sinews.
5. Cut liver into large chunks and combine with all ingredients in rectangular baking dish.
6. Roast in 400-degree oven for 30 minutes.
7. Remove eggs and coarsely chop.
8. Continue cooking livers 10 more minutes. Remove from oven and cool.
9. Coarsely chop liver mixture in food processor. Add cooked eggs.
10. Process briefly to blend.
11. Refrigerate until ready to use.
12. Serve with toast points.

J-41. Lamb and Eggplant Matzo Pie

There are many customs associated with the Jewish wedding ceremony. This is a traditional Moroccan Sephardic wedding dish.

Yield: 8 servings

Equipment needed: 2-quart heavy saucepan, wooden stirring spoon, cutting board, paring knife, French knife, colander, 2-quart wide saucepan, 13 × 9-inch baking dish, pastry brush

Ingredients

½ cup onion, chopped

2 tablespoons garlic, finely chopped

¼ cup olive oil

1½ pounds lean ground lamb

2 teaspoons salt

¼ teaspoon cumin

¼ teaspoon ginger, ground

1 teaspoon black pepper, ground

½ teaspoon cinnamon, ground

¼ teaspoon coriander, ground

½ teaspoon cayenne pepper

¼ teaspoon allspice

¼ teaspoon cloves, ground

1 teaspoon whole oregano leaves

1 teaspoon mint leaves, crushed

1 teaspoon sugar

1 can (28 ounces) crushed tomatoes

2 pounds eggplant

8 matzos

Olive oil to brush baking dish and top matzos

Method

1. Cook onions and garlic in 4 tablespoons oil until transparent; add lamb and cook over moderate heat, breaking up any lumps.
2. Add 1 teaspoon salt and all dry spices. Stir to combine.
3. Add tomatoes, bring to a slow boil, and simmer uncovered about 30 minutes.
4. Peel eggplants and cut in large cubes. Place in colander and sprinkle with remaining salt. Let stand 20 minutes.
5. Squeeze out as much moisture from eggplant as possible.
6. Put remaining oil in wide saucepan and sauté eggplants until limp. Set aside.
7. Moisten matzos until pliable but not soaking wet.
8. Set two matzos aside.
9. Put one layer of matzos in rectangular baking dish.
10. Add layers of meat, eggplant, and matzo. Top with two reserved matzos.
11. Brush with olive oil and cover with aluminum foil.
12. Bake for 15 minutes at 375 degrees.
13. Uncover and bake until matzos are brown.

J-42. Bagels

Chewy, doughnut-shaped rolls made with hard wheat dough, true bagels are preboiled in slightly alkaline water giving them a distinct flavor. Their history can be traced to a seventeenth-century Viennese baker who made stirrup-shaped rolls to thank the Polish king for defeating the Turks besieging Vienna. The German word for stirrups is *bügel*, which became *bagel* in Yiddish. Customarily, bagels are eaten after a funeral and during the first seven days of mourning, their round shape symbolizing the circle of life. New Yorkers can be quite particular about their bagels and have been known to travel to distant bakeries for the best.

Yield: 16 to 20, depending on size

Equipment needed: Electric mixer with dough hook, small bowl, flour sifter, work surface, 3-quart wide saucepan, skimmer, baking sheet

Ingredients

1 cup water
1 package yeast
1 tablespoon sugar
2 teaspoons salt
1 tablespoon oil

1 egg white
1 pound bread flour
1 teaspoon baking soda
Flour for dusting

Method

1. Warm water to about 90 degrees.
2. Add yeast, sugar, and 1 teaspoon salt. Let ferment at room temperature about 10 minutes.
3. Add oil and egg white, blend briefly with mixer at low speed.
4. Sift flour and gradually add to mixing bowl, blending ingredients at low speed.
5. Dough will be very stiff; a tablespoon of water may be added if necessary.
6. Knead dough briefly on flour-dusted work surface, cover with kitchen towel, and let rise for 40 minutes.
7. Divide dough into 16 to 20 small balls, each rolled tightly. Shape balls into strands about 7 inches long.
8. Shape strands into rings, sealing ends with water.
9. Let rings rise for 20 minutes.
10. Fill saucepan three-quarters full with water; add remaining salt and baking soda.
11. Bring to a boil. Carefully add bagels and poach for 5 minutes.
12. Lift with skimmer onto baking sheet.
13. Bake at 375 degrees for 20 minutes.

Dairy Dishes

Customarily eaten on Shavuot (the Feast of Weeks), dairy dishes are also important in everyday Jewish cuisine. According to kosher law, meat and dairy products cannot be eaten together. Any food or dish containing milk or milk products, no matter how small the quantity, is considered a dairy product. For something to be kosher, it must come from a kosher animal, contain no non-kosher ingredients, and contain no meat.

J-43. Matzo Brei

This dish is a popular breakfast food. Many cooks treat matzo brei like scrambled eggs and stir-fry the mixture.

Yield: 2 servings
Equipment needed: Two small bowls, nonstick frying pan, spatula

Ingredients

2 eggs
½ cup water or milk
Cinnamon and salt to taste
2 whole matzos

3 tablespoons vegetable oil (or
4 tablespoons butter if milk
is used)

Method

1. Combine eggs with liquid and seasoning.
2. Break matzos into little pieces and add to egg mixture.
3. Let soak 15 minutes.
4. Heat oil or butter in frying pan. Carefully add egg-matzo mixture.
5. Fry over low heat until brown on both sides.

J-44. Sephardic Leek and Feta Fritters

Since leeks grow best in a warm climate and sandy soil, many southern European and North African dishes contain them. Feta is a Mediterranean cheese made with sheep's or goat's milk preserved in brine. Many Sephardim settled in North Africa.

Yield: 20 fritters
Equipment needed: Small saucepan, colander, food processor, frying pan, tablespoon, spatula

Ingredients

2 cups leeks, diced, white part only
1 cup matzo meal
4 eggs
8 ounces feta cheese, drained and
crumbled

1 tablespoon parsley, chopped
1 teaspoon white pepper, ground
Oil for frying

Method

1. Wash leeks thoroughly to remove any sand.
2. Cover with 1 cup water in small saucepan. Leeks will float.
3. Bring to a boil, simmer 20 minutes, and drain.
4. Blend with matzo meal, eggs, feta cheese, parsley, and pepper in food processor until medium-fine consistency.
5. Let batter rest a half-hour. If too stiff, dilute with a little cold water.
6. Heat ¼ inch of oil in frying pan.
7. Drop in small fritters and fry until brown on both sides.
8. Serve with yogurt or sour cream.

J-45. Matzo Omelet

Matzo is a versatile ingredient for kosher dishes. Here is a tasty twist on a simple omelet.

Yield: 2 servings

Equipment needed: Plate to soak matzos, small bowl, whisk, 10-inch stainless steel frying pan or nonstick pan with lid, spatula, serving plate

Ingredients

2 matzos
2 tablespoons raisins
3 eggs
Pinch of salt
1 teaspoon grated lemon rind

1 tablespoon butter
2 tablespoons pine nuts
Powdered sugar
Cinnamon

Method

1. Break matzos into small pieces and soak with raisins in cold water for about 10 minutes.
2. Break eggs into small bowl, add salt, and blend thoroughly.
3. Squeeze water from raisins and matzos. Add to eggs, blending well.
4. Add grated lemon peel.
5. In medium frying pan, cook pine nuts in butter over moderate heat until light brown.
6. Add egg mixture.
7. Cover and cook over low heat, turning to cook both sides.
8. Serve sprinkled with sugar and cinnamon.

J-46. Vegetable Cutlets

Vegetable patties are popular as a main course.

Yield: 10 cutlets

Equipment needed: 3-quart heavy saucepan, wooden spoon, #10 ice cream scoop, work surface, frying pan, spatula

Ingredients

$\frac{1}{2}$ cup celery, chopped
1 cup onions, chopped
4 tablespoons butter
1 cup peas, cooked
1 cup French-style string beans, cooked
1 cup sweet potatoes, mashed

1 tablespoon parsley, chopped
$\frac{1}{2}$ cup cream cheese
3 eggs
1 teaspoon pepper, ground
$\frac{1}{2}$ teaspoon coriander, ground
1 cup matzo meal
Oil for frying

Method

1. Sauté celery and onions in butter until onions are transparent.
2. Add peas; mash with spoon.

3. Add string beans and sweet potatoes. Continue to cook, stirring constantly, until mixture is thoroughly heated.
4. Remove from heat and cool.
5. Add remaining ingredients and ¾ cup matzo meal. Mixture should be stiff. (If too soft, add more matzo meal.)
6. Sprinkle remaining matzo meal on work surface.
7. Place vegetable mixture on top and form into 10 patties. Cover evenly with matzo meal.
8. Heat ½ inch of oil in frying pan. Carefully add patties and fry on both sides until brown and heated through.

J-47. Zucchini Frittata

Since eggs are parve (neutral), this dish could be served as a hot appetizer before a meat main course or cold on a buffet.

Yield: 4 servings

Equipment needed: Paring knife, grater, 10-inch saucepan, 10 × 8-inch baking dish

Ingredients

1 pound zucchini, small	1 teaspoon salt
2 tablespoons olive oil	¼ teaspoon nutmeg
½ cup onions, chopped	1 tablespoon parmesan cheese,
6 eggs	grated
½ cup matzo meal	Pan spray

Method

1. Wash zucchini and grate into fine slivers.
2. Sauté onions in oil until transparent.
3. Add zucchini and sauté over medium heat until zucchini are hot but still crisp.
4. Cool mixture. Add remaining ingredients and mix well to blend evenly.
5. Pan-spray baking dish.
6. Pour frittata mixture into dish and bake at 300 degrees for 15 minutes.
7. Let sit for 10 minutes before serving.

J-48. Lokschen Noodle Kugel

Kugel is the German word for "sphere" or "ball" and is used to describe this dish that is traditionally baked in a round mold. Because there are many variations not prepared in the original shape, "kugel" has come to simply mean a side dish that accompanies a roast, dessert, or vegetarian main course.

Yield: 6 servings

Equipment needed: 2-quart pot, colander, mixing bowls, mixing spoon, whisk, baking dish

(*continued*)

Ingredients

8 ounces egg noodles
2 egg yolks
1 teaspoon ground cinnamon
2 tablespoons sugar
2 tablespoons vegetable oil
¼ cup chopped walnuts

½ cup raisins
¼ teaspoon salt
2 egg whites
1 tablespoon sugar
Pan spray

Method

1. Boil noodles until tender, drain, and rinse with cold water. Drain again.
2. Combine egg yolks with 2 tablespoons cold water, cinnamon, and sugar.
3. Mix to dissolve sugar. Add oil and blend.
4. Combine mixture with boiled noodles and add nuts, raisins, and salt.
5. Whip egg whites until soft peaks form, add sugar, and whip until stiff.
6. Fold egg whites into the noodle mixture.
7. Pan-spray baking dish. Pour in mixture and bake at 375 degrees until brown, about 30 minutes.

J-49. Matzo Kugel with Apples

This easy-to-make dessert is popular in New York City.
Yield: 4 to 6 dessert servings
Equipment needed: Small mixing bowl, large mixing bowl, wire whisk, peeler, paring knife, grater, baking dish

Ingredients

4 matzos
Warm water
3 Granny Smith apples
¼ cup sugar
3 eggs, separated
¼ cup sugar

3 tablespoons margarine (parve),
   melted
¼ cup raisins
Cinnamon to taste
¼ cup walnuts, chopped
Powdered sugar

Method

1. Crumble matzos and soak in warm water.
2. Drain and squeeze dry. Peel and core apples; thinly slice with grater or knife.
3. Cream sugar with egg yolks. Stir in soaked matzos.
4. Whip egg whites and sugar until stiff and foamy; blend into matzo mixture.
5. Grease baking pan and fill with half of matzo mixture.
6. Spread apples on top, then sprinkle with raisins, cinnamon, and walnuts.
7. Top off with remaining matzo mix and melted parve shortening.
8. Bake at 375 degrees for 45 minutes. Sprinkle with powdered sugar before serving.
9. Kugel may be served with a fruit sauce.

J-50. Baked Pears with Walnuts and Honey

This elegant parve (neutral) dessert may be served with either dairy or meat dishes. The pears should be ripe, but not too soft. Anjou pears are good for cooking; they are large and have greenish-yellow skin. Bartlett pears have a buttery smooth texture.

Yield: 8 servings

Equipment needed: Peeler, cutting board, French knife, melon baller, grater, small bowl, two pastry brushes, baking dish large enough to accommodate eight pear halves

Ingredients

4 ripe pears
2 tablespoons oil
1 lemon
4 tablespoons honey
1/2 cup walnuts, chopped

1 teaspoon black pepper, coarsely ground
1/2 teaspoon cardamom, ground
1/2 teaspoon coriander, ground

Method

1. Peel pears and halve lengthwise.
2. Scoop out center core and discard.
3. Brush baking dish with small amount of oil.
4. Grate lemon peel. Warm honey carefully in water bath to make it more spreadable. Blend lemon peel with honey.
5. Sprinkle baking dish with walnuts. Place pears on top, cut side down.
6. Squeeze lemon evenly over pears.
7. Blend spices and sprinkle over pears.
8. Brush pears with honey blend.
9. Drizzle remaining oil over pears.
10. Bake in 375-degree oven until pears are soft and light brown on top.

What Would Abraham Have Eaten?

The staple foods of the region where Abraham lived included olives and grapes, which were plentiful; cereal grains such as wheat, millet, and sorghum; and honey, which was used as a sweetener. Due to the scarcity of firewood, baking bread of any sort presented a challenge. Many people depended on bulghur—wheat that is steamed, hulled, and cracked and can be reconstituted by adding hot water. Bulghur was used to prepare tabbouleh, also known as *taboul* or *tabbouli*. The modern version below includes ingredients not available when Abraham lived.

J-51. Tabbouleh

Yield: 8 servings
Equipment needed: Mixing bowl, mixing spoon

(continued)

Ingredients

2 cups medium-fine bulghur

2 cups hot water

1 cup onions, chopped

½ cup olive oil

Juice of one lemon

2 tablespoons garlic, mashed

½ cup parsley, chopped

1 tablespoon mint, chopped

½ tablespoon pepper, ground

1 teaspoon cardamom seeds,
   crushed

Salt to taste

Method

1. Moisten bulghur with hot water and set aside.
2. When lukewarm, combine with remaining ingredients.

What Would Moses Have Eaten?

What constituted the diet of the ancient peoples of the Scriptures? There is a long list of foods mentioned in the Bible. However, there are no recipes or actual meals described. The "promised land" is described as the land of milk and honey and, during biblical times, ordinary people did eat a largely vegetarian diet of fruits and vegetables, grains and nuts, along with dairy products. Meat was seldom consumed. Since there was no refrigeration, milk often was fermented and made into yogurt or a soft cheese that was salted and mixed with garlic, oil, vinegar, and herbs. Olive oil was used for cooking and as lamp oil. Melons, grapes, dates, figs, and pomegranates were favorite fruits. Millet, barley, and wheat are seeds of annual grasses native to Africa and the Middle East that have been cultivated since antiquity. They were ground on stones, a technique well developed in Egypt.

During their exodus through the desert, the Israelites probably depended on flat bread baked on primitive griddles. Buttermilk from goats and sheep was readily available, and added vegetables and spices probably made the flat bread more palatable. Guinea pepper, the berries of an African tree related to cardamom, might have been available. In addition, the manna mentioned in the Bible might have come from the tamarisk shrub found on the Sinai Peninsula, as well as in Iran and Saudi Arabia. Tamarisk exudes honey-like drops during June and July, which harden during the cold nights and can be collected. The Bible also mentions locusts as being kosher. The huge locust swarms that periodically devoured the Israelites' fields were gathered and roasted.

J-52. Millet Flat Bread

Ezekiel 4:9 gives this scant recipe-like description for making bread: "Take also unto thee wheat and barley and beans and lentils and millet and spelt and put them into one vessel and make bread of it." The following recipe uses millet to make flat bread.

Yield: 20 pieces

Equipment needed: Coffee grinder or food processor, bowl, whisk, griddle, ladle

Ingredients

2 cups millet
½ cup whole-wheat flour
1 cup buttermilk
½ teaspoon cumin, crushed

½ cup sesame seeds
2 tablespoons garlic, crushed
½ cup onions, chopped
Olive oil

Method

1. Grind millet seeds in coffee grinder or food processor.
2. Combine with whole-wheat flour.
3. Add remaining ingredients and let rest at room temperature for 2 hours.
4. Lightly oil griddle and cook flat bread.

J-53. Lentil Stew

Legumes such as fava beans and lentils provided the main meal for many families. People ate sitting on the ground on an animal skin or piece of leather. Bread was used for dipping and serving instead of spoons and forks, a custom that lasted until medieval times in Europe.

Yield: 4 servings
Equipment needed: 2-quart heavy soup pot

Ingredients

2 cups lentils
1 cup onions, chopped
1 tablespoon garlic
1 teaspoon salt

1 stick cinnamon, about 2 inches
1 teaspoon mustard seeds
6 cups water
1 cup yogurt

Method

1. Combine all ingredients except yogurt.
2. Bring to a boil and simmer until lentils are soft, about an hour.
3. Remove from heat and stir in yogurt.

🖋 BIBLIOGRAPHY

Boni, Ada. *Italian Regional Cooking* (New York: Bonanza Books, 1969).

Brennan, Jennifer. *The Original Thai Cookbook* (New York: Richard Marek Publishers, 1981).

Brissenden, Rosemary. *Joys and Subtleties: South East Asian Cooking* (New York: Pantheon Books, 1970).

Bugialli, Giuliano. *Classic Techniques of Italian Cooking* (New York: Simon and Schuster, 1982).

Burt, Elinor. *Far Eastern Cookery* (Boston: Little, Brown and Company, 1947).

de Andrade, Margarette. *Brazilian Cookery* (Rio de Janeiro: A Casa do Livro Eldorado, 1978).

Fieldhouse, Paul. *Food and Nutrition: Customs and Culture* (London: Chapman Hall, 1995).

Haase, Richard. *Jewish Regional Cooking* (London: Quarto Publishing, 1985).

Harris, Marvin. *Good to Eat* (New York: Simon and Schuster, 1985).

Het Nederlands Zuivelbureau. *Dutch Cooking Today* (Inmerc: Wormer, 2002).

Hom, Ken. *Asian Vegetable Feast* (New York: William Morrow and Company, 1988).

Jaffrey, Madhur. *Invitation to Indian Cooking* (New York: Alfred A. Knopf, 1973).

———. *World Vegetarian* (New York: Clarkson Potter, 1999).

Kennedy, Dianna. *The Cuisines of Mexico* (New York: Harper & Row Publishers, 1972).

Lang, George. *The Cuisine of Hungary* (New York: Bonanza Books, 1981).

Leonard, Leah W. *Jewish Cookery* (New York: Crown Publishers, 1949).

Liakhaovskaya, Lydia. *Russian Cuisine* (St. Petersburg, Russia: Art Publishers, 2000).

Lo, Kenneth. *The Encyclopedia of Chinese Cooking* (Glasgow: William Collins & Sons, 1979).

Makela, Eero. *New Flavors from Finland* (Helsinki: Otava Publishing, 1995).

Marks, Copeland, and Aung Thein. *Burmese Kitchen* (New York: M. Evans and Company, 1994).

Ortins, Ana Patuleia. *Portuguese Home Style Cooking* (Northampton: Interlink Books, 2001).

Ortiz, Elisabeth Lambert. *Caribbean Cookery* (New York: M. Evans and Company, 1973).

Palmer, R. R. *A History of the Modern World* (New York: Alfred A. Knopf, 1963).

Romanova, Julianna, and P. Benckco-Maras. *Slovenske' Jedlo and Pennsylvania Slovak Soul Food* (New York: Morris Publishers, 1995).

Rysia. *Old Warsaw Cookbook* (New York: Roy Publishers, 1958).

Sallum, Mary. *A Taste of Lebanon* (New York: Interlink Books, 1989).

Sawyer, Edwin A. *All about Moravians* (Bethlehem, PA: Moravian Church of America, 2000).

Schmidt, Arno. *Chef's Book of Formulas, Yields and Sizes* (New York: John Wiley & Sons, 2003).

Singh, Balbir. *Indian Cookery* (London: Mills & Boon, 1975).

Slater, Mary. *Caribbean Cooking for Pleasure* (London: Hamlyn, 1972).

Souli, Sofia. *Greek Cookery and Wines* (Karela: Michael Toubi's Publications, 1997).

Stechisin, Savella. *Traditional Ukrainian Cookery* (Winnipeg, Canada: Trident Press, 1982).

Tovey, John. *Table Talk with Tovey* (London: Macdonald & Co., 1981).

Waldo, Myra. *The Complete Round the World Cookbook* (New York: Greenwich House, 1973).

Woodward, Sarah. *The Ottoman Kitchen* (New York: Interlink Books, 2001).

INDEX

Abbacchio alla Romana (Roman-Style Easter Lamb), 83

Abgooshth (Lamb and Lentil Soup), 178

Advent, 36

Adzuki Beans and Rice with Sesame, 29

Agras, 170

Aji de Gallina (Chicken Chili), 84

Al Hijra, 155

Albania

  Kabourga (Stuffed Lamb Shoulder), 151

Algerian Roast Chicken with Sweet Stuffing, 165

All Saints Day, 92

Almond(s)

  Fillet of Perch with Almonds and Avocados, 197

  German Baked Apples Filled with Almonds (*Bratäpfel mit Mandeln*), 63

  Ice cream, 154

  Iranian Almond and Pistachio Loaf, 170

  Lamb in Almond Sauce (*Roghan Josh*), 180

  Lamb with Figs, Grapes, and Almonds, 151

  Mandelbrot, 199

  Milk (*Badam Phirni*), 124

  Rice dessert (*Badam Phirni*), 139

  Sephardic Charoset, 208

  Thandai (Spiced Milk Drink), 106

Aloo Posto (Potatoes with Poppy Seeds), 141

Aloo Pulao (Potatoes and Rice), 131

Amavas, 122

Amish. *See* Christianity, Protestantism

Amish Apple Tarts on Cabbage Leaves, 37

Amish Doughnuts (*Fastnacht*), 77

Anchovy

  Italian Christmas Salad (Insalata di Rinforzo), 51

Anise Star Cookies, 44

Appetizers and snacks

  Carciofi alla Giudea, 204

  Chopped Herring, 220

  Chopped Liver, 221

  Dill-Cured Salmon (*Gravad Lax*), 49

  Dried Dates, 21

  Fried Turnovers (*Gunjiya*), 110

  Frosted Grapes, 196

  Hot and Spicy Walnuts, 9

  Lebanese Meat Turnovers (*Sambousik*), 69

  Rasstegai with Fish, 71

  Samosas, 117

  Zucchini Flower Fritters, 203

  Zucchini Frittata, 227

Apples

  Amish Apple Tarts on Cabbage Leaves, 37

  Apple Walnut Cake, 73

  Ashkenazic Charoset, 207

  German Baked Apples Filled with Almonds (*Bratäpfel mit Mandeln*), 63

Apples *(continued)*
  Matzo Kugel with Apples, 228
  Pork Chops Baked with Apples and
    Sauerkraut, 72
Apple Walnut Cake, 73
Apricots
  Bosnian Apricot Soup, 172
Arjan Dev, 121
Arni Psito Sto Hart (Greek Roast Leg of
    Lamb in Paper), 86
Artichokes
  Carciofi alla Giudea, 204
Asalha Puja, 27
Ashkenazic Charoset, 207
Ashura, 159
Austria
  Kaiserschmarren (Emperor's Shredded
    Pancake), 79
  Kletzenbrot (Tyrolean Dried Fruit Bread),
    36
Avial (Vegetable Puree), 122
Avocado
  Fillet of Perch with Almonds and
    Avocados, 197
Azerbaijani Roasted Eggs, 211
Azores
  Sopa do Espírito Santo (Holy Spirit Soup),
    88

Baba Ghannooj (Smoked Eggplant Puree),
    149
Badam Phirni (Almond Milk), 124
Badam Phirni (Almond Rice Dessert), 139
Bagels, 223
Baked Goat and Rice (*Gosht Biryani*), 148
Baked Pears with Walnuts and Honey,
    229
Baked Virginia Ham, 55
Banana(s)
  Banana Fudge (*Kele Ka Halwa*), 131
  Butter-Broiled Bananas, 126
  Pineapple and Banana Dessert (*Cajeta de
    Piña y Plátano*), 43
Bandhakopir Dalna (Bengali Cabbage
    Curry), 133
Baptists. *See* Christianity, Protestantism
Bar (Bat) Mitzvah, 219
Barbecued Lamb Breast, 153
Barley Bread, 94
Barley with Mushrooms and Onions, 14
Basbousa (Semolina Cake), 175
Basic Soup Stock (*Dashi*), 5
Basmati Rice (*Chawal*), 103
Basmati Rice with Spices and Saffron
    (*Chawal Pullao*), 103

Bean and Goose Cholent (*Sólet*), 216
Beans. *See also* Lentils; Peas
  Adzuki Beans and Rice with Sesame, 29
  Bean and Goose Cholent (*Sólet*), 216
  Cholent, 215
  Egyptian Chickpea Fritters (*Falafel*), 178
  Fava Bean Fritters (*Taamiya*), 174
  Five-Jewel Creamed Legumes, 136
  Lima, in Vegetable Puree (*Avial*), 122
  Serbian Beans in Tomato Sauce, 40
  Vegetable Cutlets, 226
Beef
  Bean and Goose Cholent (*Sólet*), 216
  Beef Sukiyaki, 24
  Bulgarian Beef Soup with Meatballs
    (*Supa Topcheta*), 69
  Braised Brisket with Pomegranate, 192
  Cholent, 215
  Stuffed Cabbage (*Holishkes*), 196
  Unstuffed Cabbage, 197
Beef Sukiyaki, 24
Beet Horseradish, 208
Bengali Cabbage Curry (*Bandhakopir
    Dalna*), 133
Ben Zohor, 218
Benne Cookies, 168
Besan Flour Chapattis (*Papri*), 112
Besan ka Cheela (Chickpea Flour Pancakes),
    121
Besan Ke Ladoo (Diwali Ladoos), 140
Beverages
  Agras, 170
  Cumin Seed Cooler (*Jal Jeera*), 107
  Pomegranate Mint Tea, 159
  Spiced Milk Drink (*Thandai*), 106
Bil Pollo (Mayan Mexican Graveyard Pie),
    92
Blintzes, 213
Bodhi Day, 31
Bodhidarma Day, 29
Bosnia
  Bosnian Apricot Soup, 172
  Cherry Bread Pudding, 154
Braised Brisket with Pomegranate, 192
Bratäpfel mit Mandeln (German Baked
    Apples Filled with Almonds), 63
Brazilian Cashew and Guava Cake, 212
Brazilian Seafood Pie, 78
Breads and buns
  Bagels, 223
  Barley Bread, 94
  Besan Flour Chapattis (*Papri*), 112
  Challah, 214
  Day of the New Bread (*Kalács*), 90
  Fig and Date Bread, 169

Flat Bread (*paratha*), 105
Honey-Baked Shredded Dough (*Tel Kadayif*), 158
Mandelbrot, 199
Millet Flat Bread, 230
Monastery Bread, 13
Mormon Baptism Buns, 87
Punjab Fried Wheat Bread (*Poori* or *Puri*), 113
Russian Easter Cheese Bread *(Syrnyk)*, 85
Split Pea-Filled Griddle Breads (*Puranpoli*), 109
Syrian Flatbread, 169
Tunisian Terabilesi Bread, 156
Tyrolean Dried Fruit Bread (*Kletzenbrot*), 36
Breakfast Matzo Fritters, 207
Brith Millah, 219
Broiled Oysters, 48
Bûche de Noël (French Christmas Log), 60
Buddha Purnima. *See* Vesak
Buddhism
    Beliefs, 1
    Demographics, 2
    Dietary practices, 2–3
    History, 1–2
Buddhist Mindfulness Days, 9
Bulgarian Beef Soup with Meatballs (*Supa Topcheta*), 69
Burdock Pickle (*Tataki Gobo*), 7
Butter-Broiled Bananas, 126

Cabbage
    Bengali Cabbage Curry (*Bandhakopir Dalna*), 133
    Stuffed Cabbage *(Holishkes)*, 196
    Unstuffed Cabbage, 197
Cactus. *See* Mexican Cactus Salad
Cajeta de Piña y Plátano (Pineapple and Banana Dessert), 43
Cake. *See also* Desserts
    Apple Walnut Cake, 73
    Brazilian Cashew and Guava Cake, 212
    Eastern European Seed Cake, 212
    French Alsatian Easter Cake (*Gateau de Paque*), 84
    Greek Christmas Cake (*Vassilopitta*), 66
    Honey Cake, 219
    Norwegian Christmas Cake (*Julakaka*), 64
    Semolina Cake (*Basbousa*), 175
    Three Kings Sweet Bread *(Roscón de Reyes)*, 67
Caldo de Pollo (Mexican Chicken Broth), 42
Caldo Tlalpeño (Mexican Chicken and Vegetable Soup), 41

Canada
    French Canadian Pork Pie (*Tourtière*), 55
Candy and Sweets
    Candy Crisps (*Zuckerstangen*), 38
    Dried Nut Toffee (*Gajjac*), 115
    Hais, 186
    Sesame Halwa, 138
    Sweets (*Pedhas*), 118
Carciofi alla Giudea, 204
Carribean
    Barbecued Lamb Breast, 153
Caribbean Black-Eyed Peas (*Urhad Dal Sabat*), 138
Caribbean Lamb Curry with Pecans, 112
Carrot Halwa, 125
Carrots
    Carrot and Prunes Tzimes, 193
    Carrot Halwa, 125
    Pickled Daikon, Cucumber, and Carrot, 6
    Pineapple Carrot Soufflé, 210
Carrots and Prunes Tzimes, 193
Cashew(s)
    Brazilian Cashew and Guava Cake, 212
Catholicism. *See* Christianity
Cauliflower with Ginger and Cilantro (*Dum Gobi*), 101
Cerkez Tavuğu (Chicken in Nut Sauce), 176
Chaamp Masala (Lamb Masala), 119
Challah, 214
Chana Masaledar (Chickpea Dal), 134
Channa Masaleda (Spiced Chickpeas), 106
Chard and Lentil Soup, 163
Chawal (Basmati Rice), 103
Chawal Pullao (Basmati Rice with Spices and Saffron), 103
Cheese
    Blintzes, 213
    Cottage Cheese and Fruit Dessert, 127
    Greek Cheese Pie (*Tiropitta*), 76
    Peas with Farmer Cheese *(Mattar Paneer)*, 120
    Ricotta Dessert (*Roshogolla Rasgulla*), 139
    Rugelach, 199
    Russian Easter Cheese Bread *(Syrnyk)*, 85
    Sephardic Leek and Feta Fritters, 225
    Spanish Fried Cheese (*Queso Frito*), 78
Cherry Bread Pudding, 154
Chicken
    Algerian Roast Chicken with Sweet Stuffing, 165
    Chicken and Date Patties, 191
    Chicken Chili (*Aji de Gallina*), 84
    Chicken Curry with Tomatoes (*Murgha Kari*), 123

Chicken *(continued)*
   Chicken Dilruba, 133
   Chicken in Foil, 125
   Chicken in Nut Sauce (*Cerkez Tavuğu*), 176
   Chicken Legs with Kumquats, 201
   Garam-Spiced Chicken Strips, 104
   Iranian Lemon Chicken with Roasted Garlic (*Tahsreeb Dijaj*), 180
   Lemon Chicken, 157
   Mexican Chicken and Vegetable Soup (*Caldo Tlalpeño*), 41
   Stuffed Chicken, 209
   Tandoori Baked Chicken (*Tandoori Murgha*), 110
Chicken and Date Patties, 191
Chicken Chili (*Aji de Gallina*), 84
Chicken Curry with Tomatoes (*Murgha Kari*), 123
Chicken Dilruba, 133
Chicken in Foil, 125
Chicken in Nut Sauce (*Cerkez Tavuğu*), 176
Chicken Legs with Kumquats, 201
Chickpea Dal (*Chana Masaledar*), 134
Chickpea Dip (*Nahit*), 209
Chickpea Flour Pancakes (*Besan ka Cheela*), 121
Chickpea Soup (*Karhi*), 101
Chilled Buckwheat Noodles (*Toshikoshi Soba*), 8
China
   Aromatic Fried Rice, 30
   Crispy Duck Breast with Vegetables, 16
   Dumpling Dipping Sauce, 17
   Jao Tze (Steamed Dumpling), 17
   Nnian Gao (Eight Precious Pudding), 18
   Rice Soup, 15
   Stir-Fried Shrimp with Jasmine Tea Leaves, 31
Chinese Aromatic Fried Rice, 30
Chinese New Year, 14
Chocolate Icing, 61
Cholent, 215
Chopped Herring, 220
Chopped Liver, 221
Christianity
   Beliefs, 33
   Catholicism, 34
   Dietary practices, 35–36
   Food traditions, 33–36
   History, 33
   Orthodoxy, 35
   Protestantism, 34–35
Christmas Day, 48
Christmas Eve, 45

Christmas, Orthodox, 69
Christmas Sauerkraut Soup (*Kapustnica*), 52
Church of Jesus Christ of Latter-Day Saints, The. *See* Christianity, Protestantism
Coconut
   Coconut Rice (*Kheer Ade*), 129
   Malaysian Chicken in Coconut Cream (*Rendan Santan*), 166
   Malaysian Coconut, Tapioca, and Melon Soup, 23
   Rainbow Rice Dessert, 181
Collard Greens (*Haak*), 143
Cookies
   Anise Star Cookies, 44
   Benne Cookies, 168
   German Gingerbread (*Lebkuchen*), 39
   Hamantaschen, 205
   Honey Cakes (*Petruska*), 72
   Moravian Christmas Cookies, 65
   Rugelach, 199
   Santa Claus Almond Cookies, 40
   Spanish Honey Cakes (*Galletas de Miel*), 89
   Spanish Shortcakes (*Polverones Navideña*), 47
Conversion of St. Paul, 74
Corpus Christi, 88
Cottage Cheese and Fruit Dessert, 127
Crisp Cornmeal Waffles, 214
Crispy Duck Breast with Vegetables, 16
Cucumber
   Pickled Daikon, Cucumber, and Carrot, 6
   Stir-Fried Scallops with Chicken, Mushrooms, and Cucumbers, 179
Cumin Seed Cooler (*Jal Jeera*), 107
Curry
   Bengali Cabbage Curry (*Bandhakopir Dalna*), 133
   Caribbean Lamb Curry with Pecans, 112
   Chicken Curry with Tomatoes (*Murgha Kari*), 123
   Lamb Curry (*Lamb Korma*), 152
   Sweet Pumpkin Curry (*Kaddu Ki Sabzi*), 132
Czech Bread Dumplings (*Knedliki*), 57
Czech Republic
   Knedliki (Czech Bread Dumplings), 57
   Moravian Christmas Cookies, 65
   Moravian Clear Beef Soup with Cream of Wheat Dumplings, 74
   Powidltascherln, 217

Dairy dishes: in kosher cookery, 224
Dal Shorba (Green and Red Lentil Soup), 114
Dashi (Basic Soup Stock), 5

Date Nut Loaf, 198
Dates
    Ashkenazic Charoset, 207
    Chicken and Date Patties, 191
    Chinese, red, in dumplings, 27
    Date Nut Loaf, 198
    Date Sweetmeat (Holwar Tamar), 167
    Dried Dates, 21
    English Steamed Date and Fig Pudding, 62
    Fig and Date Bread, 169
    Fruit Refreshment, 186
    Hais, 186
    Red seedless, in rice soup, 15
    Sephardic Charoset, 208
    Stuffed Dates, 95
Date Sweetmeat (Holwar Tamar), 167
Day of the New Bread (Kalács), 90
Death Day of George Fox, 73
Denmark. See Scandinavia
Dessert Dumplings (Modakas), 129
Desserts and Puddings. See also Fritters; Pancakes
    Almond Ice Cream, 154
    Almond Milk (Badam Phirni), 124
    Almond Rice Dessert (Badam Phirni), 139
    Baked Pears with Walnuts and Honey, 229
    Banana Fudge (Kele Ka Halwa), 131
    Butter-Broiled Bananas, 126
    Carrot Halwa, 125
    Cherry Bread Pudding, 154
    Cottage Cheese and Fruit Dessert, 127
    Dessert Dumplings (Modakas), 129
    Diwali Ladoos (Besan Ke Ladoo), 140
    Eight Precious Pudding (Nian Gao), 18
    English Steamed Date and Fig Pudding, 62
    French Christmas Log (Bûche de Noël), 60
    Frozen Milk (Kulfi), 135
    Gingerbread Pudding, 62
    Iranian Almond and Pistachio Loaf, 170
    Lemon Curd, 63
    Malaysian Rice Flour Dessert 184
    Matzo Kugel with Apples, 228
    Mawa Ladoos, 141
    New Year Sweet Potato Balls (Kuri Kinton), 8
    Pineapple and Banana Dessert (Cajeta de piña y Plátano), 43
    Quince Sorbet, 182
    Rainbow Rice Dessert, 181
    Ricotta Dessert (Roshogolla Rasgulla), 139
    Sweet Cardamom Rice (Sevaiyya Kheer), 171

Sweet Vermicelli Pudding (Seviyan/Savia/Sewian), 153
Sweetened Semolina (Kahara Prasad), 142
Dia de Senora Nuestra de Guadelupe, 41
Dietary practices. See individual religions
Dill-Cured Salmon (Gravad Lax), 49
Dips and spreads
    Chickpea Dip (Nahit), 209
    Egyptian Mazza Dip, 177
    Fish Roe Dip (Tarama), 150
    Hilbeh Dip, 177
    Scandinavian Liver Spread (Leverpastej), 49
    Smoked Eggplant Puree (Baba Ghannooj), 149
Diwali, 136
Diwali Ladoos (Besan Ke Ladoo), 140
Dom Yam Gung (Hot and Sour Shrimp Soup), 28
Doughnuts
    Amish Doughnuts (Fastnacht), 77
    Sufganiyot, 200
Dragon Boat Celebration, 26
Draniki (Potato Fritters), 80
Dresi (Sweet Saffron Rice), 12
Dried Dates, 21
Dried fruit
    Kletzenbrot (Tyrolean Dried Fruit Bread), 36
Dried Nut Toffee (Gajjac), 115
Drinks. See Beverages
Droma (Rice and Potato Stew), 11
Duck
    Crispy Duck Breast with Vegetables, 16
Dum Alu (Potato Stew), 19
Dum Gobi (Cauliflower with Ginger and Cilantro), 101
Dumpling Dipping Sauce, 17
Dumplings
    Cream of Wheat, 75
    Czech Bread Dumplings (Knedliki), 57
    Dessert Dumplings (Modakas), 129
    Gefilte Fish, 220
    Powidltascherln, 217
    Steamed Dumpling (Jao Tze), 17
    Stuffed Kishke or Derma, 202
    Tibetan New Year's Eve Soup with Dumplings (Guthuk), 10
    Ukrainian Dumplings with Sour Cream (Varenyky), 45
    Zongzi, 27
Dussehra, 133

Easter, 80–86
Eastern European Seed Cake, 212
Eggplant
    Lamb and Eggplant Matzo Pie, 223
    Smoked Eggplant Puree (*Baba Ghannooj*),
        149
Eggs
    Azerbaijani Roasted Eggs, 211
    Matzo Brei, 224
    Matzo Omelet, 226
    Meringue, 61
    Ukrainian Easter Eggs, 81
Egypt. *See also* North Africa
    Falafel (Egyptian Chickpea Fritters), 178
    Fig and Date Bread, 169
    Basbousa (Semolina Cake), 175
    Mazza Dip, 177
Egyptian Chickpea Fritters (*Falafel*), 178
Egyptian Mazza Dip, 177
Eid-al-Adha, 147
Eid-al-Fitr, 177
Eight Precious Pudding (*Nian Gao*), 18
Elizabethan Venison with Fennel, 56
Emperor's Shredded Pancake
        (*Kaiserschmarren*), 79
England
    Elizabethan Venison with Fennel, 56
    English Steamed Date and Fig Pudding,
        62
Ensalada de Nopales (Mexican Cactus
        Salad), 50
Epiphany, 67
Episcopalian church. *See* Christianity,
        Protestantism

Falafel (Egyptian Chickpea Fritters), 178
Farfel, 195
Fastnacht (Amish Doughnuts), 77
Fava Bean Fritters (*Taamiya*), 174
Feast of San Gennero, 91
Festivals and celebrations
    Advent, 36
    Al Hijra, 155
    All Saints Day, 92
    Amavas, 122
    Arjan Dev, 121
    Asalha Puja, 27
    Ashura, 159
    Bodhi Day, 31
    Bodhidarma Day, 29
    Buddhist Mindfulness Days, 9
    Chinese New Year, 14
    Christmas Day, 48
    Christmas Eve, 45
    Christmas, Orthodox, 69

Conversion of St. Paul, 74
Corpus Christi, 88
Death Day of George Fox, 73
Dia de Senora Nuestra de Guadelupe, 41
Diwali, 136
Dragon Boat Celebration, 26
Dussehra, 133
Easter, 80–86
Eid-al-Adha, 147
Eid-al-Fitr, 177
Epiphany, 67
Feast of San Gennero, 91
Ganesha Chaturti, 127
Guru Nanek Dev, 141
Guru Purnima, 123
Gutor, 10
Hanamatsuri, 24
Hanukkah, 200
Holi, 108
Installation of the Guru Granth Sahib,
    131
Janmashtami, 124
Karva Chauth, 135
Las Posadas, 42
Lent, 76
Losar, 11
Maha Shivarati, 106
Maka Puja, 20
Maka Sankranti, 100
Mawlid-al-Nabi, 162
Monlam, 13
Moravian Unitas Fratrum, 74
Navrati, 132
Nirvana Day, 18
Onam, 125
Passover, 205
Pentecost, 87
Pooram, 121
Purim, 204
Raksha Bandhan, 126
Ramadan, 167
Rosh Hashanah, 191
St. Basil's Day, 66
St. James Day, 89
St. Nicholas' Day, 39
St. Stephens' Day, 90
Shab-E-Barat, 162
Shavuot, 213
Shogatsu (Japanese New Year's Festival),
    3
Sikh New Year, 113
Sikh Vaisakhi, 119
Songkran, 20
Submersion of the Holy Cross, 68
Sukkot, 195

Thai Raek Na, 26
Tu Bishvat, 203
Vaisakhi, 115
Vara Lakshmi, 130
Vasant Panchami, 103
Vasanta, 115
Vesak, 25
Yom Kippur, 194
Fig and Date Bread, 169
Figs
    Fig and Date Bread, 169
    English Steamed Date and Fig Pudding,
        62
    Hais, 186
    Lamb with Figs, Grapes and Almonds,
        151
Fillet of Perch with Almonds and
        Avocados, 197
Fish
    Brazilian Seafood Pie, 78
    Chopped Herring, 220
    Dill-Cured Salmon (*Gravad Lax*), 49
    Fillet of Perch with Almonds and
        Avocados, 197
    Gefilte Fish, 220
    Iranian Fruit Rice with Fish, 166
    Polish Sweet Sour Carp, 46
    Rasstegai with Fish, 71
    Scandinavian Poached Preserved Cod
        (*Lutfisk*), 59
    Sea Bass in Green Chutney, 127
    Stewed Fish over Rice and Noodles, 164
Fish Roe Dip (*Tarama*), 150
Five-Jewel Creamed Legumes, 136
Flat Bread (*Paratha*), 105
France
    Bûche de Noël (French Christmas Log), 60
    Gateau de Paque (French Alsatian Easter
        Cake), 84
    Pot au feu (French Hearty Soup), 53
French Alsatian Easter Cake (*Gateau de
        Paque*), 84
French-Canadian Pork Pie (*Tourtière*), 55
French Christmas Log (*Bûche de Noël*), 60
French Hearty Soup (*Pot au Feu*), 53
Fried Turnovers (*Gunjiya*), 110
Fritters. *See also* Desserts; Pancakes
    Breakfast Matzo Fritters, 207
    Fava Bean Fritters (*Taamiya*), 174
    Kapse Fritters, 12
    Sephardim Leek and Feta Fritters, 225
    Sfingi Fritters, 91
    Sweet Fritters (*Malpuas*), 111
    Zucchini Flower Fritters, 203
    Zucchini Frittata, 227

Fritters in Syrup (*Gulab Jamin*), 162
Frosted Grapes, 196
Frozen Milk (*Kulfi*), 135
Fruit and Mint Chutney (*Podina Chutney*),
    116
Fruit Refreshment, 186

Gaeng Chud No Ma Thai (Pork and Bamboo
    Shoot Soup), 21
Gajjac (Dried Nut Toffee), 115
Galletas de Miel (Spanish Honey Cakes), 89
Ganesha Chaturti, 127
Garam Masala (Punjabi Mixed Spice), 119
Garam Spiced Chicken Strips, 104
Gateau de Paque (French Alsatian Easter
    Cake), 84
Gefilte Fish, 220
German Baked Apples Filled with Almonds
    (*Bratäpfel mit Mandeln*), 63
German Gingerbread (*Lebkuchen*), 39
Germany
    Anise Star Cookies, 44
    Bratäpfel mit Mandeln (German Baked
        Apples Filled with Almonds), 63
    Lebkuchen (German Gingerbread), 39
    Mandelbrot, 199
    Zuckerstangen (Candy Crisps), 38
Ginger snaps
    Hais, 186
Gingerbread Pudding, 62
Goat
    Baked Goat and Rice (*Gosht Biryani*),
        148
Goose
    Bean and Goose Cholent (*Sólet*), 216
Gosht Biryani (Baked Goat and Rice), 148
Grapes
    Frosted Grapes, 196
    Lamb with Figs, Grapes, and Almonds,
        151
Gravad Lax (Dill-Cured Salmon), 49
Gravlaxsås (Mustard and Dill Sauce), 50
Greece
    Arni Psito Sto Hart (Greek Roast Leg of
        Lamb in Paper), 86
    Tiropitta (Greek Cheese Pie), 76
    Vassilopitta (Greek Christmas Cake), 66
    Zalatina (Greek Pork in Lemon and
        Vinegar Jelly), 68
Greek Cheese Pie (*Tiropitta*), 76
Greek Christmas Cake (*Vassilopitta*), 66
Greek Pork in Lemon and Vinegar Jelly
    (*Zalatina*), 68
Greek Roast Leg of Lamb in Paper (*Arni
    Psito Sto Hart*), 86

Green and Red Lentil Soup (*Dal Shorba*), 114

Green Mint and Cilantro Chutney (*Podina Dhania Ki*), 128

Guava
Brazilian Cashew and Guava Cake, 212

Gulab Jamin (Fritters in Syrup), 162

Gunjiya (Fried Turnovers), 110

Guru Nanek Dev, 141

Guru Purnima, 123

Guthuk (Tibetan New Year's Eve Soup with Dumplings), 10

Gutor (Day before Tibetan New Year's Eve), 10

Haak (Collard Greens), 143

Hais, 186

Halal. *See* Islam, dietary practices

Ham
Baked Virginia Ham, 55

Hamantaschen, 205

Hanamatsuri, 24

Hanukkah, 200

Haram. *See* Islam, dietary practices

Harira (Moroccan Lentil Soup), 173

Hazlenuts
Chicken in Nut Sauce (*Cerkez Tavuğu*), 176

Hilbeh Dip, 177

Hinduism
Beliefs, 97–98
Demographics, 98
Dietary practices, 98–99
History, 97–98

Holi, 108

Holishkes (Stuffed Cabbage), 196

Holland
Santa Claus Almond Cookies, 40

Holwar Tamar (Date Sweetmeat), 167

Holy Spirit Soup (*Sopa do Espírito Santo*), 88

Honey Baked Shredded Dough (*Tel Kadayif*), 158

Honey Cake, 219

Honey Cakes (*Petruska*), 72

Hot and Sour Shrimp Soup (*Dom Yam Gung*), 28

Hot and Spicy Walnuts, 9

Hungarian Stuffed Kohlrabi (*Töltött Kalarábá*), 58

Hungary
Kalács (Day of the New Bread), 90
Sólet (Bean and Goose Cholent), 216
Töltött kalarábá (Hungarian Stuffed Kohlrabi), 58

İç Pilâl (Turkish Spiced Liver Rice), 175

Iftar. *See* Ramadan

Imli Ke Chutney (Tamarind Sauce), 135

India
Aloo Posto (Potatoes with Poppy Seeds), 141
Aloo Pulao (Potatoes and Rice), 131
Avial (Vegetable Puree), 122
Badam Phirni (Almond Milk), 124
Bandhakopir Dalna (Bengali Cabbage Curry), 133
Besan ka Cheela (chickpea flour pancakes), 121
Besan Ke Ladoo (Diwali Ladoos), 140
Carrot Halwa, 125
Chaamp Masala (Lamb Masala), 119
Chana Masaledar (Chickpea Dal), 134
Channa Masaledar (Spiced Chickpeas), 106
Chawal (Basmati Rice), 103
Chawal Pullao (Basmati Rice with Spices and Saffron), 103
Chicken Dilruba, 133
Chicken in Foil, 125
Cottage Cheese and Fruit Dessert, 127
Dal Shorba (Green and Red Lentil Soup), 114
Dum Alu (Potato Stew), 19
Dum Gobi (Cauliflower with Ginger and Cilantro), 101
Five-Jewel Creamed Legumes, 136
Gajjac (Dried Nut Toffee), 115
Garam Masala (Punjabi Mixed Spice), 119
Garam-Spiced Chicken Strips, 104
Gosht Biryani (Baked Goat and Rice), 148
Gulab Jamin (Fritters in Syrup), 162
Gunjiya (Fried Turnovers), 110
Haak (Collard Greens), 143
Imli Ke chutney (Tamarind Sauce), 135
Jal Jeera (Cumin Seed Cooler), 107
Kaddu Ki Sabzi (Sweet Pumpkin Curry), 132
Kahara Prasad (Sweetened Semolina), 142
Karhi (Chickpea Soup), 101
Kheer Ade (Coconut Rice), 129
Kulfi (Frozen Milk), 135
Lamb Korma (Lamb Curry*)*, 152
Malpuas (Sweet Fritters), 111
Malupa (Indian pancakes), 20
Mampazhapachadi (Sour Mango Soup), 116
Masur Dal (Stewed Lentils), 108, 122

Mattar Paneer (Peas with Farmer Cheese), 120

Mawa Ladoos, 141

Modakas (Dessert Dumplings), 129

Papri (Besan Flour Chapattis), 112

Paratha (Flat Bread), 105

Pedhas (Sweets), 118

Podina (Chutney Fruit and Mint Chutney), 116

Podina Dhania Ki (Green Mint and Cilantro Chutney), 128

Poori or *puri* (Punjab Fried Wheat Bread), 113

Potali (Steamed Rice in Banana Leaves), 130

Potato Stew with Asafetida, 29

Puranpoli (Split Pea-Filled Griddle Breads), 109

Samosas, 117

Sarkkarai Pongal (Saffron Rice Cooked in Milk), 100

Sea Bass in Green Chutney, 127

Sweet Tomato Chutney, 107

Tandoori Murgha (Tandoori Baked Chicken), 110

Thandai (Spiced Milk Drink), 106

Indonesia

   Sambal Goreng Undang (Indonesian Spiced Shrimp), 157

Indonesian Spiced Shrimp (*Sambal Goreng Undang*), 157

Installation of the Guru Granth Sahib, 131

Insalata di Rinforzo (Italian Christmas Salad), 51

Iran

   Amond and Pistachio Loaf, 170

   Fruit Rice with Fish, 166

   Tahsreeb Dijaj (Iranian Lemon Chicken with Roasted Garlic), 180

Iranian Almond and Pistachio Loaf, 170

Iranian Fruit Rice with Fish, 166

Iranian Lemon Chicken with Roasted Garlic (*Tahsreeb Dijaj*), 180

Iraq

   Moujadara (Lentils with Rice), 160

   Persian Lamb Stew, 160

   Persian Sweet Rice (*Shekar Polo*), 161

Islam

   Beliefs, 145–46

   Demographics, 146

   Dietary practices, 146–47

   History, 145

Israel

   Breakfast matzo fritters, 207

   Challah, 214

   Chicken and Date Patties, 191

   Cholent, 215

   Date Nut Loaf, 198

   Lamb and Eggplant Matzo Pie, 223

   Matzo Kugel with Apples, 228

   Matzo Omelet, 226

   Zucchini Flower Fritters, 203

Italian Christmas Salad (*Insalata di Rinforzo*), 51

Italy

   Abbacchio alla Romana (Roman-Style Easter Lamb), 83

   Carciofi alla Giudea, 204

   Insalata di Rinforzo (Italian Christmas Salad), 51

   Risi e Bisi (Venetian Rice and Peas), 82

   Sfingi Fritters, 91

Jal Jeera (Cumin Seed Cooler), 107

Janmashtami, 124

Jao Tze (Steamed Dumpling), 17

Japan

   Adzuki Beans and Rice with Sesame, 29

   Beef Sukiyaki, 24

   Dashi (Basic Soup Stock), 5

   Kanot-Style New Year's Day Soup, 6

   Kuri Kinton (New Year Sweet Potato Balls), 8

   Omochi (Pounded Rice Cakes), 4

   O-zoni (New Year's Day Soup), 5

   Pickled Daikon, Cucumber, and Carrot, 6

   Tataki Gobo (Burdock Pickle), 7

   Toshikoshi Soba (Chilled Buckwheat Noodles), 8

   Udon miso, 19

Judaism

   Beliefs, 189

   Demographics, 190

   Dietary practices, 190–91

   History, 189

Julakaka (Norwegian Christmas Cake), 64

Kabourga (Stuffed Lamb Shoulder), 151

Kaddu Ki Sabzi (Sweet Pumpkin Curry), 132

Kahara Prasad (Sweetened Semolina), 142

Kaiserschmarren (Emperor's Shredded Pancake), 79

Kalács (Day of the New Bread), 90

Kanot-Style New Year's Day Soup, 6

Kapse Fritters, 12

Kapustnica (Christmas Sauerkraut Soup), 52

Karhi (Chickpea Soup), 101

Karva Chauth, 135
Kasha Varnitchekes, 194
Kele Ka Halwa (Banana Fudge), 131
Kheer (Rice Cooked in Milk), 25
Kheer Ade (Coconut Rice), 129
Kletzenbrot (Tyrolean Dried Fruit Bread), 36
Knedliki (Czech Bread Dumplings), 57
Kohlrabi
    Hungarian Stuffed Kohlrabi (*Töltött Kalarábá*), 58
Kosher. *See* Judaism, dietary practices
Kulfi (Frozen Milk), 135
Kumquats
    Chicken Legs with Kumquats, 201
    New Year Sweet Potato Balls (*Kuri Kinton*), 8
Kuri Kinton (New Year Sweet Potato Balls), 8

Lââssida (Semolina Cooked in Water), 163
Lamb
    Barbecued Lamb Breast, 153
    Caribbean Lamb Curry with Pecans, 112
    Chard and Lentil Soup, 163
    Greek Roast Leg of Lamb In Paper (*Arni Psito Sto Hart*), 86
    Lamb and Eggplant Matzo Pie, 223
    Lamb and Lentil Soup (*Abgooshth*), 178
    Lamb Curry (*Lamb Korma*), 152
    Lamb in Almond Sauce (*Roghan Josh*), 180
    Lamb in Sour Mango Soup (*Mampazhapachadi*), 116
    Lamb with Figs, Grapes and Almonds, 151
    Lebanese Meat Turnovers (*Sambousik*), 69
    Malaysian Roast Lamb, 156
    Masala (*Chaamp Masala*), 119
    Moroccan Lentil Soup (*Harira*), 173
    Persian lamb Stew, 160
    Roman-Style Easter Lamb (*Abbacchio alla Romana*), 83
    Stuffed Lamb Shoulder (*Kabourga*), 151
    Sweet Lamb Stew (*Mrouzia Tajine*), 149
Lamb and Eggplant Matzo Pie, 223
Lamb and Lentil Soup (*Abgooshth*), 178
Lamb Curry (*Lamb Korma*), 152
Lamb in Almond Sauce (*Roghan Josh*), 180
Lamb *Korma* (Lamb Curry), 152
Lamb Masala (*Chaamp Masala*), 119
Lamb with Figs, Grapes and Almonds, 151
Laotian Papaya Salad, 74
Las Posadas, 42
Lebanese Meat Turnovers (*Sambousik*), 69

Lebkuchen (German Gingerbread), 39
Leeks
    Sephardim Leek and Feta Fritters, 225
Lemon
    Carciofi alla Giudea, 204
    Iranian Lemon Chicken with Roasted Garlic (*Tahsreeb Dijaj*), 180
    Lemon chicken, 157
    Lemon Curd, 63
Lemon Chicken, 157
Lemongrass
    Hot and sour Shrimp Soup (*Dom Yam Gung*), 28
    Myanmar Tomato Soup with Lemongrass, 22
Lent, 76
Lentils. *See also* Beans; Peas
    Chard and Lentil Soup, 163
    Green and Red Lentil Soup (*Dal Shorba*), 114
    Lamb and Lentil Soup (*Abgooshth*), 178
    Moroccan Lentil Soup (*Harira*), 173
    Stewed Lentils (*Masur Dal*), 108, 122
    Lentils with Rice (*Moujadara*), 160
Lentil Stew (*Masoor Dal*), 122
Lentil Stew, 231
Lentils with Rice (*Moujadara*), 160
Leverpastej (Scandinavian Liver Spread), 49
Libya. *See also* North Africa
    Hilbeh dip, 177
Liver
    Chopped Liver, 221
    Turkish Spiced Liver Rice (*Iç Pilâl*), 174
Lokschen Noodle Kugel, 227
Losar, 11
Lotus
    Lotus seeds, in rice soup, 15
    Lotus Spiced Rice with Lotus Root and Mango, 32
Louisiana Gumbo with Sassafras, 53
Lutfisk (Scandinavian Poached Preserved Cod), 59
Lutherans. *See* Christianity, Protestantism

Maha Shivarati, 106
Maka Puja, 20
Maka Sankranti, 100
Malaysian Chicken in Coconut Cream (*Rendan Santan*), 166
Malaysian Coconut, Tapioca, and Melon Soup, 23
Malaysian Rice Flour Dessert, 184
Malaysian Roast Lamb, 156
Malpuas (Sweet Fritters), 111

Malupa (Indian Pancakes), 20
Mampazhapachadi (Sour Mango Soup), 116
Mandelbrot, 199
Mango
  Sour Mango Soup (*Mampazhapachadi*), 116
  Spiced Rice with Lotus Root and Mango, 32
Masoor Dal (Lentil Stew), 122
Masur Dal (Stewed Lentils), 108
Mattar Paneer (Peas with Farmer Cheese), 120
Matzo, 206
  Breakfast Fritters, 207
  Lamb andie, 223
Matzo Brei, 224
Matzo Kugel with Apples, 228
Matzo Omelet, 226
Mawa Ladoos, 141
Mawlid-al-Nabi, 162
Mayan Mexican Graveyard Pie (*Bil Pollo*), 92
Melon
  Fruit Refreshment, 186
  Malaysian Coconut, Tapioca, and Melon Soup, 23
Mennonites. *See* Christianity, Protestantism
Meringue, 61
Methodists. *See* Christianity, Protestantism
Mexican Cactus Salad (*Ensalada de Nopales*), 51
Mexican Chicken and Vegetable Soup (*Caldo Tlalpeño*), 41
Mexican Chicken Broth (*Caldo de Pollo*), 42
Mexican Pork Soup (*Pozole*), 42
Mexican Squash Flower Soup (*Sopa de Flor de Calabacita*), 81
Mexico
  Bil Pollo (Mayan Mexican Graveyard Pie), 92
  Cajeta de Piña y Plátano (Pineapple and Banana Dessert), 43
  Caldo de Pollo (Mexican Chicken Broth), 42
  Caldo Tlalpeño (Mexican Chicken and Vegetable Soup), 41
  Ensalada de Nopales (Mexican Cactus Salad), 50
  Sopa de Flor de Calabacita (Mexican Squash Flower Soup), 81
Millet Flat Bread, 230
Millet Pancakes, 159
Millet Porridge, 155
Mint
  Agras, 170
  Fruit refreshment, 186

Modakas (Dessert Dumplings), 129
Monastery Bread, 13
Monlam, 13
Moravian Christmas Cookies, 65
Moravian Church. *See* Christianity, Protestantism
Moravian Clear Beef Soup with Cream of Wheat Dumplings, 74
Moravian Unitas Fratrum, 74
Mormon Baptism Buns, 87
Mormons. *See* Christianity, Protestantism
Morocco. *See also* North Africa
  Harira (Moroccan Lentil Soup), 173
  Lââssida (Semolina Cooked in Water), 163
  Lamb and Eggplant Matzo Pie, 223
  Mrouzia Tajine (Sweet Lamb Stew), 149
Moroccan Lentil Soup *(Harira)*, 173
Moujadara (Lentils with Rice), 160
Mrouzia Tajine (Sweet Lamb Stew), 149
Mushbooh. *See* Islam, dietary practices
Mushrooms
  Stir-fried Scallops with Chicken, Mushrooms, And Cucumbers, 179
  Stuffed Chicken, 209
Mustard and Dill Sauce (*Gravlaxsås*), 50
Myanmar Tomato Soup with Lemongrass, 22

Nahit (Chickpea Dip), 209
Nahit with Rice, 218
Navrati, 132
New Year Sweet Potato Balls (*Kuri Kinton*), 8
New Year's Day Soup (*O-zoni*), 5
Nian Gao (*Eight Precious Pudding*), 18
Nirvana Day, 18
Noodles
  Chilled Buckwheat Noodles (*Toshikoshi Soba*), 8
  Farfel, 195
  Kasha Varnitchekes, 194
  Lokschen Noodle Kugel, 227
  Stewed Fish over Rice and Noodles, 164
  Sweet Vermicelli Pudding (*Seviyan/Savia/ Sewian*), 153
  Udon Miso, 19
North Africa. *See also* Egypt; Libya; Morocco
  Millet Pancakes, 159
  Millet Porridge, 155
  Sephardic Leek and Feta Fritters, 225
Norway. *See* Scandinavia
Norwegian Christmas Cake (*Julakaka*), 64
Nuts. *See* individual nuts

Okra
  Oxtail and Okra Soup, 172
Olives
  Tunisian Terabilesi Bread, 156
Oman
  Taamiya (Fava Bean Fritters), 174
Omochi (Pounded Rice Cakes), 4
Onam, 125
Oranges
  Scallops with Anise and Oranges, 89
Orthodox Christmas, 69
Orthodoxy. *See* Christianity, Orthodox
Oxtail and Okra Soup, 172
O-zoni (New Year's Day Soup), 5

Pakistan
  Abgooshth (Lamb and Lentil Soup), 178
Pancakes. *See also* Desserts; Fritters
  Blintzes, 213
  Chickpea Flour Pancakes *(Besan Ka
    Cheela)*, 121
  Emperor's Shredded Pancake
    (Kaiserschmarren), 79
  Indian Pancakes *(Malupa)*, 20
  Millet Pancakes, 159
  Potato Latkes, 202
Papaya
  Laotian Papaya Salad, 74
Papri (Besan Flour Chapattis), 112
Paratha (Flat Bread), 105
Parinirvana. See Nirvana Day
Parve. *See* Judaism, dietary practices
Passover, 205
Pastries and tarts
  Amish Apple Tarts on Cabbage Leaves, 37
  Shiebiat Pastry, 184
Peach Condiment, 183
Peanut Stew, 175
Peas. *See also* Beans; Lentils
  Caribbean Black-Eyed Peas *(Urhad Dal
    Sabat)*, 138
  Chickpea Dal *(Chana Masaledar)*, 134
  Chickpea Dip *(Nahit)*, 209
  Egyptian Chickpea Fritters *(Falafel)*, 178
  Nahit with Rice, 218
  Peas with Farmer Cheese *(Mattar Paneer)*,
    120
  Spiced Chickpeas *(Channa Masaledar)*,
    106
  Split-Pea Filled Griddle Breads
    (Puranpoli), 109
  Vegetable Cutlets, 226
  Venetian Rice And Peas *(Risi e Bisi)*, 82
Peas with Farmer Cheese *(Mattar Paneer)*,
  120

Pears
  Baked Pears with Walnuts and Honey,
    229
Pecans
  Caribbean Lamb Curry with Pecans, 112
Pedhas (Sweets), 118
Pentecost, 87
Persian Lamb Stew, 160
Persian Sweet Rice *(Shekar Polo)*, 161
Peru
  Aji de Gallina (Chicken Chili), 84
Pesach. *See* Passover
Petruska (Honey Cakes), 72
Pickled Daikon, Cucumber, and Carrot, 6
Pies
  Brazilian Seafood Pie, 78
  French Canadian Pork Pie *(Tourtière)*, 55
  Greek Cheese Pie *(Tiropitta)*, 76
  Mayan Mexican Graveyard Pie *(Bil
    Pollo)*, 92
Pineapple and Banana Dessert *(Cajeta de
  Piña y Plátano)*, 43
Pineapple Carrot Soufflé, 210
Pistachio
  Iranian Almond and Pistachio Loaf, 170
  Rainbow Rice Dessert, 181
  Sweet Cardamom Rice *(Sevaiyya Kheer)*,
    171
Podina (Chutney Fruit and Mint Chutney),
  116
Podina Dhania Ki (Green Mint and Cilantro
  Chutney), 128
Polish Sweet Sour Carp, 46
Polverones Navideña (Spanish Shortcakes), 47
Pomegranate
  Pomegranate Mint Tea, 159
  Braised Brisket with Pomegranate, 192
  Sephardic Charoset, 208
Pongol. See Maka Sankranti
Pooram, 121
Poori or *Puri* (Punjab Fried Wheat Bread),
  113
Pork
  French Canadian Pork Pie *(Tourtière)*, 55
  Greek Pork in Lemon and Vinegar Jelly
    (Zalatina), 68
  in Hungarian Stuffed Kohlrabi *(Töltött
    Kalarábá)*, 58
  Mayan Mexican Graveyard Pie *(Bil
    Pollo)*, 92
  Mexican Pork Soup *(Pozole)*, 42
  Pork Chops Baked with Apples and
    Sauerkraut, 72
  Thai Pork and Bamboo Shoot Soup
    (Gaeng Chud No Ma), 21

Pork Chops Baked with Apples and Sauerkraut, 72
Pot au Feu (French Hearty Soup), 53
Potali (Steamed Rice in Banana Leaves), 130
Potato Fritters (*Draniki*), 80
Potato Latkes, 202
Potato Stew (*Dum Alu*), 19
Potato Stew with Asafetida, 29
Potatoes and Rice *(Aloo Pulao)*, 131
Potatoes with Poppy Seeds (*Aloo Posto*), 141
Pounded Rice Cakes (*Omoch*i), 4
Powidltascherln, 217
Pozole (Mexican Pork Soup),
Protestantism. *See* Christianity
Prunes
    Carrots and Prunes Tzimes, 193
    Powidltascherln, 217
Pumpkin
    Sweet Pumpkin Curry (*Kaddu Ki Sabzi*), 132
Punjab Fried Wheat Bread (*Poori* or *Puri*), 113
Punjabi Mixed Spice (*Garam Masala*), 119
Puranpoli (Split Peas Filled Griddle Breads), 109
Purim, 204

Quakers. *See* Christianity, Protestantism
Queso Frito (Spanish Fried Cheese), 78
Quince Sorbet, 182

Raksha Bandhan, 126
Rainbow Rice Dessert, 181
Ramadan, 167
Rasstegai with Fish, 71
Relishes and condiments
    Beet Horseradish, 208
    Burdock Pickle (*Tataki Gobo*), 7
    Fruit and Mint Chutney *(Podina Chutney)*, 116
    Green Mint and Cilantro Chutney (*Podina Dhania Ki*), 128
    Peach Condiment, 183
    Pickled Daikon, Cucumber, And Carrot, 6
    Sweet Tomato Chutney, 107
    Tamarind Sauce (*Imli Ke Chutney*), 135
Rendan Santan (Malaysian Chicken in Coconut Cream), 166
Rice
    Adzuki Beans and Rice with Sesame, 29
    Baked Goat and Rice (*Gosht Biryani*), 148
    Basmati Rice (*Chawa*l), 103
    Basmati Rice with Spices and Saffron (*Chawal Pullao*), 103

Chinese Aromatic Fried Rice, 30
Coconut Rice (*Kheer Ade*), 129
Eight Precious Pudding (*Nian Gao*), 18
Iranian Fruit Rice with Fish, 166
Lentils with Rice (*Moujadara*), 160
Nahit with Rice, 218
Persian Sweet Rice (*Shekar Polo*), 161
Potatoes and Rice *(Aloo Pulao)*, 131
Pounded Rice Cakes (*Omoch*i), 4
Rice and Potato Stew (*Droma*), 11
Rice Cooked in Milk *(Kheer)*, 25
Rainbow Rice Dessert, 181
Rice Soup, 15
Saffron rice Cooked in Milk (*Sarkkarai Pongal*), 100
Spiced Rice with Lotus Root and Mango, 32
Steamed Rice in Banana Leaves (*Potali*), 130
Sweet Cardamom Rice (*Sevaiyya Kheer*), 171
Sweet Saffron Rice (*Dresi*), 12
Symbolism of, 3
Turkish Spiced Liver Rice (*Iç Pilâl*), 174
Venetian Rice and Peas (*Risi e Bisi*), 82
Zongzi, 27
Rice and Potato Stew (*Droma*), 11
Rice Cooked in Milk *(Kheer)*, 25
Rice Soup, 15
Ricotta Dessert (*Roshogolla Rasgulla*), 139
Risi e Bisi (Venetian Rice and Peas), 82
Roghan Josh (Lamb in Almond Sauce), 181
Roman-Style Easter Lamb (*Abbacchio alla Romana*), 83
Romania
    Nahit with Rice, 218
Roscón de Reyes (Three Kings Sweet Bread), 67
Rosh Hashanah, 191
Roshogolla Rasgulla (Ricotta Dessert), 139
Rugelach, 199
Russia
    Draniki (Potato Fritters), 80
    Petruska (Honey Cakes), 72
    Rasstegai with Fish, 71
    Syrnyk (Russian Easter Cheese Bread), 85
Russian Easter Cheese Bread *(Syrnyk)*, 85

Saffron Rice Cooked in Milk (*Sarkkarai Pongal*), 100
Sabbath, 214
Salad
    Italian Christmas Salad (*Insalata di Rinforzo*), 51

Salad *(continued)*
  Laotian Papaya Salad, 74
  Mexican Cactus Salad (*Ensalada de
    Nopales*), 50
  Tabbouleh, 229
Sambal Goreng Undang (Indonesian Spiced
    Shrimp), 157
Sambousik (Lebanese Meat Turnovers), 69
Samosas, 117
Santa Claus Almond Cookies, 40
Sarkkarai Pongal (Saffron Rice Cooked in
    Milk), 100
Sauces
  Chinese Dumpling Dipping Sauce, 17
  Mustard and Dill Sauce (*Gravlaxsås*), 50
Saudi Arabia
  Lemon Chicken, 157
Sauerkraut
  Christmas Soup (*Kapustnica*), 52
  Pork Chops Baked with Apples and
    Sauerkraut, 72
Scallops
  Stir-fried with Chicken, Mushrooms,
    and Cucumbers, 179
  with Anise and Oranges, 89
Scallops with Anise and Oranges, 89
Scandinavia
  Gravad Lax (Dill-Cured Salmon), 49
  Gravlaxsås (Mustard and Dill Sauce), 50
  Julakaka (Norwegian Christmas Cake), 64
  Lleverpastej (Scandinavian Liver Spread),
    49
  Lutfisk (Scandinavian Poached Preserved
    Cod), 59
Scandinavian Liver Spread (*Leverpastej*), 49
Scandinavian Poached Preserved Cod
    (*Lutfisk*), 59
Schmaltz, 221–22
Sea Bass in Green Chutney, 127
Seder meal, 206
Semolina Cake (*Basbousa*), 175
Semolina Cooked in Water (*Lââssida*), 163
Sephardic Charoset, 208
Sephardic Leek and Feta Fritters, 225
Serbian Beans in Tomato Sauce, 40
Sesame
  Benne Cookies, 168
  Date Sweetmeat (*Holwar Tamar*), 167
  Egyptian mazza dip, 177
  Sesame Halwa, 138
  Sesame Seeds with Adzuki Beans and
    Rice, 29
Sesame Halwa, 138
Sevaiyya Kheer (Sweet Cardamom Rice),
    171

Seventh Day Adventists. *See* Christianity,
    Protestantism
Seviyan/Savia/Sewian (Sweet Vermicelli
    Pudding), 153
Sfingi Fritters, 91
Shab-E-Barat, 162
Shavuot, 213
Shekar Polo (*Persian Sweet Rice*), 161
Shellfish
  Brazilian Seafood Pie, 78
  Broiled Oysters, 48
  Indonesian Spiced Shrimp (*Sambal
    Goreng Undang*), 157
  Scallops with Anise and Oranges, 89
  Stir-Fried Scallops with Chicken,
    Mushrooms, and Cucumbers, 179
Shiebiat Pastry, 184
Shintoism
  Beliefs, 2
  Dietary practices, 3
  History, 2
Shogatsu, 3
Shrimp
  Hot and sour Shrimp Soup (*Dom Yam
    Gung*), 28
  Indonesian Spiced Shrimp (*Sambal
    Goreng Undang*), 157
  Shrimp with Spices, 26
  Stir-Fried Shrimp with Jasmine Tea
    Leaves, 31
Shrimp with Spices, 26
Sikhism, 98–99
Sikh New Year, 113
Sikh Vaisakhi, 119
Singapore
  Stir-fried Scallops with Chicken,
    Mushrooms, and Cucumbers, 179
Slovakia
  Kapustnica (Christmas Sauerkraut Soup),
    52
  Velija lokšy (Slovakian Bread Soup), 45
Smoked Eggplant Purée (*Baba Ghannooj*),
    149
Sólet (Bean and Goose Cholent), 216
Songkran, 20
Sopa de Flor de Calabacita (Mexican Squash
    Flower Soup), 81
Sopa do Espírito Santo (Holy Spirit Soup), 88
Soups and stocks
  Basic Soup Stock (*Dashi*), 5
  Bosnian Apricot Soup, 172
  Bulgarian Beef Soup with Meatballs
    (*Supa Topcheta*), 69
  Chard and Lentil Soup, 163
  Chickpea Soup (*Karhi*), 101

Christmas Sauerkraut Soup (*Kapustnica*), 52

French Hearty Soup (*Pot Au Feu*), 53

Green and Red Lentil Soup (*Dal Shorba*), 114

Holy Spirit Soup (*Sopa Do Espírito Santo*), 88

Hot and Sour Shrimp Soup (*Dom Yam Gung*), 28

Kanot-Style New Year's Day Soup, 6

Lamb and Lentil Soup (*Abgooshth*), 178

Malaysian Coconut, Tapioca, and Melon Soup, 23

Mexican Chicken and Vegetable Soup (*Caldo Tlalpeño*), 41

Mexican Chicken Broth (*Caldo De Pollo*), 42

Mexican Pork Soup (*Pozole*), 42

Mexican Squash Flower Soup (*Sopa De Flor De Calabacita*), 81

Moravian Clear Beef Soup with Cream-of-Wheat Dumplings, 74

Moroccan Lentil Soup (*Harira*), 173

Myanmar Tomato Soup with Lemongrass, 22

New Year's Day Soup (*O-Zoni*), 5

Oxtail and Okra Soup, 172

Rice Soup, 15

Slovakian Bread Soup (*Velija Lokšy*), 45

Sour Mango Soup (*Mampazhapachadi*), 116

Southeast Asian Vegetable Stock for Soup, 22

Thai Pork and Bamboo Shoot Soup (*Gaeng Chud No Ma*), 21

Tibetan New Year's Eve Soup with Dumplings (*Guthuk*), 10

Sour Mango Soup (*Mampazhapachadi*), 116

Spain

  Galletas de Miel (Spanish Honey Cakes), 89

  Polverones Navideña (Spanish Shortcakes), 47

  Queso Frito (Spanish Fried Cheese), 78

  Roscón de Reyes (Three Kings Sweet Bread), 67

  Scallops with Anise and Oranges, 89

Spanish Fried Cheese (*Queso Frito*), 78

Spanish Honey Cakes (*Galletas de Miel*), 89

Spanish Shortcakes (*Polverones Navideña*), 47

Spiced Chickpeas (*Channa Masaledar*), 106

Spiced Milk Drink (*Thandai*), 106

Spiced Rice with Lotus Root and Mango, 32

Split Pea–Filled Griddle Breads (*Puranpoli*), 109

St. Basil's Day, 66

St. James Day, 89

St. Nicholas's Day, 39

St. Stephen's Day, 90

Steamed Dumpling (*Jao Tze*), 17

Steamed Rice in Banana Leaves (*Potali*), 130

Stews

  Barley with Mushrooms and Onions, 14

  Chicken Chili (*Aji de Gallina*), 84

  Lentil Stew (*Masoor Dal*), 122

  Lentil Stew, 231

  Louisiana Gumbo with Sassafras, 53

  Peanut Stew, 175

  Persian Lamb Stew, 160

  Potato Stew (*Dum Alu*), 19

  Rice and Potato Stew (*Droma*), 11

  Stewed Fish over Rice and Noodles, 164

  Sweet Lamb Stew (*Mrouzia Tajine*), 149

  Tharid, 185

Stewed Fish over Rice and Noodles, 164

Stewed Lentils (*Masur Dal*), 108

Stir-Fried Scallops with Chicken, Mushrooms, and Cucumbers, 179

Stir-Fried Shrimp with Jasmine Tea Leaves, 31

Stuffed Cabbage (*Holishkes*), 196

Stuffed Chicken, 209

Stuffed Dates, 95

Stuffed Kishke or Derma, 202

Stuffed Lamb Shoulder (*Kabourga*), 151

Submersion of the Holy Cross, 68

Sufganiyot, 200

Suhoor. *See* Ramadan

Sukkot, 195

Supa Topcheta (Bulgarian Beef Soup with Meatballs), 69

Sweden. *See* Scandinavia

Sweet Cardamom Rice (*Sevaiyya Kheer*), 171

Sweet Fritters (*Malpuas*), 111

Sweet Lamb Stew (*Mrouzia Tajine*), 149

Sweet Potato

  New Year Sweet Potato Balls (*Kuri Kinton*), 8

  Vegetable Cutlets, 226

Sweet Pumpkin Curry (*Kaddu Ki Sabzi*), 132

Sweet Saffron Rice (*Dresi*), 12

Sweet Tomato Chutney, 107

Sweet Vermicelli Pudding (*Seviyan/Savia/ Sewian*), 153

Sweetened Semolina (*Kahara Prasad*), 142

Sweets (*Pedhas*), 118
Syria
    Flatbread, 169
    Shiebiat Pastry, 184
Syrian Flatbread, 169
Syrnyk (Russian Easter Cheese Bread), 85

Taamiya (Fava Bean Fritters), 174
Tabbouleh, 229
Tahsreeb Dijaj (Iranian Lemon Chicken
    with Roasted Garlic), 180
Tamarind Sauce (*Imli Ke Chutney*), 135
Tandoori Baked Chicken (*Tandoori
    Murgha*), 110
Tandoori Murgh (Tandoori Baked Chicken),
    110
Tapioca
    Malaysian Coconut, Tapioca, and Melon
        Soup, 23
Tarama (Fish Roe Dip), 150
Tataki Gobo (Burdock Pickle), 7
Tel Kadayif (Honey Baked Shredded
    Dough), 158
Thai Pork and Bamboo Shoot Soup (*Gaeng
    Chud No Ma*), 21
Thai Raek Na, 26
Thailand
    Dried dates, 21
    Gaeng Chud No Ma (Pork and Bamboo
        Shoot Soup), 21
    Shrimp with Spices, 26
Thandai (Spiced Milk Drink), 106
Tharid, 185
Three Kings Sweet Bread (*Roscón de Reyes*),
    67
Tibet
    Barley with Mushrooms and Onions, 14
    Dresi (Sweet Saffron Rice), 12
    Droma (Rice and Potato Stew), 11
    Guthuk (Tibetan New Year's Eve Soup
        with Dumplings), 10
    Kapse Fritters, 12
    Monastery Bread, 13
Tibetan New Year's Eve Soup with
    Dumplings (*Guthuk*), 10
Tiropitta (Greek Cheese Pie), 76
Töltött Kalarábá (Hungarian Stuffed
    Kohlrabi), 58
Tomato
    Myanmar Tomato Soup with
        Lemongrass, 22
Toshikoshi Soba (Chilled Buckwheat
    Noodles), 8
Tu Bishvat, 203
Tunisia. *See also* North Africa

Agras, 170
    Baba Ghannooj (Smoked Eggplant Purée),
        149
Tunisian Terabilesi Bread, 156
Turkey
    Cerkez Tavuğu (Chicken in Nut Sauce),
        176
    İç Pilâl (Turkish Spiced Liver Rice), 175
    Peach Condiment, 183
    Tarama (Fish Roe Dip), 150
    Tel Kadayif (Honey Baked Shredded
        Dough), 158
Turkish Spiced Liver Rice (*İç Pilâl*), 174
Trinidad and Tobago
    Urhad dal Sabat (Caribbean Black-Eyed
        Peas), 138
Tyrolean Dried Fruit Bread (*Kletzenbrot*), 36

Udon Miso, 19
Ukraine
    Holishkes (Stuffed Cabbage), 196
    Ukrainian Easter Eggs, 81
    Varenyky (Ukrainian Dumplings with
        Sour Cream), 45
Ukrainian Dumplings with Sour Cream
    (*Varenyky*), 45
Ukrainian Easter Eggs, 81
United States
    Amish Apple Tarts on Cabbage Leaves, 37
    Amish doughnuts (*Fastnacht*), 77
    Apple Walnut Cake, 73
    Baked Virginia Ham, 55
    Benne Cookies, 168
    Braised Brisket with Pomegranate, 192
    Broiled Oysters, 48
    Gingerbread Pudding, 62
    Louisiana Gumbo with Sassafras, 53
    Mormon Baptism Buns, 87
    Oxtail and Okra Soup, 172
    Peanut Stew, 175
    Rainbow Rice Dessert, 181
    Stewed Fish over Rice and Noodles, 164
    Yam Patties, 164
Unstuffed Cabbage, 197
Urhad Dal Sabat (Caribbean Black-Eyed
    Peas), 138

Vara Lakshmi, 130
Varenyky (Ukrainian Dumplings with Sour
    Cream), 45
Vaisakhi, 115
Vasant Panchami, 103
Vasanta, 115
Vassilopitta (Greek Christmas Cake), 66
Vegetable Cutlets, 226

Vegetable Puree (*Avial*), 122
Vegetable Stock for Soup, 22
Velija Lokšy (Slovakian Bread Soup), 45
Venetian Rice and Peas (*Risi e Bisi*), 82
Venison
   Elizabethan Venison with Fennel, 56
Vesak, 25
Visakah Puja. *See Vesak*
Visakha Pucha. *See Vesak*

Walnuts
   Apple Walnut Cake, 73
   Ashkenazic Charoset, 207
   Baked Pears with Walnuts and Honey, 229
   Date Nut Loaf, 198
   Date Sweetmeat (*Holwar Tamar*), 167

Hot and Spicy Walnuts, 9
New Year's Sweet Potato Balls (*Kuri Kinton*), 8
Rugelach, 199
Waisak. *See Vesak*
Wesak. *See Vesak*

Yam Patties, 164
Yom Kippur, 194

Zalatina (Greek Pork in Lemon and Vinegar Jelly), 68
Zen
Zongzi, 27
Zucchini Flower Fritters, 203
Zucchini Frittata, 227
Zuckerstangen (Candy Crisps), 38

ABOUT THE AUTHORS

ARNO SCHMIDT is a former executive chef and has written a number of books on various aspects of food and drink management in the hotel industry.

PAUL FIELDHOUSE is Adjunct Professor of Nursing at the University of Manitoba, and a nutrition research and policy analyst for Manitoba Health. He is the author of *Food and Nutrition: Customs and Culture* (1995) and other books and essays on nutrition, religion, and food practices.